LUNDY ISLAND
THROUGH TIME

Simon Dell

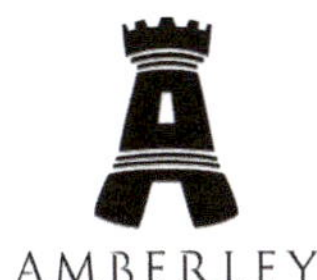

AMBERLEY

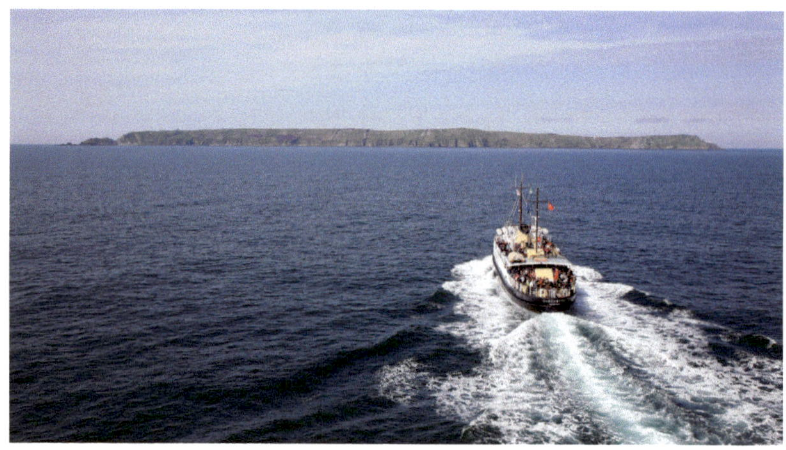

Oldenburg on the way to the island.

For Sylvia Maureen
Who spent many happy years gazing upon this glorious isle.

First published 2011
Reprinted 2011

Amberley Publishing
The Hill, Stroud
Gloucestershire, GL5 4EP

www.amberley-books.com

ISBN 978 1 4456 0074 1

British Library Cataloguing in Publication Data.
A catalogue record for this book is available from
the British Library.

Typeset in 9.5pt on 12pt Celeste.
Typesetting by Amberley Publishing.
Map illustration by User design.
Printed in the UK.

Appointed GPSR EU Representative: Easy Access
System Europe Oü, 16879218
Address: Mustamäe tee 50, 10621, Tallinn, Estonia
Contact Details: gpsr.requests@easproject.com,
+358 40 500 3575

Introduction

Lundy Island lies approximately ten miles off the North Devon coast in the mouth of the Bristol Channel. Just three miles long and about half a mile wide, it is a significant mass of granite, which has stood witness to an interesting and often turbulent history. Stories of pirates and smugglers are rife, of convicts bound for the Americas kept as slave labour, and of treason and plot against the King. All these tales, and more beside, weave themselves into the very fabric and soul of this isolated haven for wildlife and those seeking its idyllic solitude. Much has been written about this unique isle by its residents, academics, archaeologists and naturalists alike, but this small volume in no way intends to repeat those informative accounts. Instead, it is a collection of photographs, many dating back to the nineteenth century. They are juxtaposed with modern-day images, in order to explore the many and varied changes that this island has undergone over the last one and a half centuries. This book tells a photographic tale of the way the island has evolved since its time as the 'Kingdom of Heaven', to the present day in the ownership of the National Trust. Lundy remains a place of beauty, of tranquillity, and of such interest that many visitors return year upon year, to seek that which the mainland is unable to offer.

Lundy is accessible in spring, summer and autumn, from the ports of Bideford and Ilfracombe aboard the island ship – the *Oldenburg*. During the winter months, access for those staying on the island is by helicopter from Hartland Point.

Full details of the island, daytrips and accommodation are available at the island website www.lundyisland.co.uk or by telephone to the Lundy Shore Office on 01271 863636.

If the turn of each page brings a smile of long-forgotten recognition or a desire to visit for the first time, then I consider the undertaking worthwhile indeed.

Simon Dell MBE
The Radio Room, Lundy, 2011

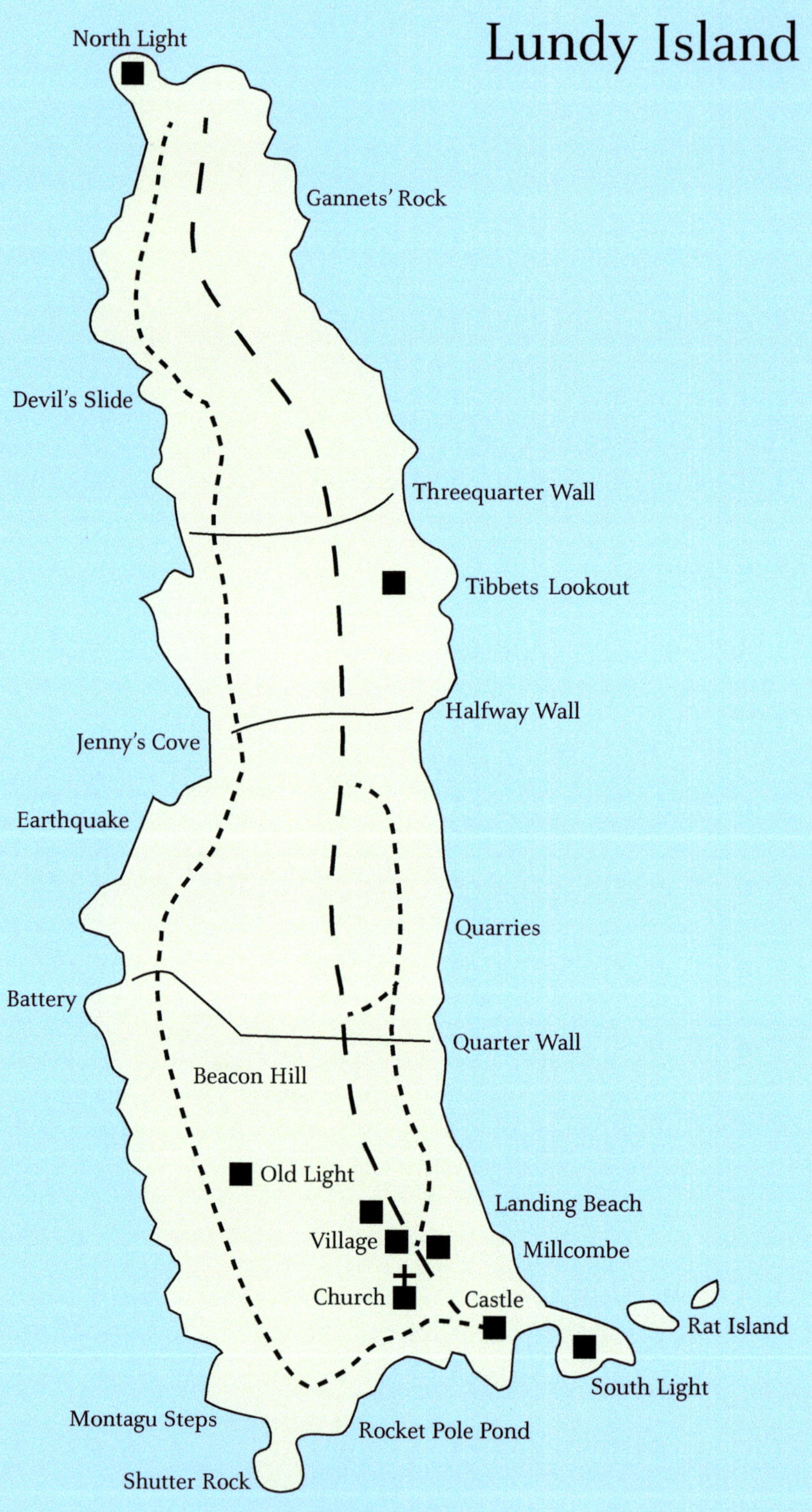

Lundy Island
North Light
Gannets' Rock
Devil's Slide
Threequarter Wall
Tibbets Lookout
Halfway Wall
Jenny's Cove
Earthquake
Quarries
Battery
Quarter Wall
Beacon Hill
Old Light
Landing Beach
Village
Millcombe
Church
Castle
Rat Island
South Light
Montagu Steps
Rocket Pole Pond
Shutter Rock

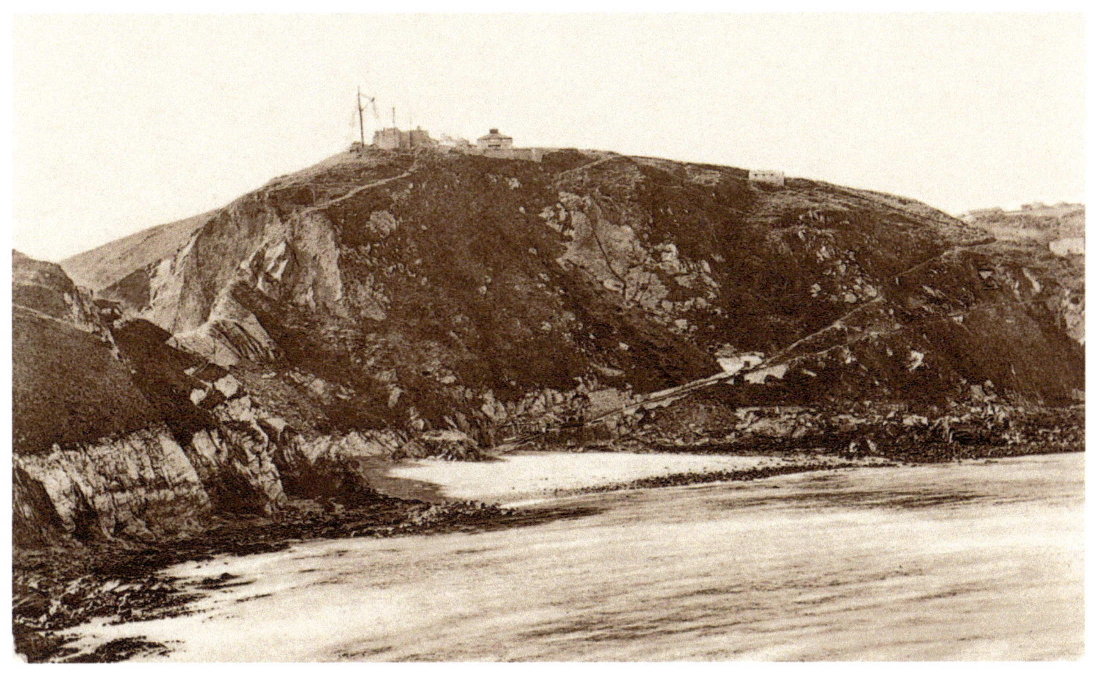

The Landing Bay

Above is the island landing bay, pictured between 1884 and 1896, in the time when Lloyds had a signalling station high up on the castle parade ground. This photograph also shows the semi-detached houses used for the signal station staff, situated to the rear of the castle. The beach road leading up to the island plateau is also evident, along with the much older track now known as 'the goat track', which is slightly higher than the road and less obvious in the newer image below, taken from the new landing jetty.

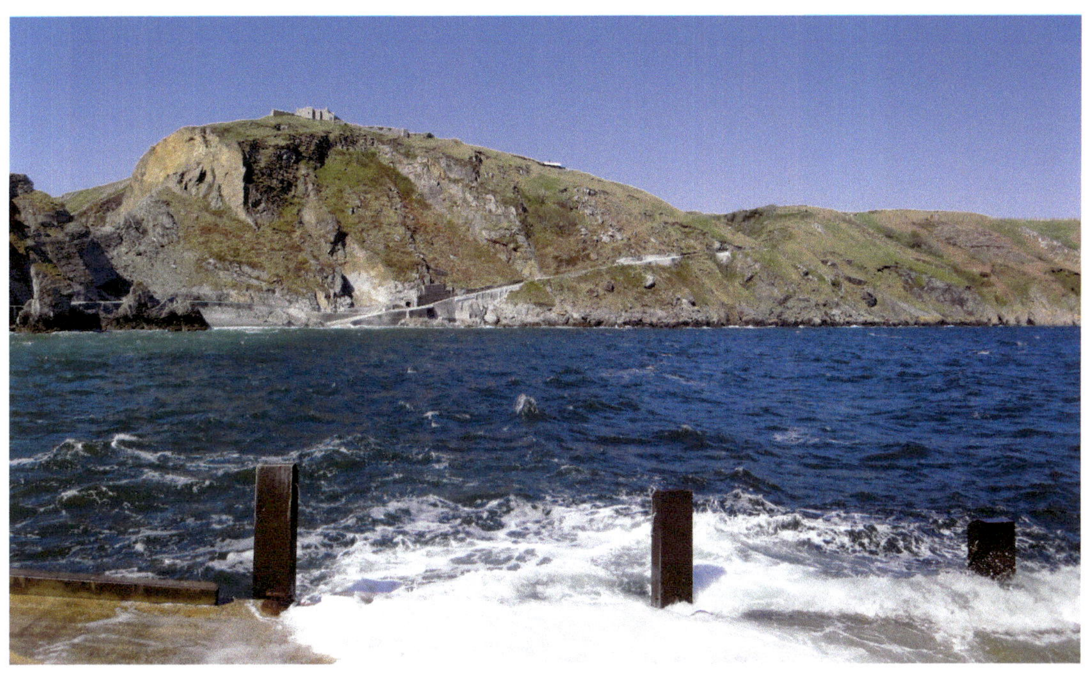

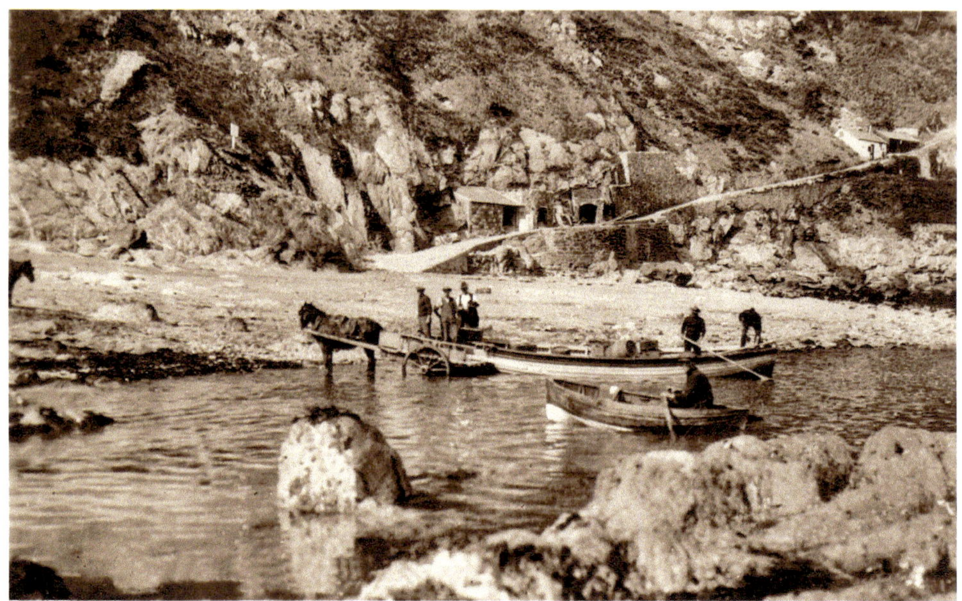

Unloading Stores

Above, unloading stores onto Lundy in the 1920s was a physically demanding and time-consuming operation. Today, the *Oldenburg* moors up at the jetty, and a single tractor driver can unload a whole cargo in very little time at all. The view above clearly shows much of the slipway area, which was devastated by a landslip in 1954 when the limekiln and bait store building were destroyed. Further up the beach road, to the right, is the little white fisherman's shelter known as 'Sea View'.

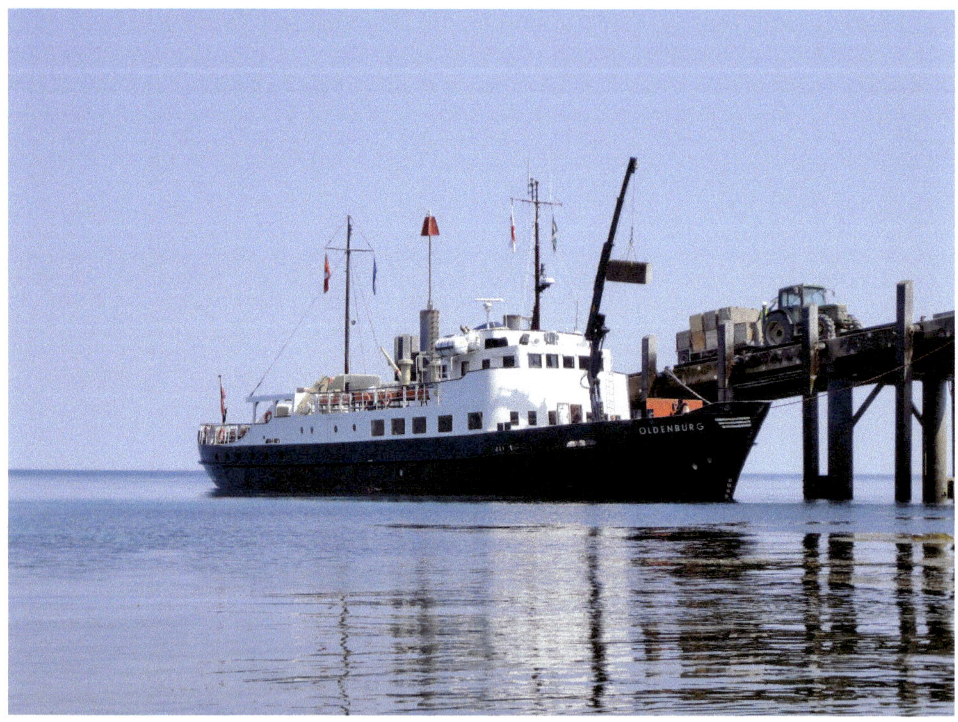

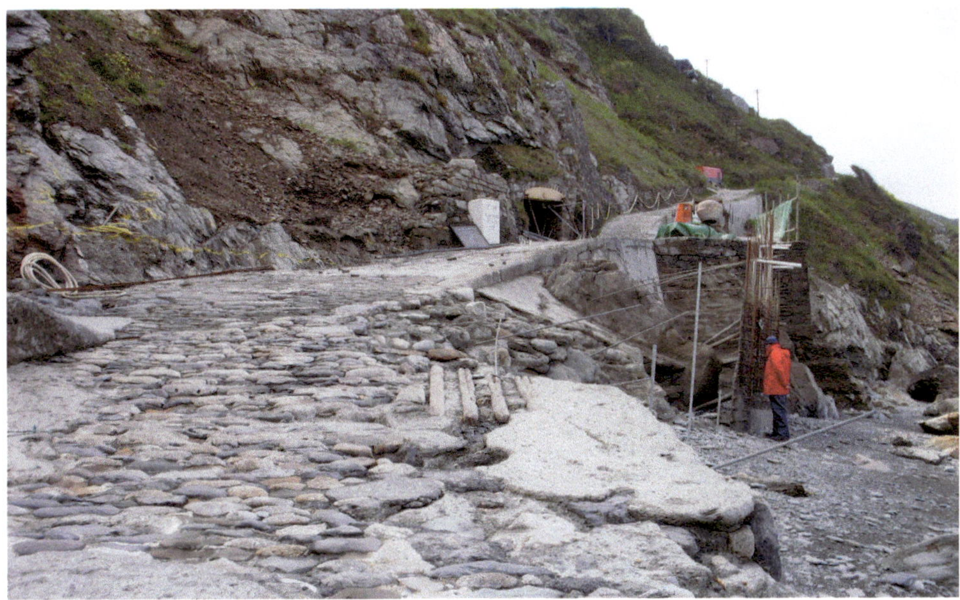

The Slipway and Beach Road

Repair work to the crumbling beach road in 2010 has secured the future of the island. The large red generator, pictured on the road above the concrete mixer, is located at the site once occupied by the old 'Sea View' fisherman's building, pictured below. It was here that the last red deer stag on the island took up nightly residence prior to the Second World War. He evidently enjoyed scaring passing lighthouse keepers as they stumbled their way home from the island tavern to the South Light!

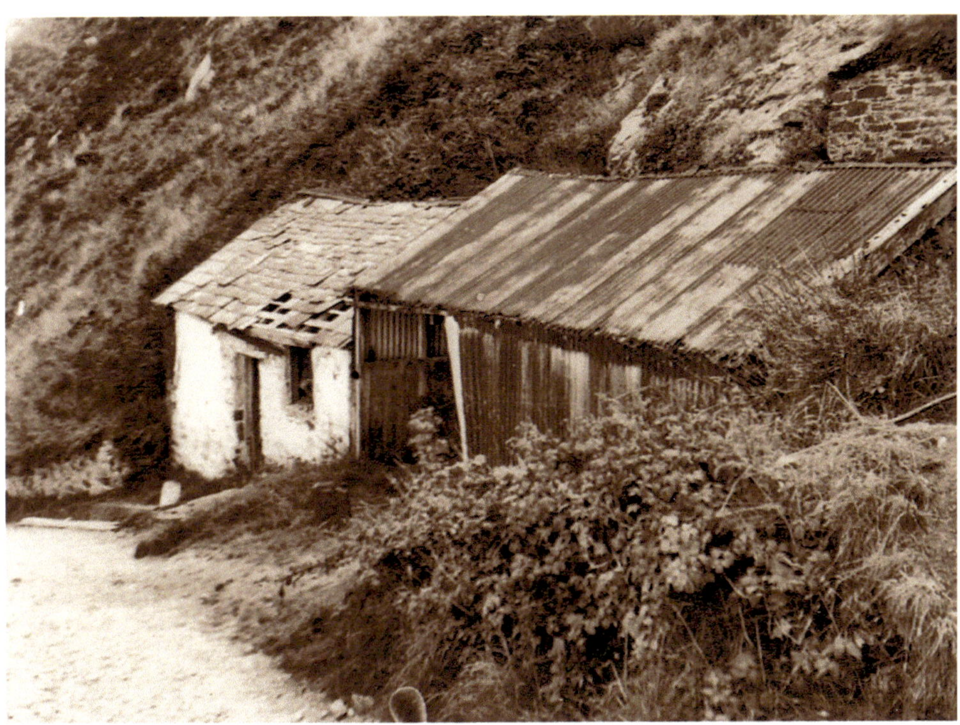

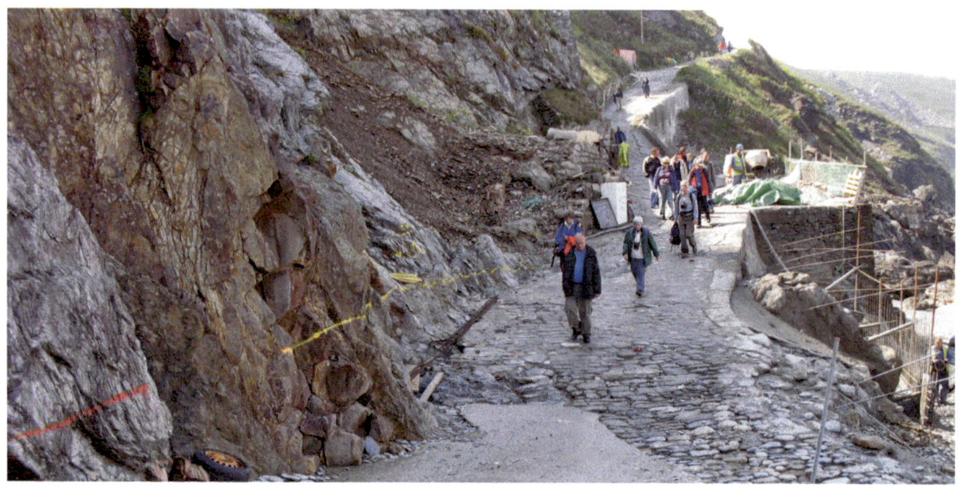

The Trinity House Stone, 1819

In 1819, the Engineers of Trinity House landed to make a survey of the most suitable location to build their magnificent new lighthouse. They arrived here in the bay and commemorated the occasion by erecting a T. H. Landing Place stone (*below*) next to the long-lost limekiln. The stone, now newly whitewashed, still stands at the head of the slipway, and has survived the upheaval of the beach road restoration works, in full swing above. The yellow line on the left, incidentally, shows the level of the current-day beach road surface following its reconstruction in 2010.

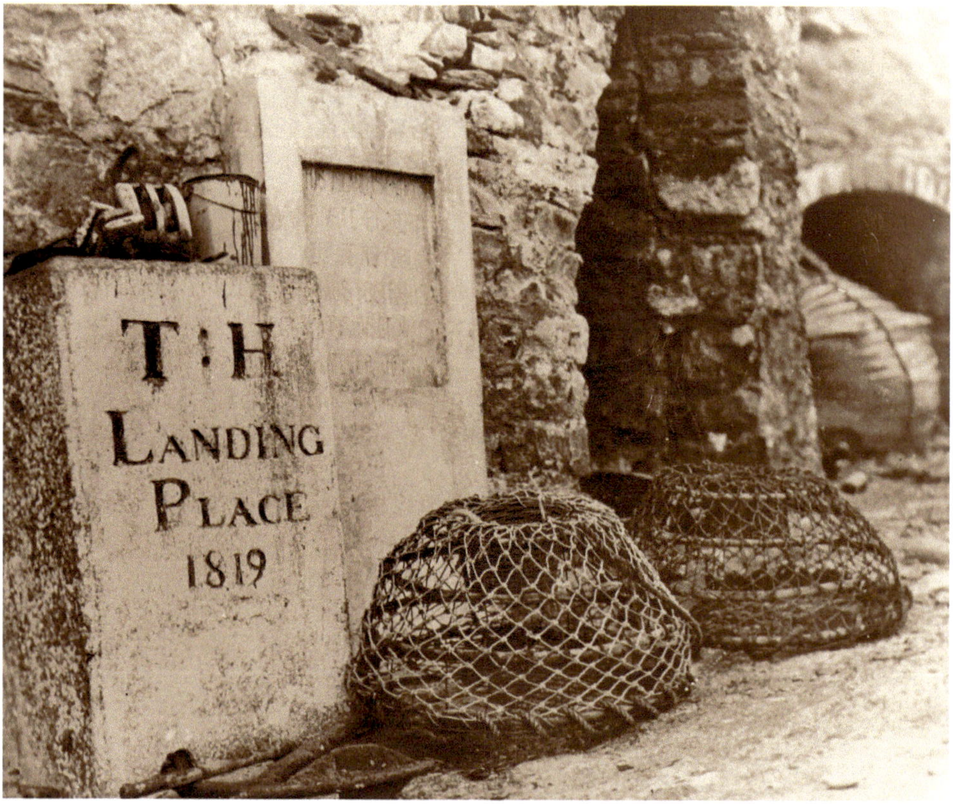

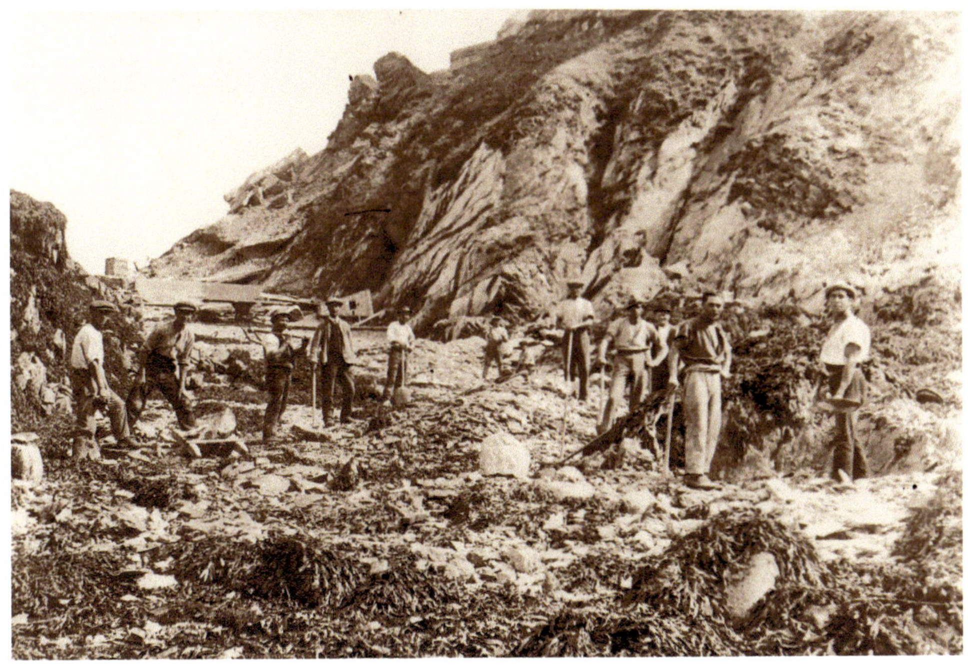

The Christie Quay

In the early 1920s, Lundy was purchased by the Christie family from Tapeley House at Instow. During their ownership, it was decided to have a more sheltered landing place and small quayside built to house the island vessel the *Lerina*. A large workforce was employed (*above*) to construct the sea defences. The quayside still provides a sheltered landing place for smaller vessels, in front of the wooden divers' building at the head of the newly constructed jetty, in the shadow of Rat Island.

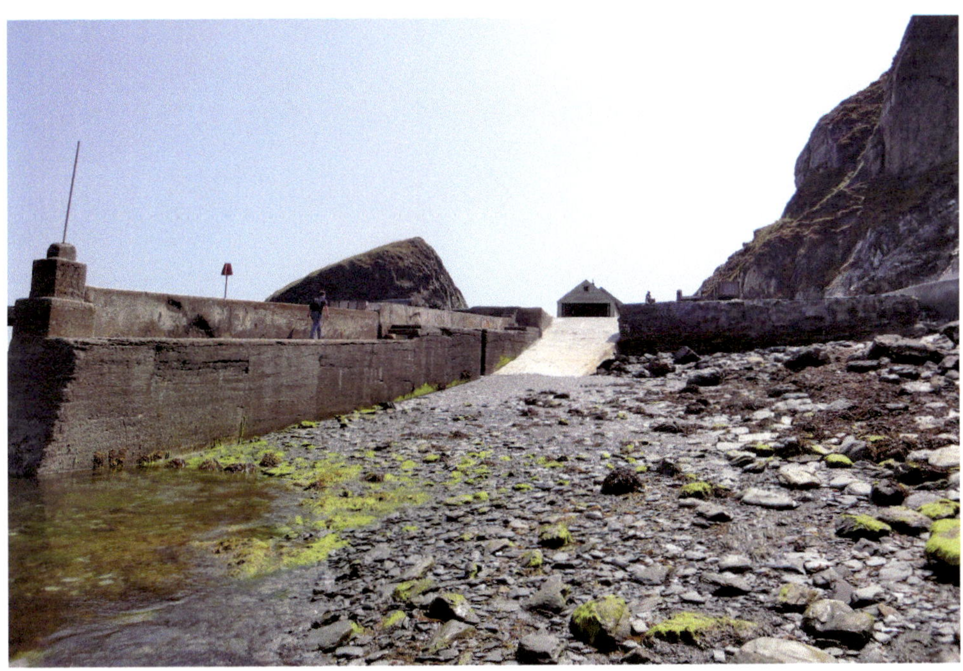

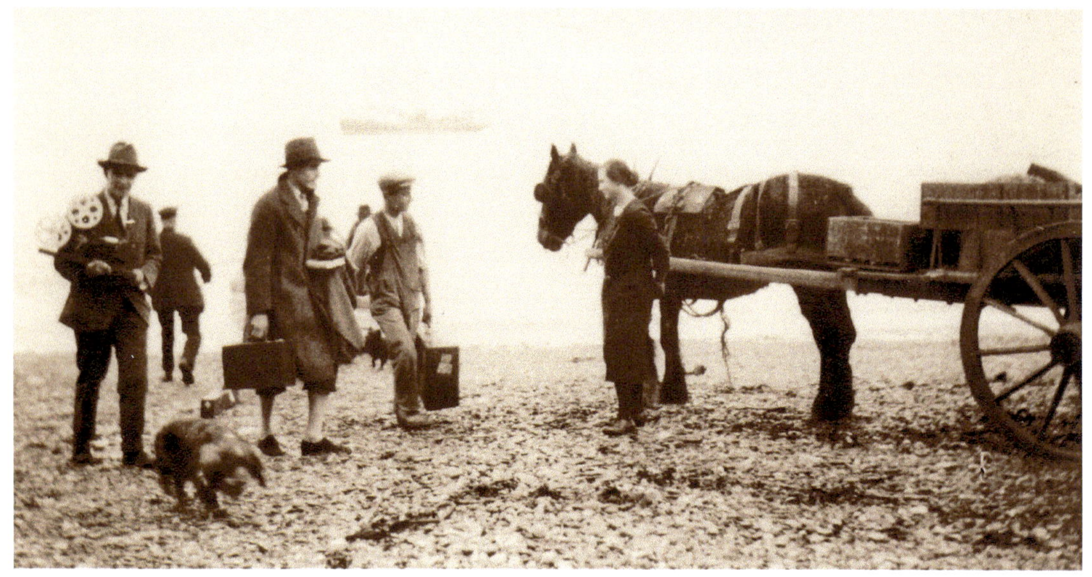

Beach Landings

The British Pathé Newsreel cameraman arrives on Lundy in 1931, having been brought over from Instow aboard the *Lerina*, which is seen above in the background moored offshore. Landings in those days were carried out by small rowing boat, directly onto the beach. Even now, as can be seen below, visiting yacht crews still arrive by dinghy onto the newly refurbished landing slipway, constructed in 2010, when the work to restore the beach road was completed.

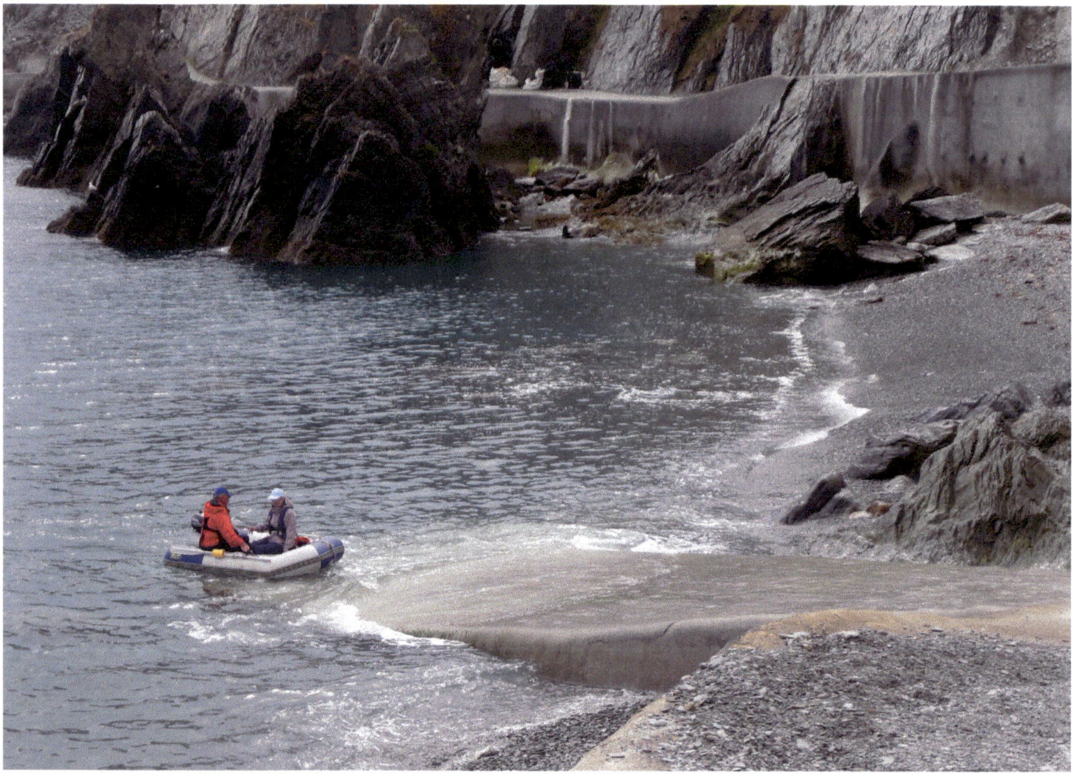

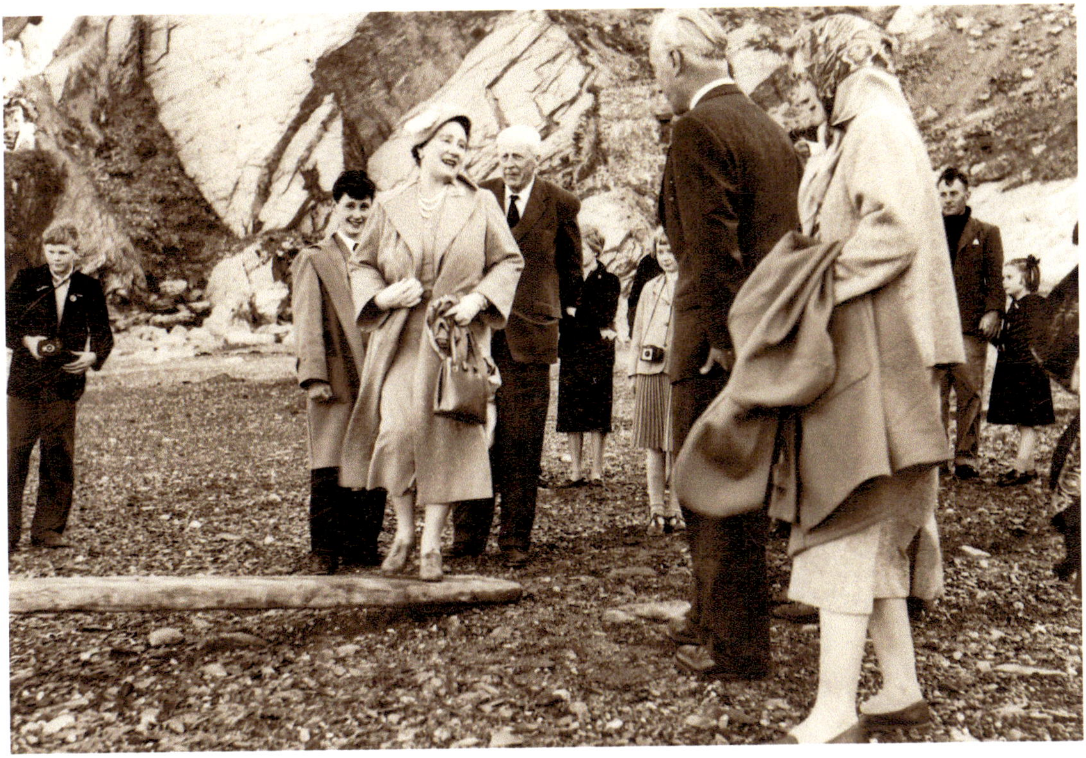

The Queen Mother's visit to Lundy in 1958

On Sunday 11 May 1958, Her Majesty The Queen Mother landed on Lundy on her journey home from Northern Ireland, on the Royal Yacht *Britannia* – a rare visit by royalty. She was entertained for a few hours, and is pictured above leaving the island. Seeing her off is Mr Albion Harman, the owner of Lundy, along with his sister Ruth, pictured in the foreground. Behind the Queen Mother is the very tall figure of Felix Gade, the Island Agent for Mr Harman and resident of Lundy almost continuously for over fifty years. While on the island, Her Majesty kindly signed an illuminated souvenir (*right*) which now hangs in Millcombe House.

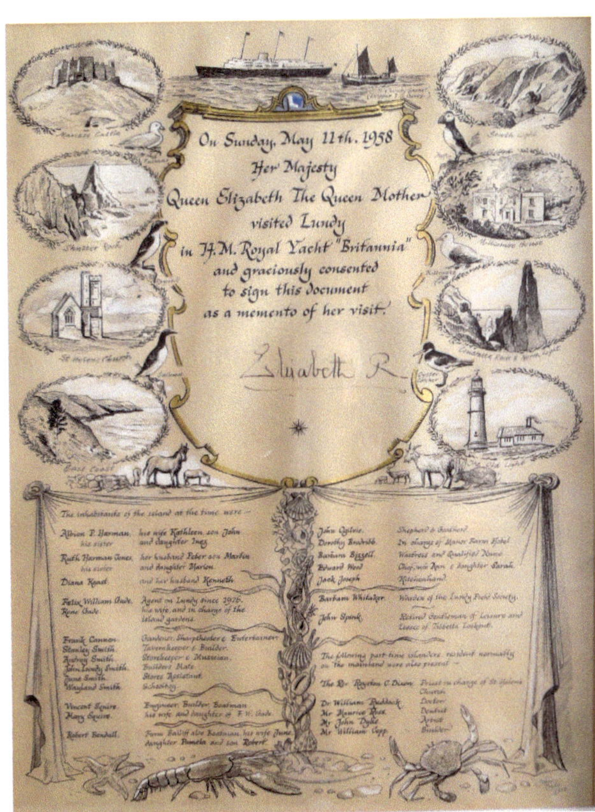

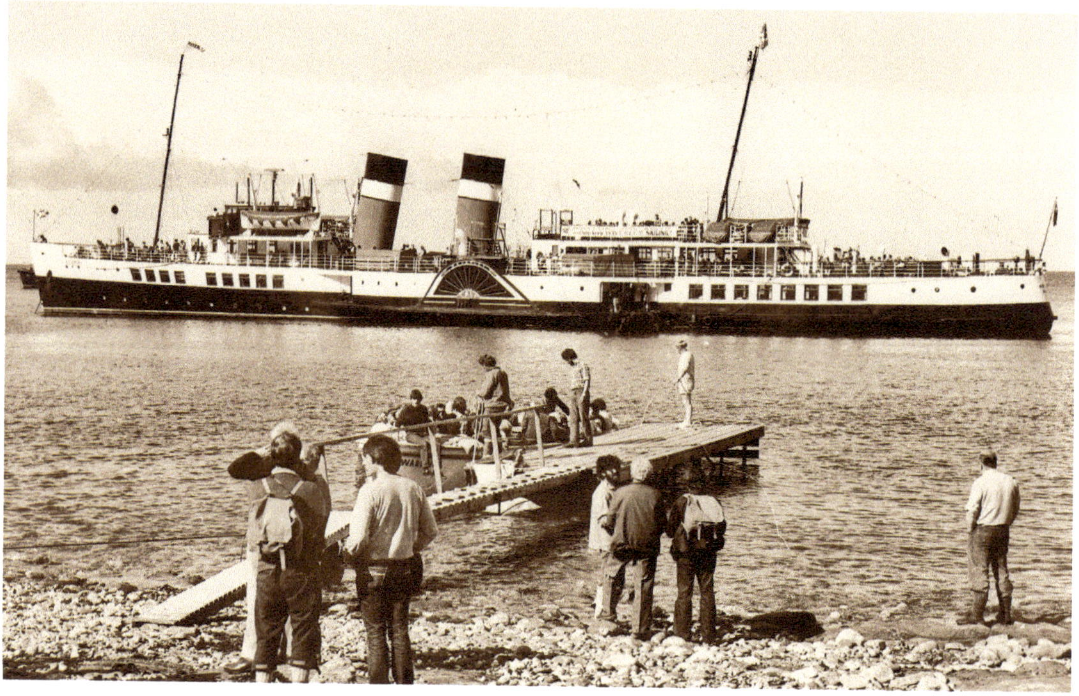

Visitors Arriving on Lundy

Lundy has received tourist visitors since Victorian times. The paddle steamer the *Waverley,* pictured above, is unloading passengers in the 1980s on the small, portable, landing-stage. However, a much quicker journey (*below*) is undertaken in the modern-day winter months by helicopter service from Hartland Point in about 7 minutes! The *Waverley* was built in 1946 as a Clyde ferry and cruise ship but is now operated by the Waverley Steam Navigation Company, and is the only ocean-going paddle steamer in the world, still making visits to the island.

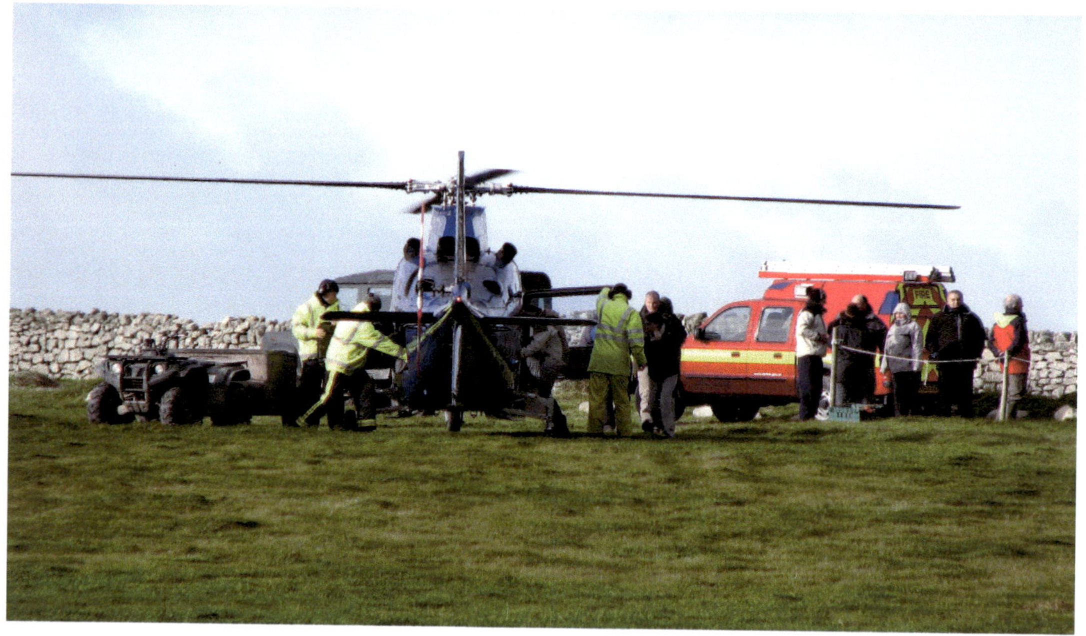

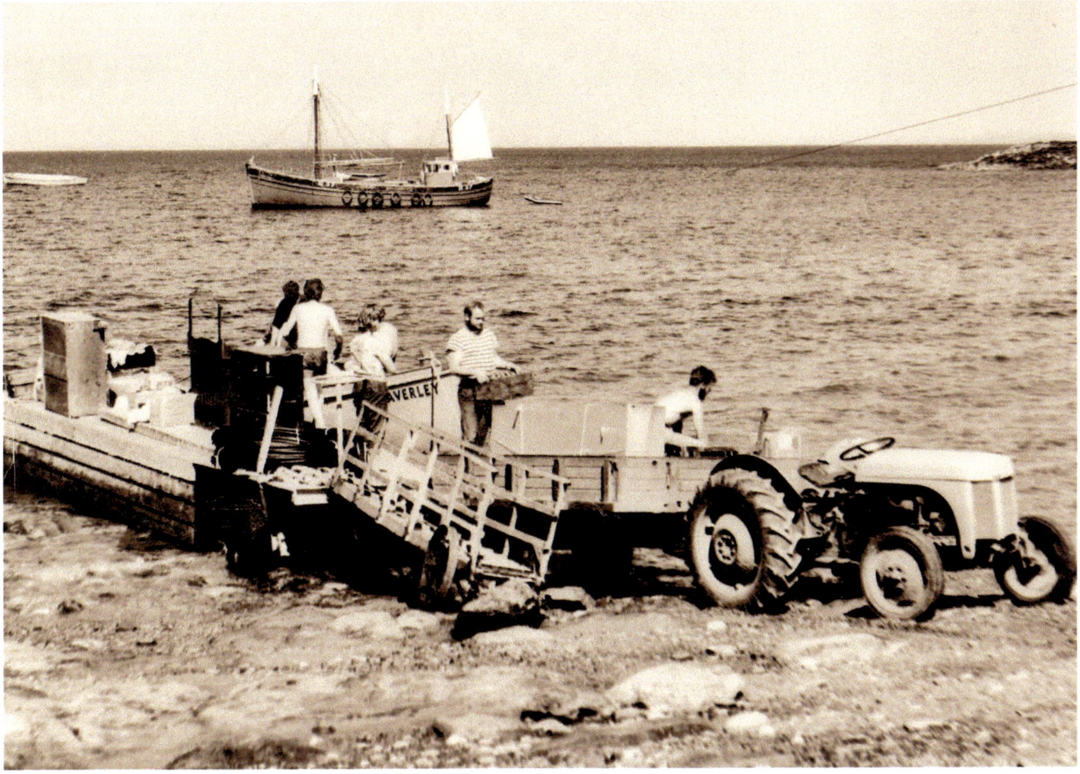

The Arrival of Stores on Lundy

Until comparatively recently, as pictured above, stores were manhandled several times on their journey to Lundy. Here, furniture and possessions of newly arrived residents have been delivered by the *Lundy Gannet*, seen in the landing bay. It seems, however, that one of the small tenders from the *Waverley* is being used for the final shuttle to the beach, so possibly the huge *Waverley* is lurking somewhere out of shot! Campbell's Steamers used to lodge two or three employees for the summer season on the island to assist in transporting visitors, and these men used to help out wherever they could on non-sailing days. The modern method of transportation (*right*) is equally challenging on the narrow and precipitous beach road, as shown by the skilful tractor-driver's ability!

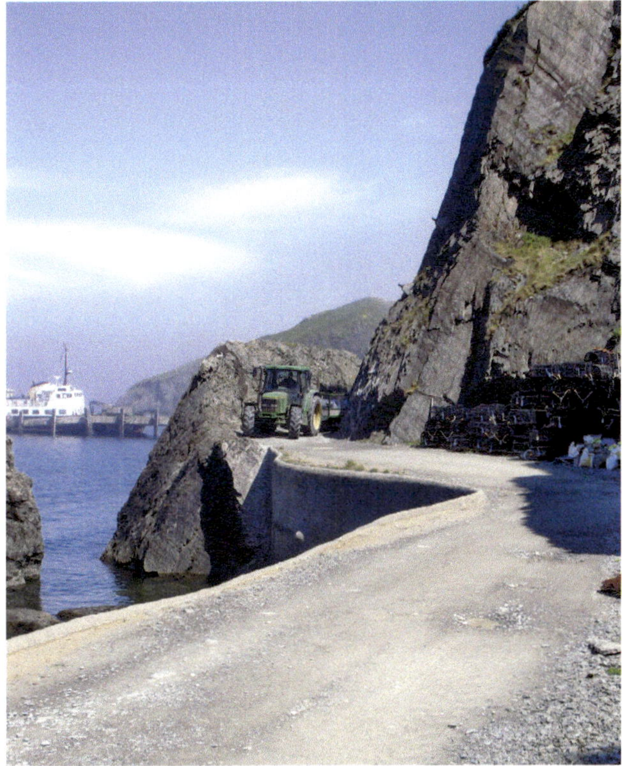

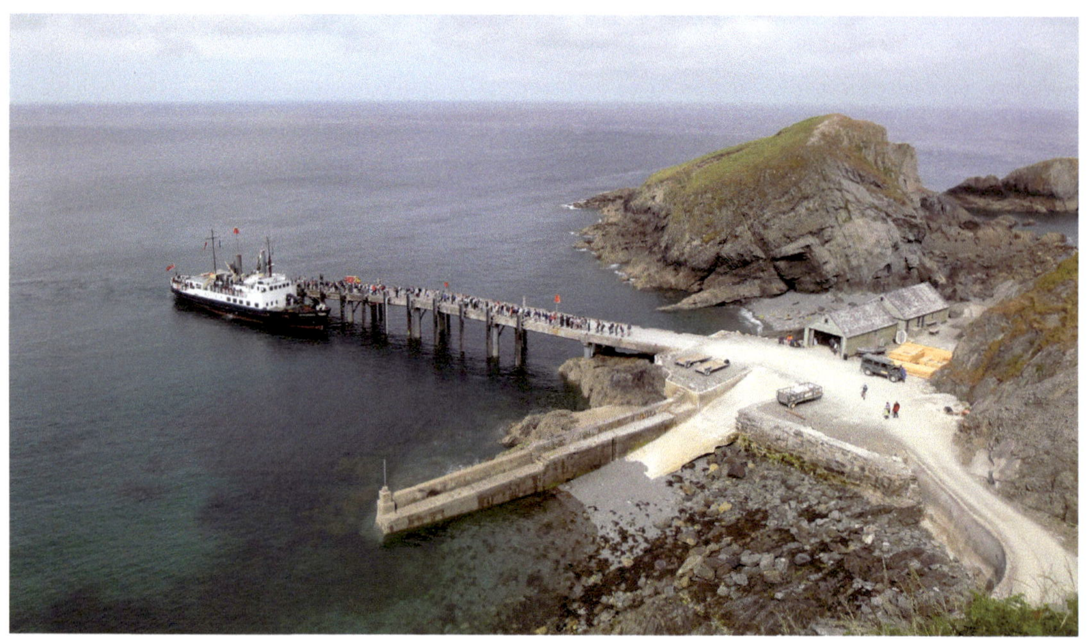

Departure Queues – Just the Size Varies!

The queue of day-trippers on the jetty, as seen from high above at the South Light. The lower photograph shows what it used to be like before the construction of the new jetty. It would take a considerable time to load everyone on board using the smaller tender and the portable landing stage, which was hauled down by tractor to the water's edge. This older photograph clearly shows the former steps and path up to the South Light. This pathway slipped away during the construction of the new road to the Christie's Quay area in the late 1980s in preparation for the building of the new jetty. Modern-day passengers can board the *Oldenburg* in a fraction of the time nowadays.

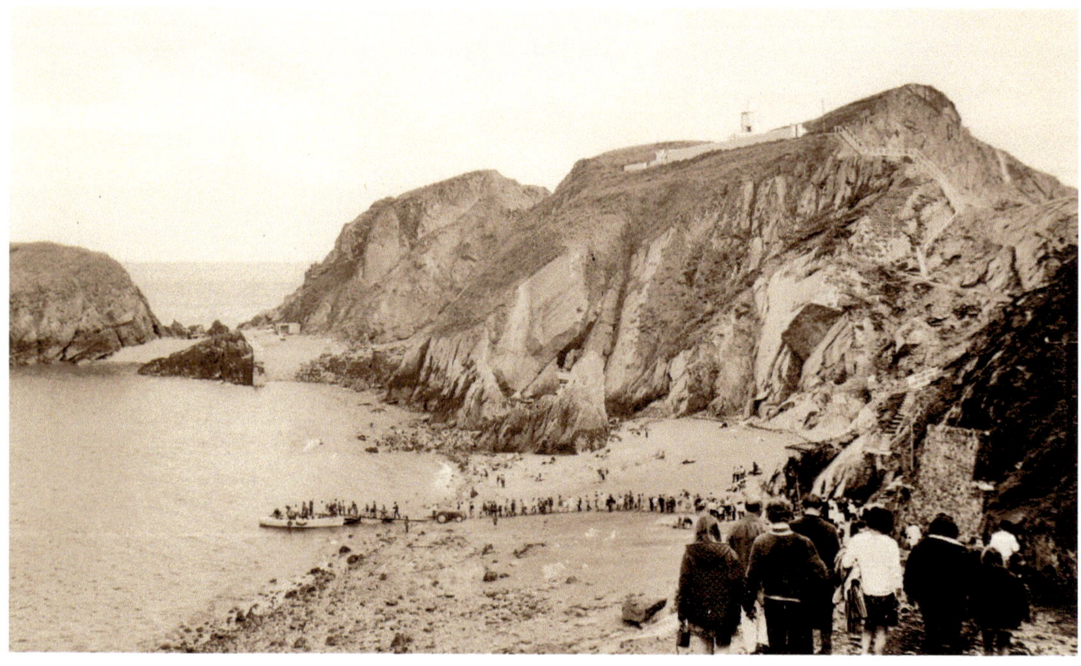

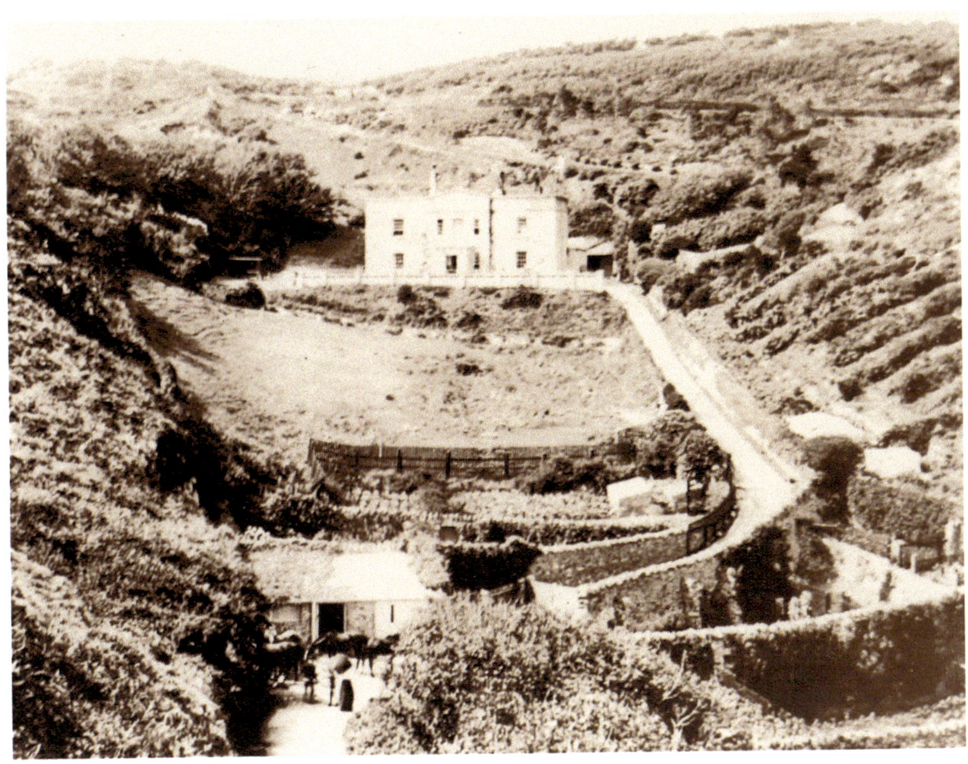

Millcombe House

When William Heaven bought Lundy in 1836, he designed a fine Georgian mansion as his residence. Originally called 'The Villa', it stands in the Millcombe valley, hence its modern name. The house has an ingeniously inward-sloping roof in order to catch rainwater in great tanks in the basement. The modern-day Millcombe House offers accommodation for a dozen people in very elegant surroundings. During its Victorian life, it boasted well-kept kitchen gardens and a stable at the entrance gateway.

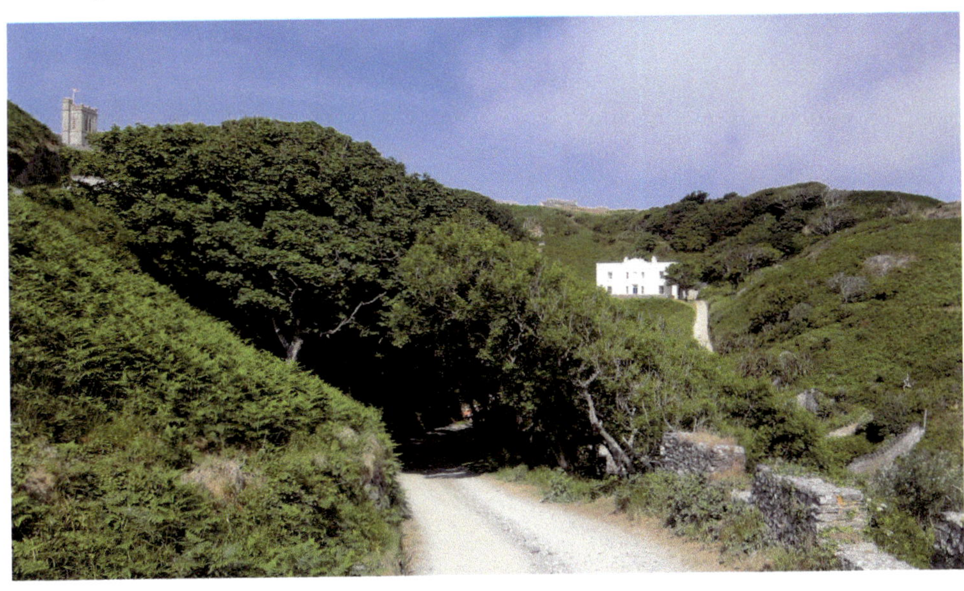

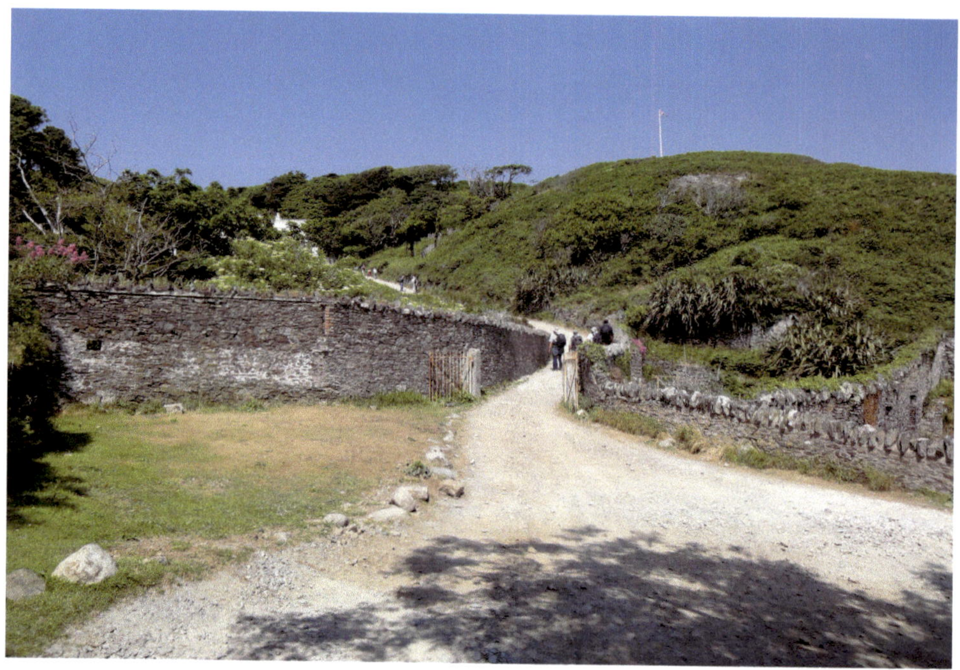

The Gateway to Millcombe House

Beside the original gateway to Millcombe House stood a building that housed the carriage of Mr William Heaven, owner of the island, along with a stable for his horse. The massive granite gateposts were cut from the capstone cover of a huge ancient burial chamber, located on the south end of the island. The gates stood as a division between the private grounds of the Heaven family and that of the rest of the island, but today the public footpath goes right up the main driveway and past the white-painted mansion to the village beyond. In 1886, human remains were located, buried under the site of the gatehouse building.

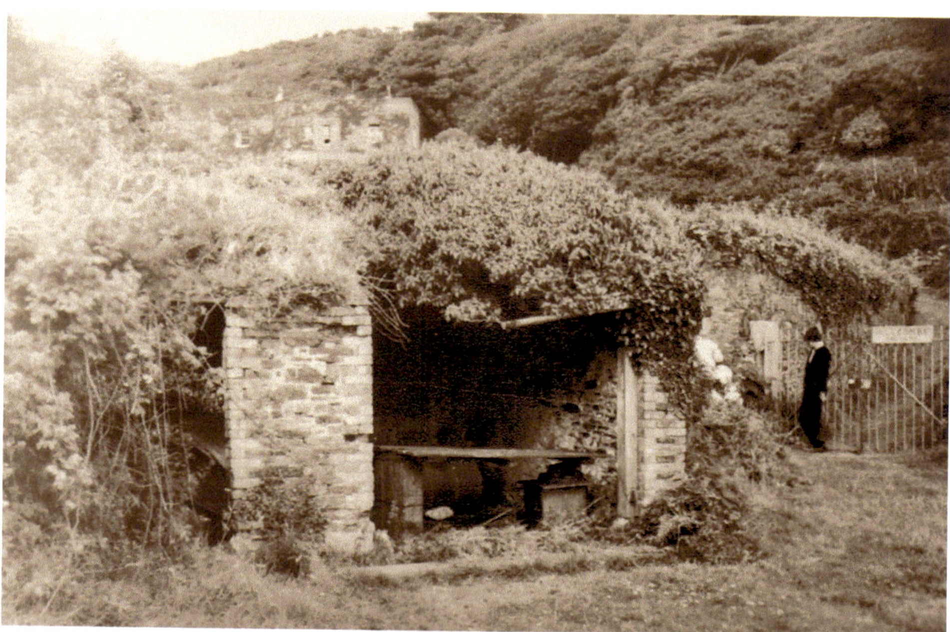

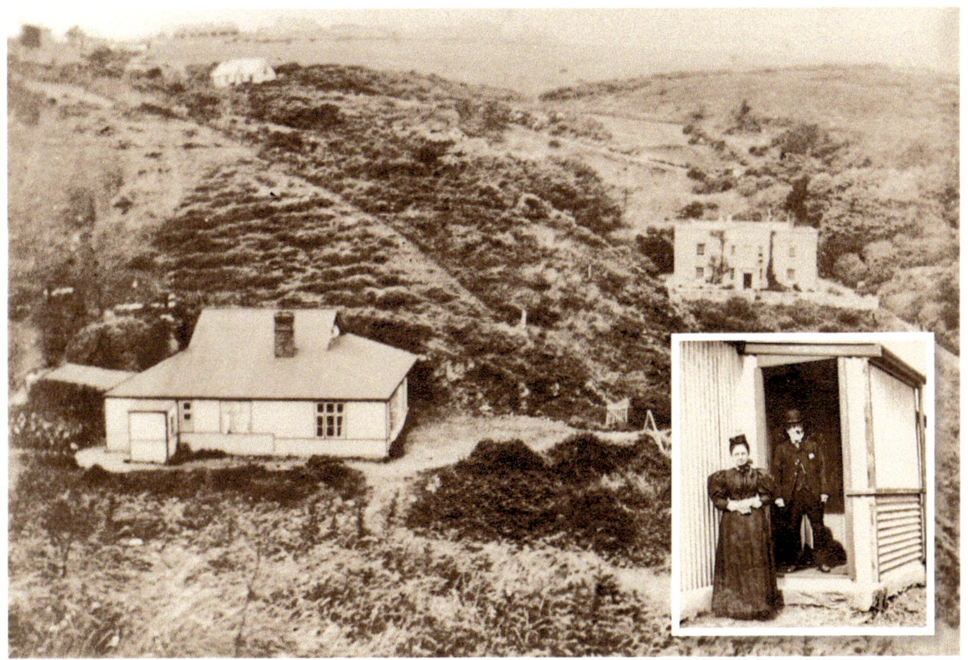

The Bungalow – Bramble Villas

The original wooden bungalow was built in a colonial style familiar to Mr Heaven from his time as a sugar plantation owner. It was originally the residence of his staff, as pictured in the smaller photograph (*above*) – Mr Ward was the coachman gardener and Mrs Ward was the cook at Millcombe House. The new Bramble Villa bungalow was constructed for the Landmark Trust Island Manager in 1971 and is now divided into two properties – Brambles East and Brambles West with fine views over the landing bay and the North Devon coast in clear weather.

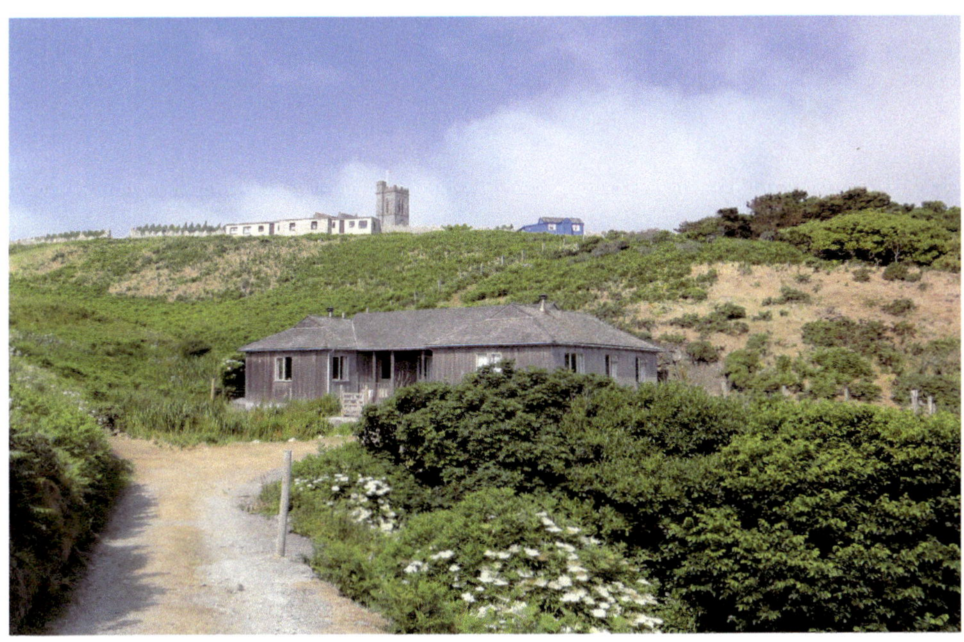

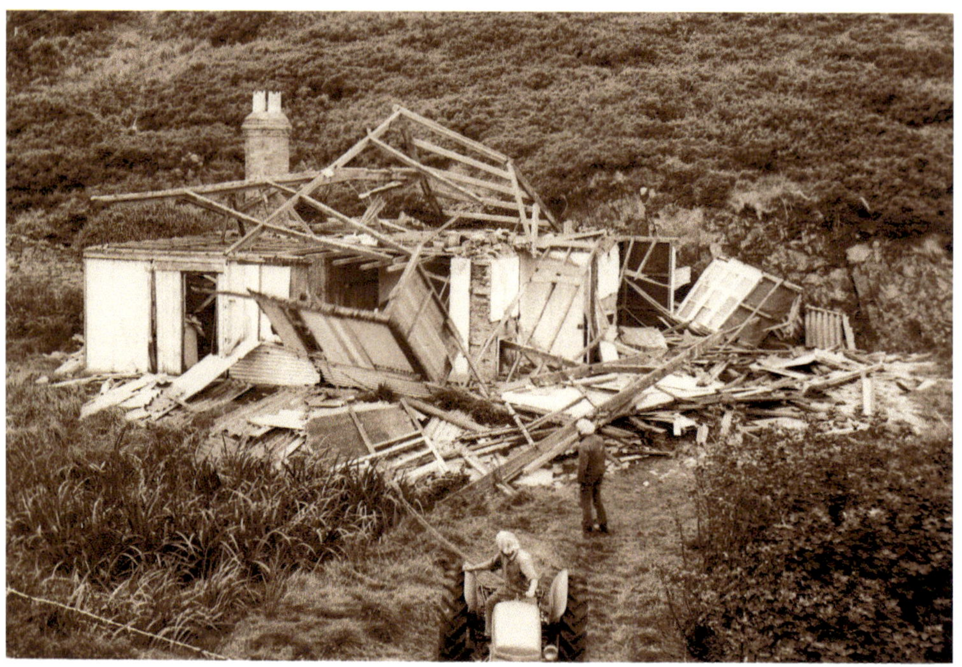

The Replacement of the Bungalow

In 1971, the old bungalow had deteriorated greatly and required replacement. It was pulled down with a tractor and chain in very little time and was converted to firewood just as quickly! The replacement was prefabricated and speedily constructed as the residence for the Island Manager at that time, although not occupied for long in that capacity. The modern building is now divided into two separate holiday units and nestles in a sheltered spot beneath the village. Millcombe House is seen to the right, with the Church of St Helen high above. The blue building is the school room, which was built as a Sunday school in the time of the Heaven family ownership.

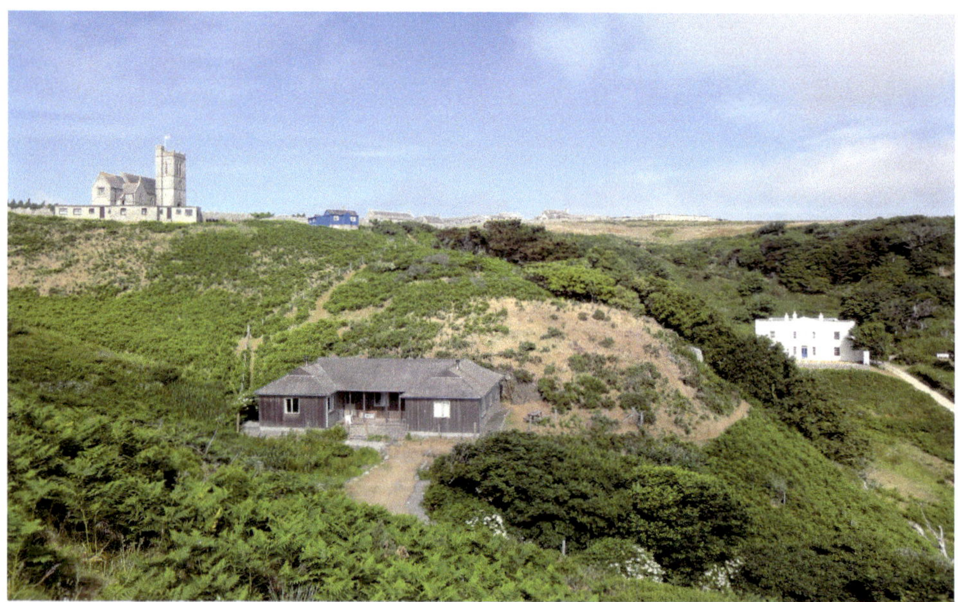

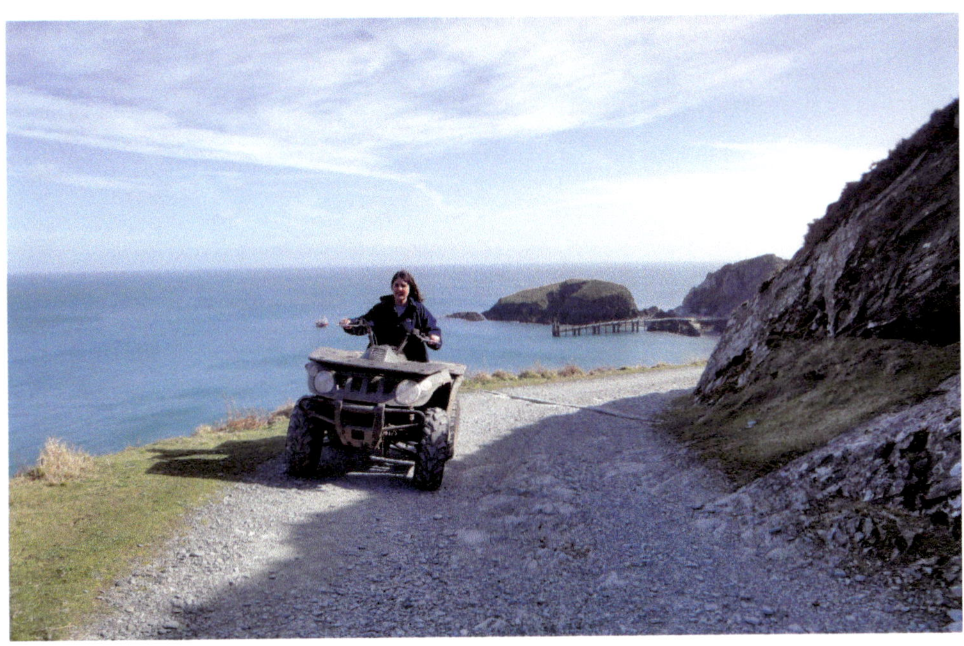

Above, the Lundy Island Warden, Nicola Saunders, makes her way up the beach road at a point known as 'windy corner'. If you stand there in an easterly gale, you'll find out why it gets this name! In modern times, the transport of island staff is generally a quad bike, but in former times a horse and cart was the only means of getting about, as shown below. To negotiate the road with a mechanical vehicle must seem easy compared with the vagaries involved in horse-drawn transportation!

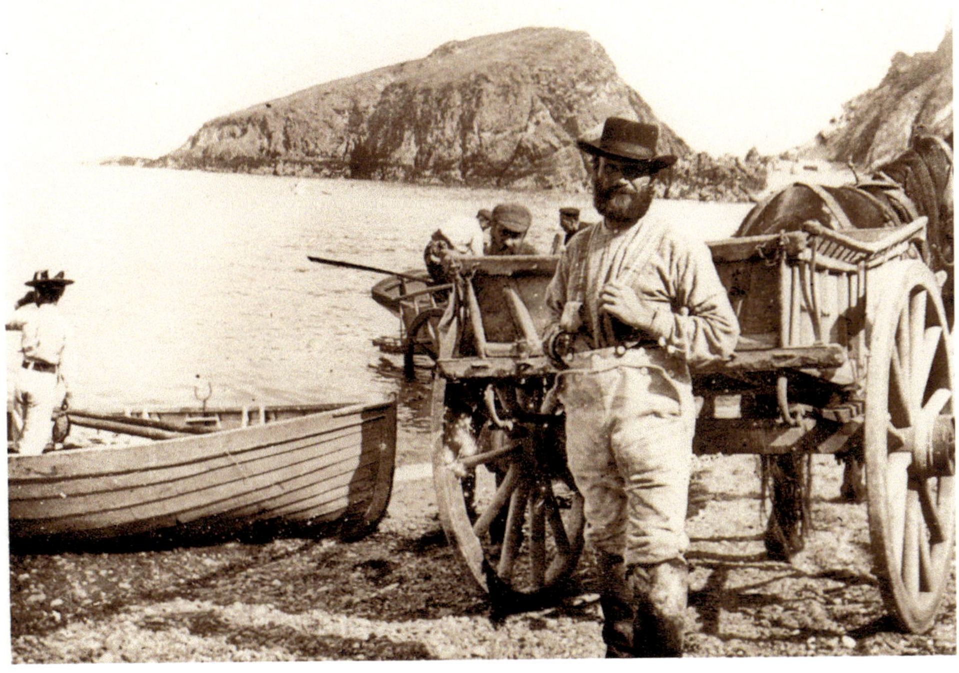

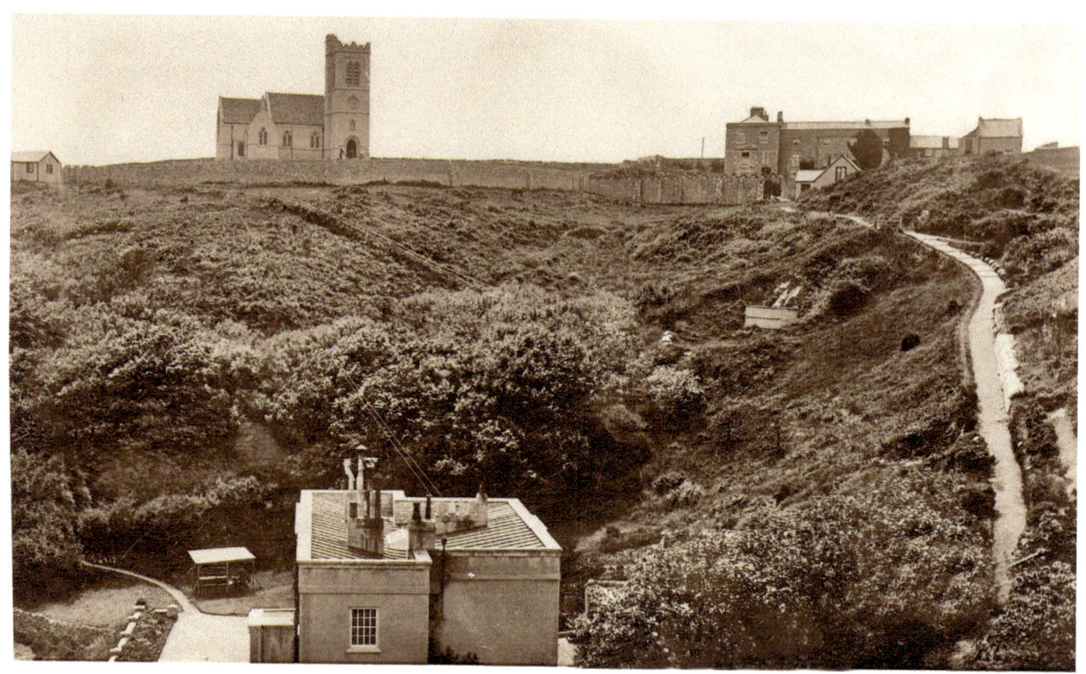

The Village above Millcombe House

Millcombe House nestles quietly below the village and church. Initially, things might not seem to have changed very much, as the older photograph was taken after 1896. However, Government House, the last building to be constructed on the island, is seen in the colour image dominating the top of the valley. The former prefabricated iron church is still seen at the top of the footpath in the older picture. It is also interesting to note the telephone wires in the older photograph, which linked Millcombe House to the village above – cutting-edge technology at the time!

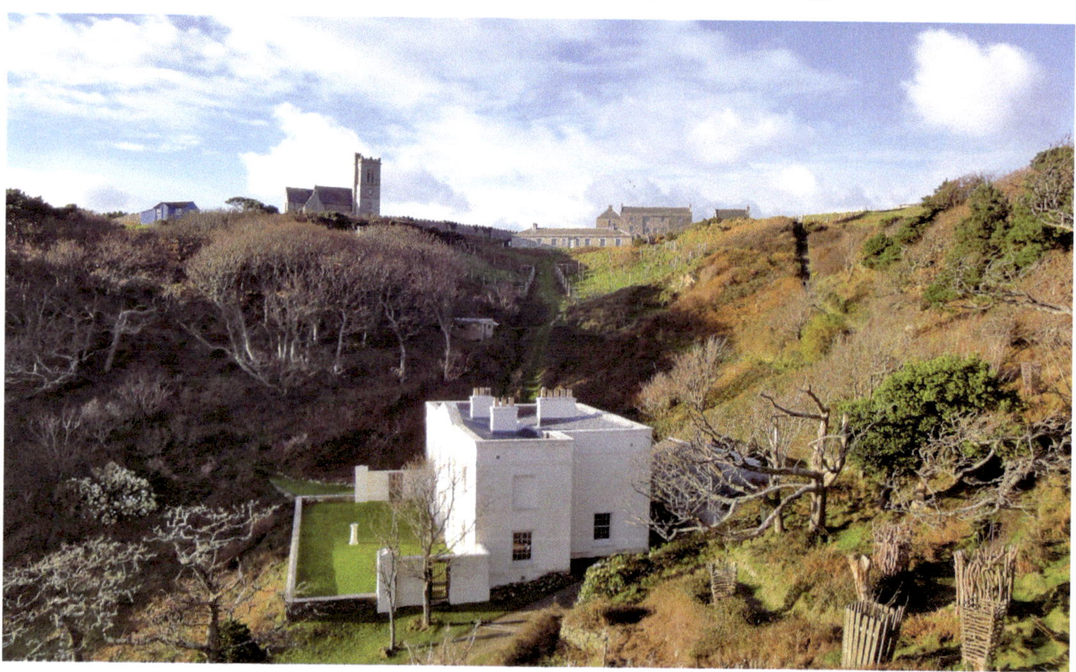

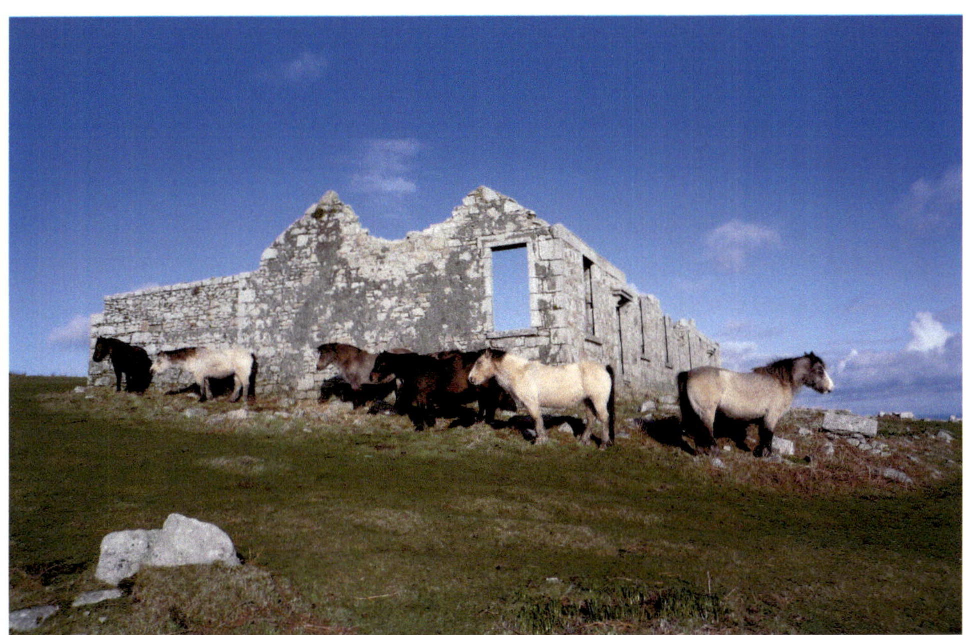

Belle Vue Cottages

Sometimes erroneously referred to as Quarter Wall Cottages, these three dwellings were once the home to the Manager and staff of the quarrying industry, which was somewhat short-lived on Lundy in the 1860s. The nearest cottage was still occupied in 1916, but now they all lie in ruins, high on the east side of the island overlooking the North Devon coast. They are, as can be seen, a favourite and sheltered spot for the Lundy Ponies when the wind is blowing from the west. The door lintel from the centre cottage was removed in the 1980s to be reused as the lintel over the front door of Government House.

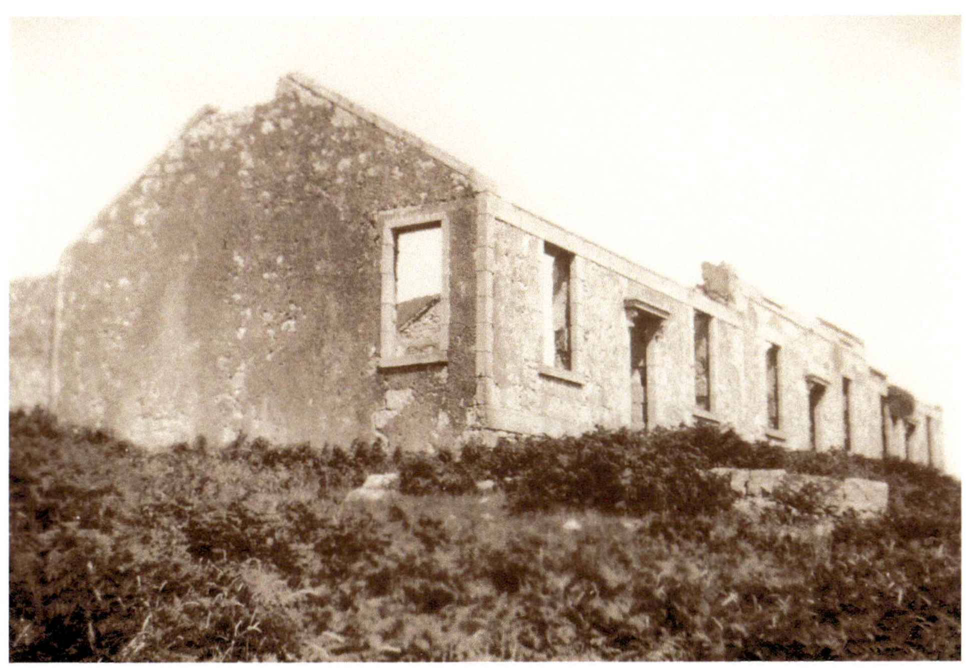

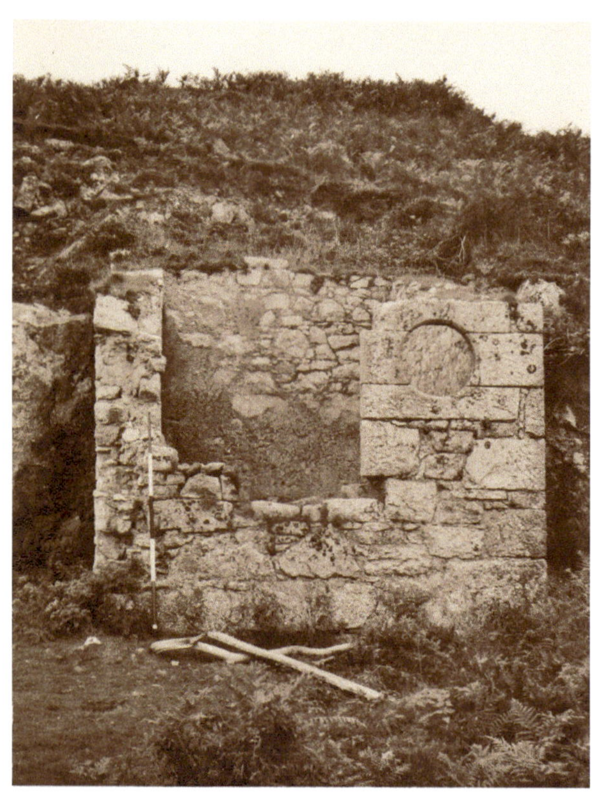

The Time Keeper's Hut

This small granite building, high above the quarries, was the office of the Quarry Timekeeper, and in the round window recess once stood the time-clock. The clock, long since gone, has been replaced by a slate memorial to Felix Gade, who lived for over fifty years on Lundy as Mr Harman's land agent.

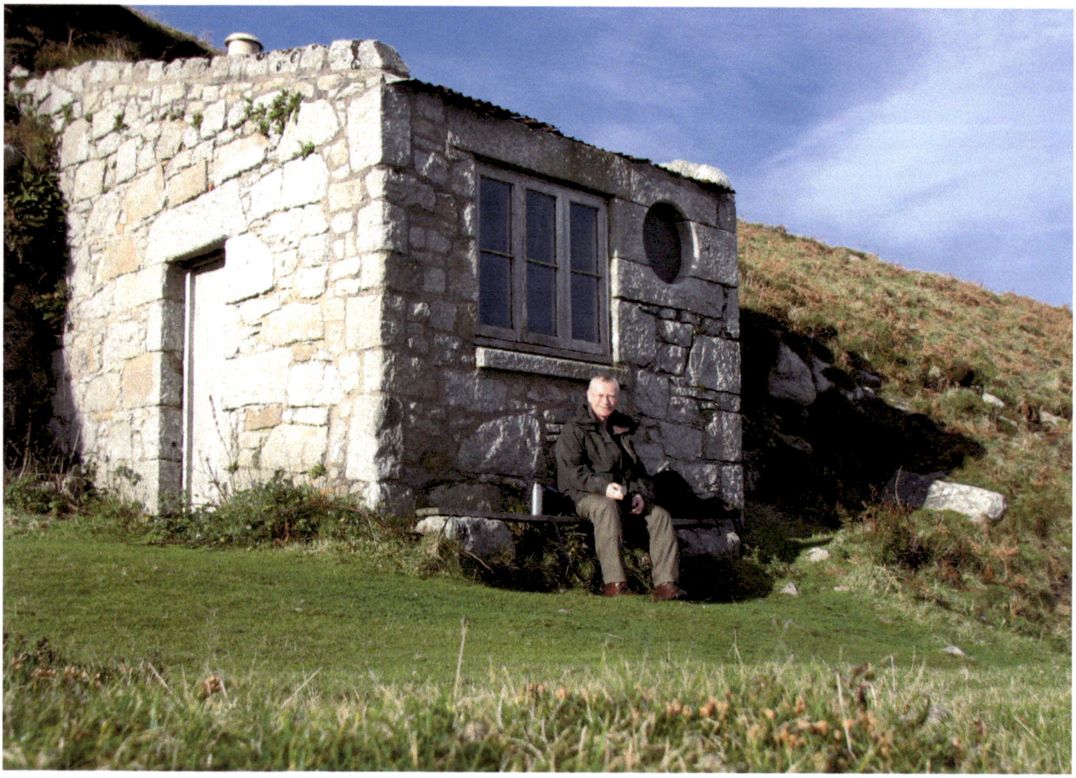

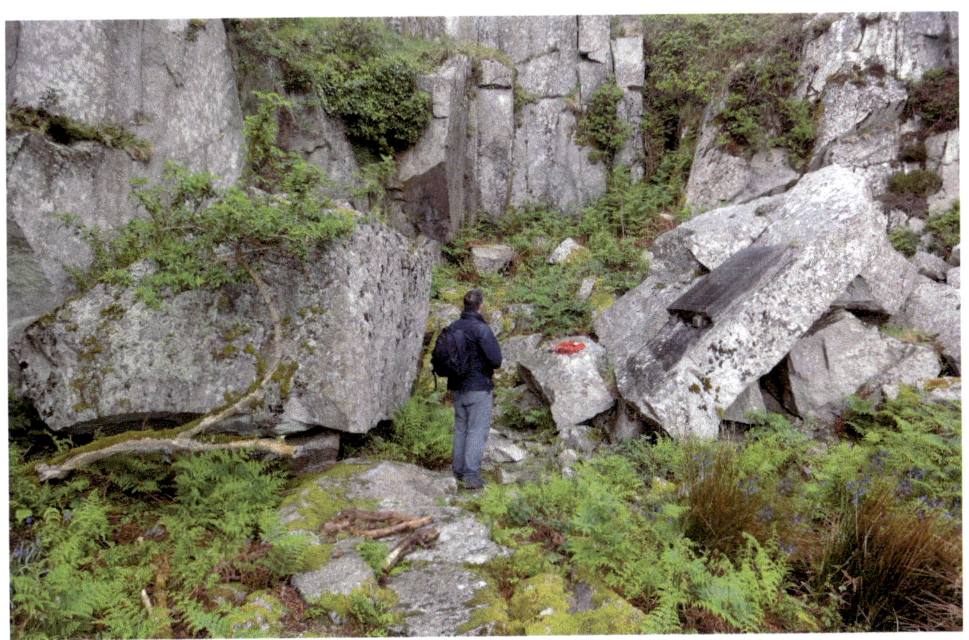

VC Quarry – John Pennington Harman's Memorial

On the tranquil eastern side of the island lies a memorial to a brave young man, John Harman. He was the son of Martin Coles Harman, who owned Lundy during the period of the Second World War. John lost his life at the Battle of Kohima in April 1944, and as a result of his gallantry, he was awarded a posthumous Victoria Cross. A memorial to John Harman was unveiled in 1949, on the fifth anniversary of his death, by his family. His father is pictured (*below, left*) at the ceremony. The quarry, where John played as a boy, is now subsequently known as VC Quarry.

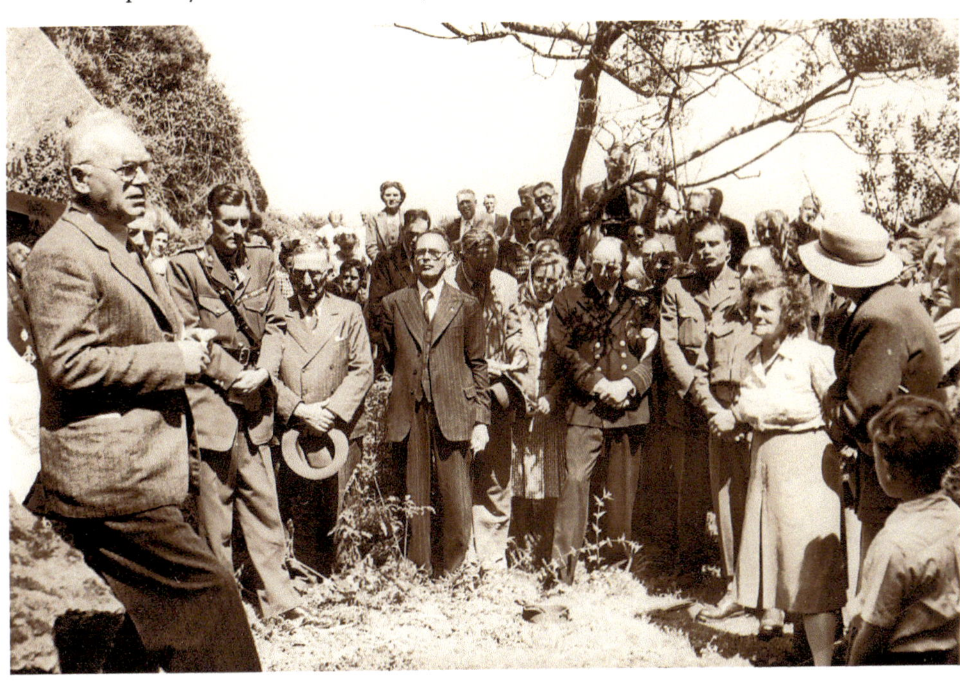

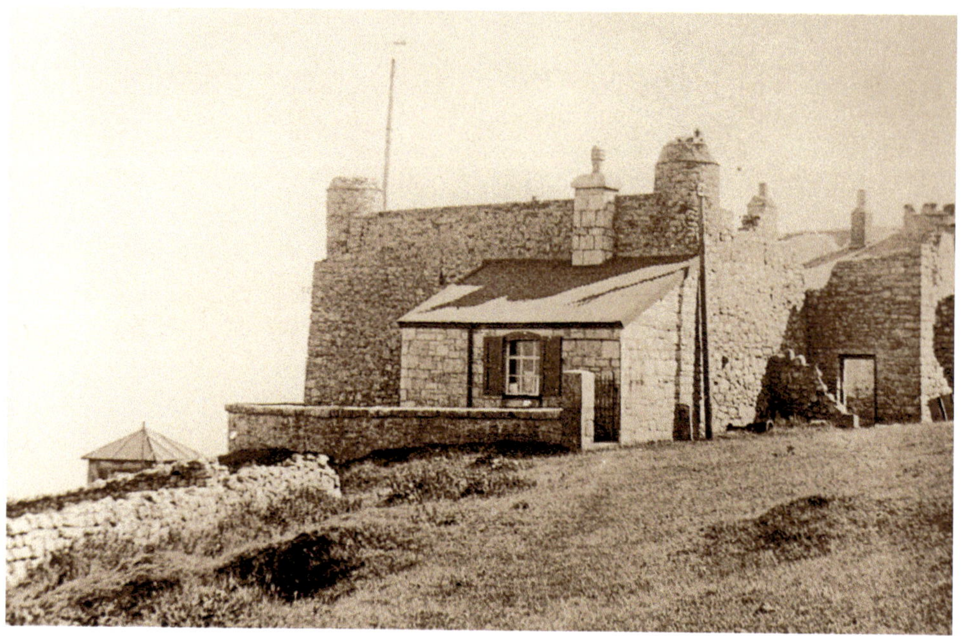

Castle Cottage – the Cable Hut

The Post Office had a granite hut built against the north wall of the Castle Keep in the late nineteenth century to house the terminal of the new submarine-telegraph cable from Croyde. The telephone instrument was in one of the two Signal Cottages behind the castle. The one-roomed cable hut has since been refurbished and extended, and is now known as Castle Cottage, with wonderful views across to North Devon. In the above photograph, the small Signal Station hut can also be seen on the castle parade ground, where Lloyds housed a signal station to pass messages to ships as they voyaged up the Bristol Channel.

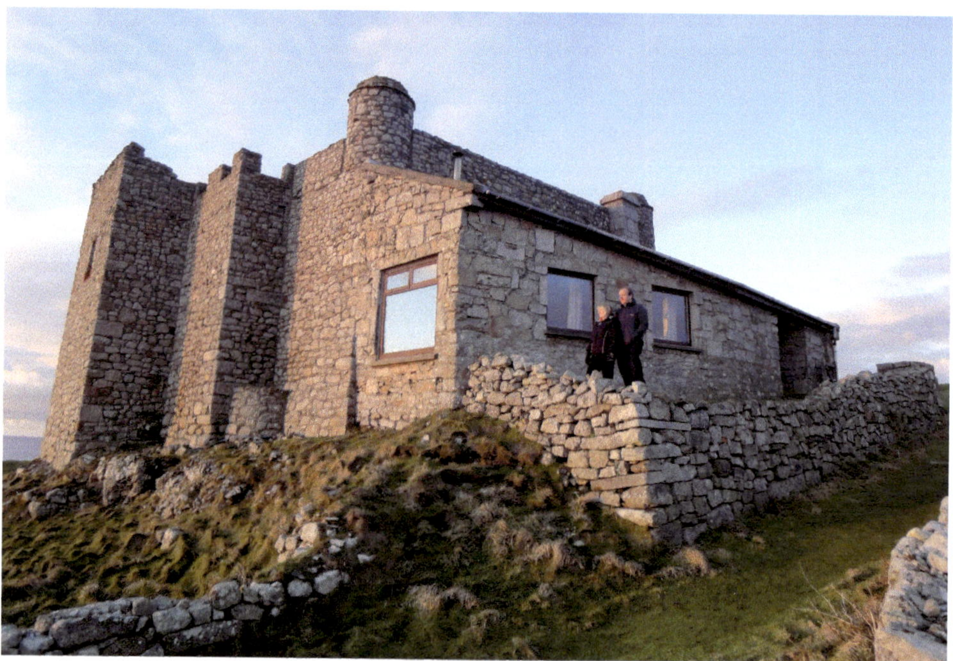

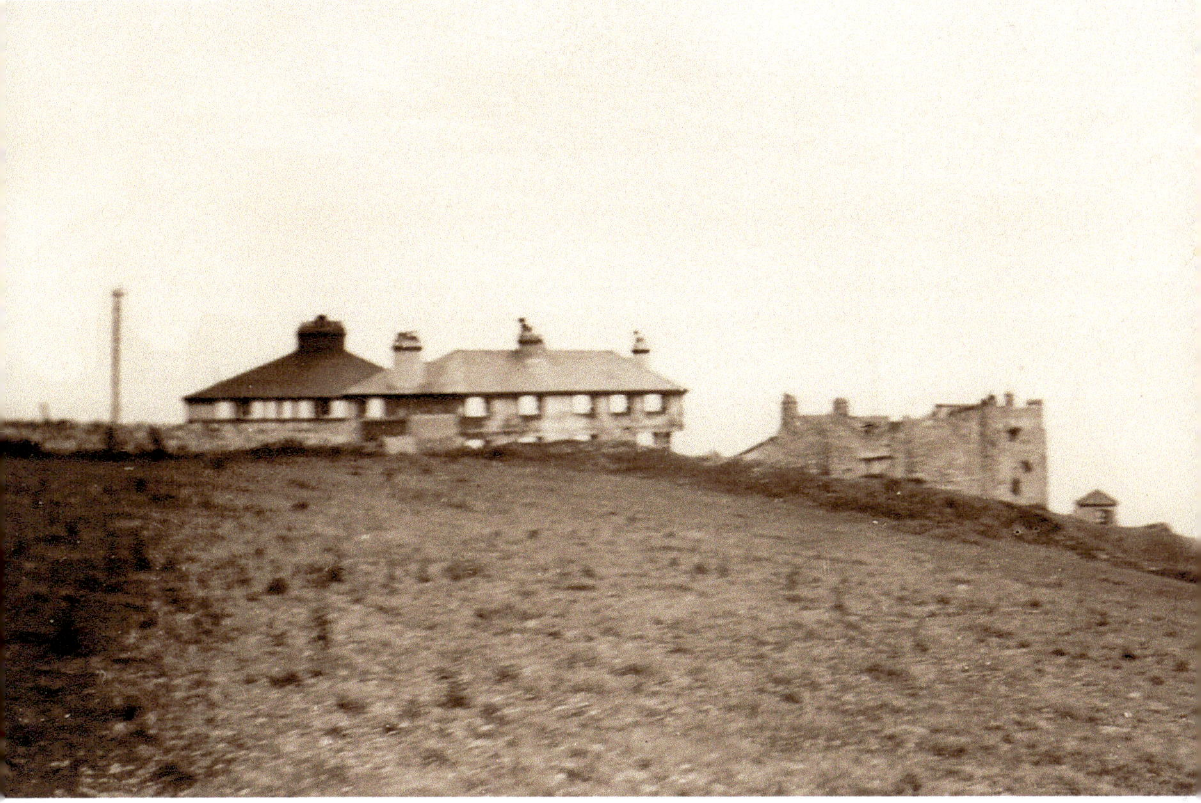

Castle, Signal Cottages and Coastguard Cottages

Very few photographs exist of the old Coastguard Cottages and Signal Cottages, which stood beside the castle overlooking the landing bay. The Lloyds Signal Hut can be seen to the right of the castle (*above*). The only building still remaining is the much-refurbished castle, which comprises four cottages, for rent by holiday-makers. The photograph below clearly shows the far-reaching views across to the North Devon coast in the distance.

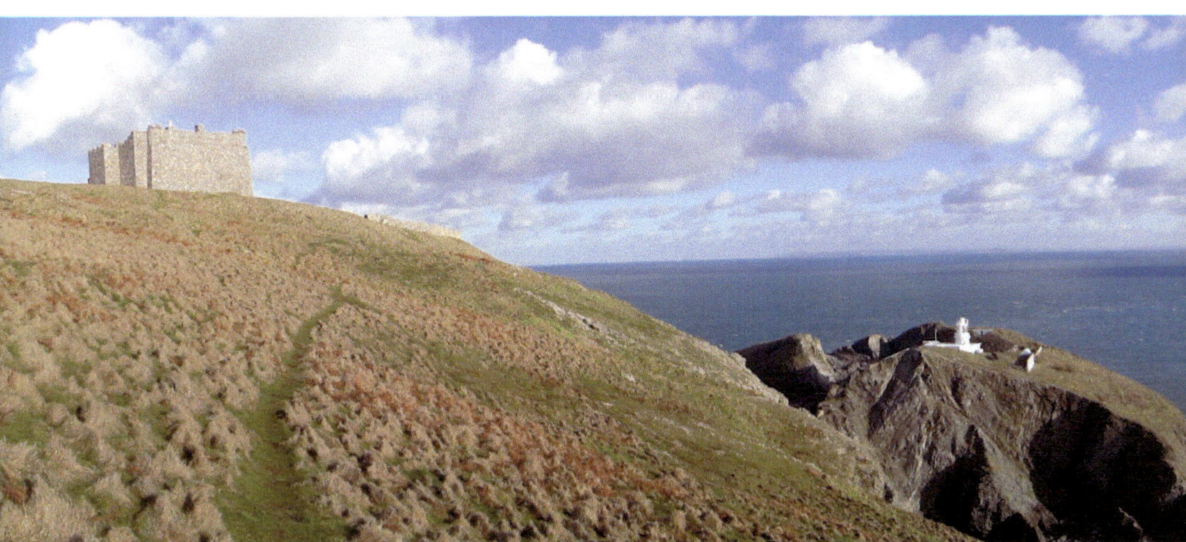

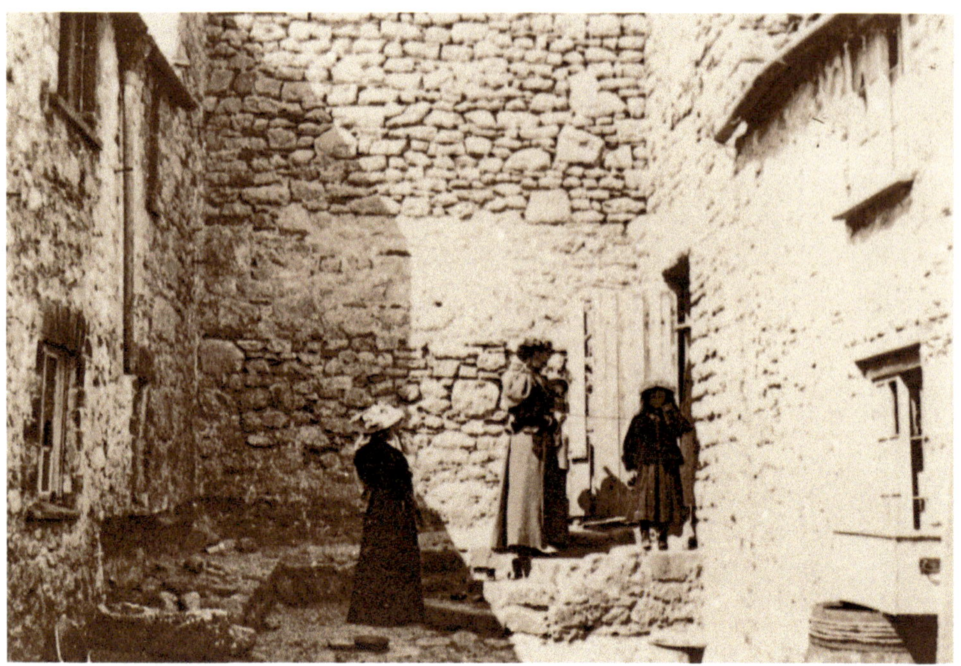

The Castle Keep Interior

The above photograph was taken when The Revd Hudson Heaven owned the island. The Castle Keep cottages were frequently used to house shipwrecked mariners and also used by visiting fishermen. In the 1980s, the cottages were refurbished to provide three dwellings for rental. In the small group pictured above, on the steps leading out of the castle confines, is (on the far right) Sylvia Heaven the great-granddaughter of William Heaven.

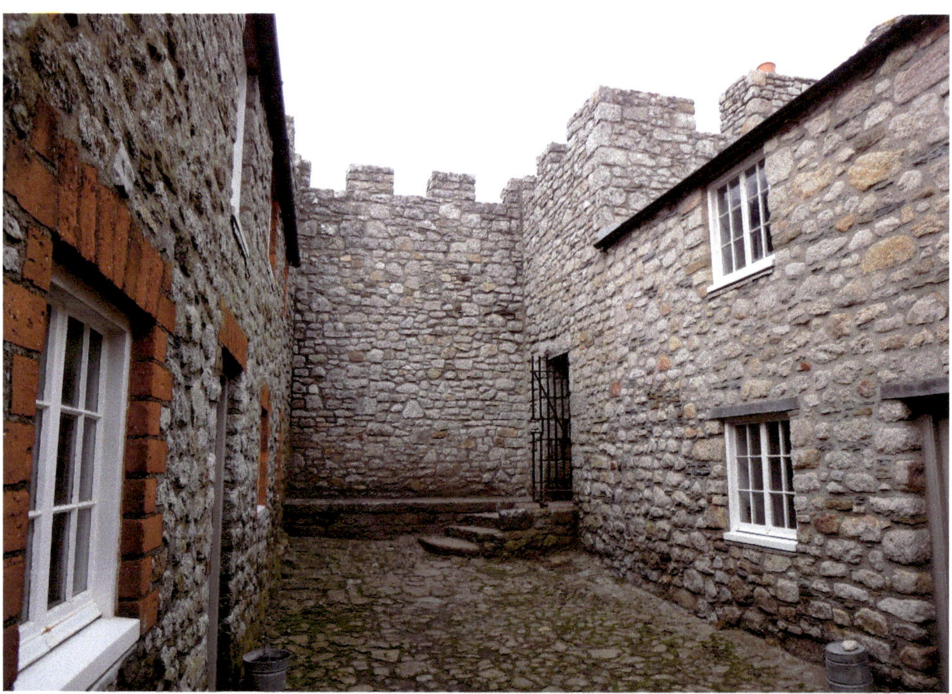

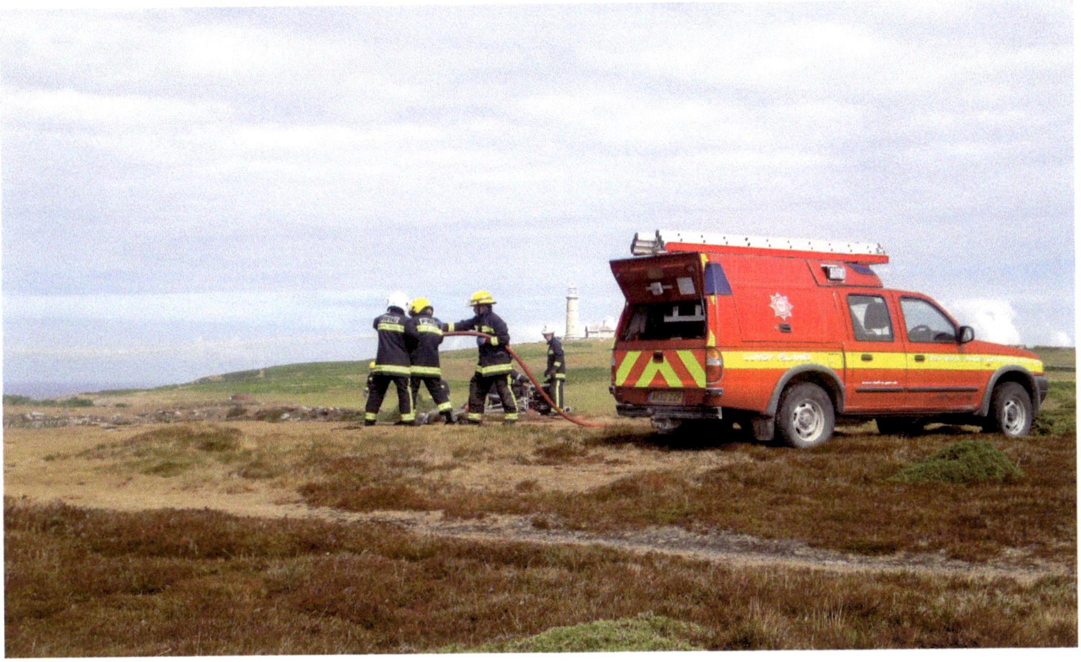

Firefighters and Rescue Equipment

The photograph above shows the Lundy crew of the Devon & Somerset Fire & Rescue Service on one of their regular practice training days at Rocket Pole Pond, with the Old Light in the background. Rescue equipment has been housed on the island since the nineteenth century, when breeches-buoy equipment was used to save the lives of shipwrecked sailors. In the lower picture, Mr Gade, second from the right, is seen supervising the rescue rocket apparatus training.

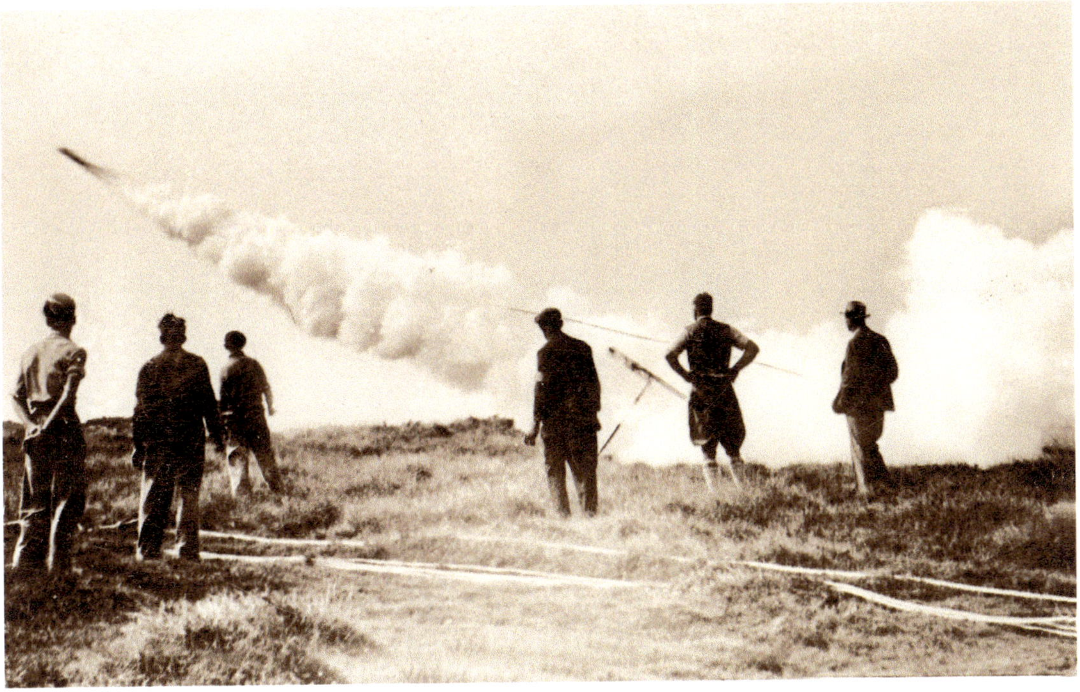

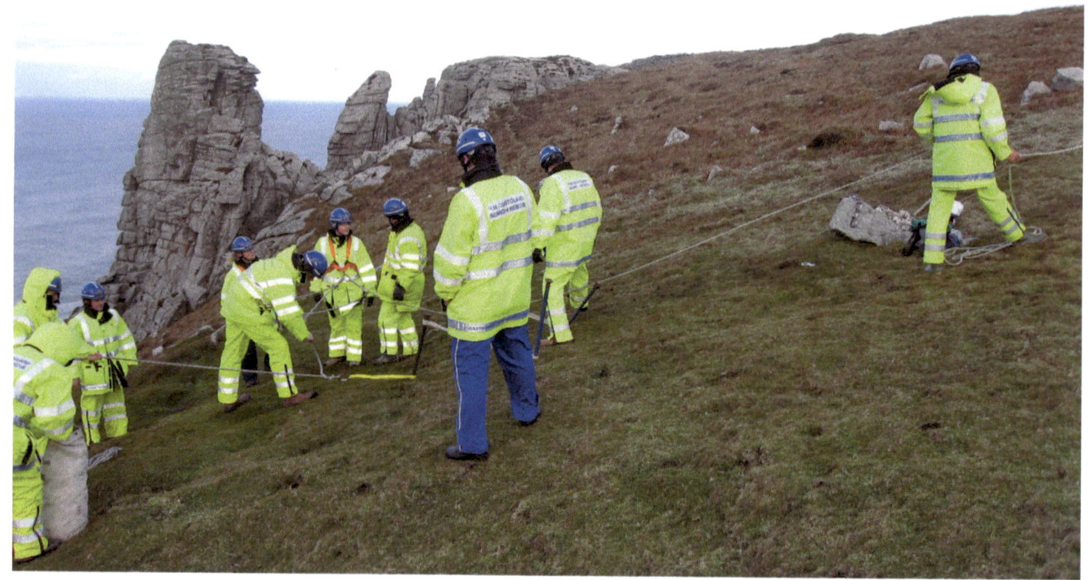

The Coastguard, Old and New

The Coastguard has watched over our shores for many years in various guises. The photograph above shows the modern-day island coastguard section practising cliff rescue techniques. The team is made up from volunteer island staff. Below, island inhabitants also took on the responsibilities, as seen in this late-nineteenth-century image of the coastguard rescue rocket apparatus team. Their equipment was housed in the village, in the shed now used as the visitor exhibition building.

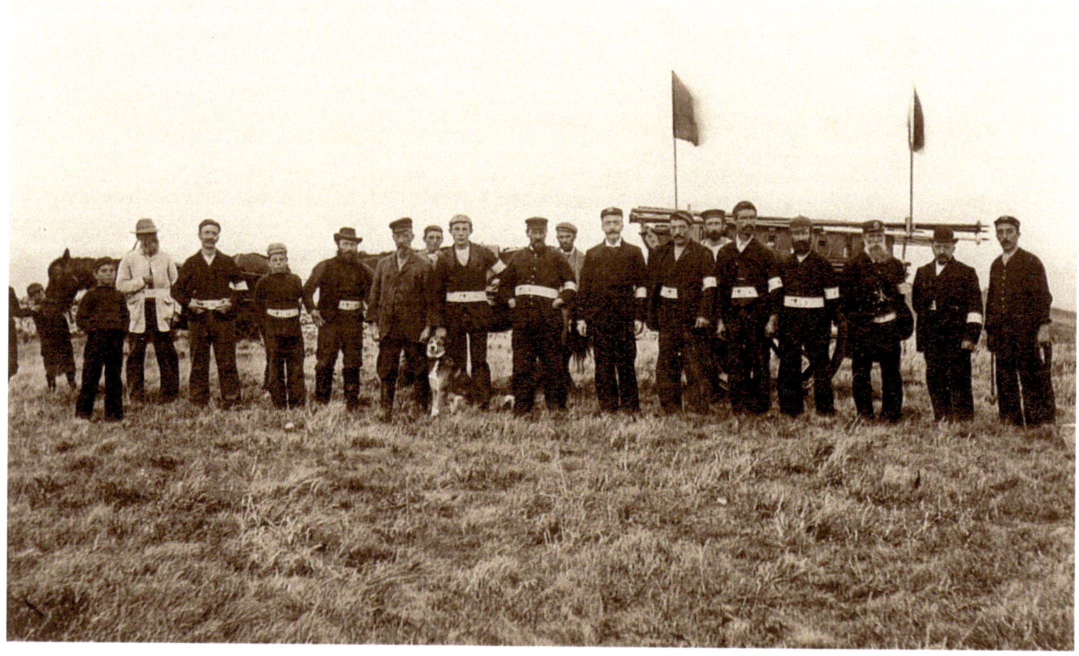

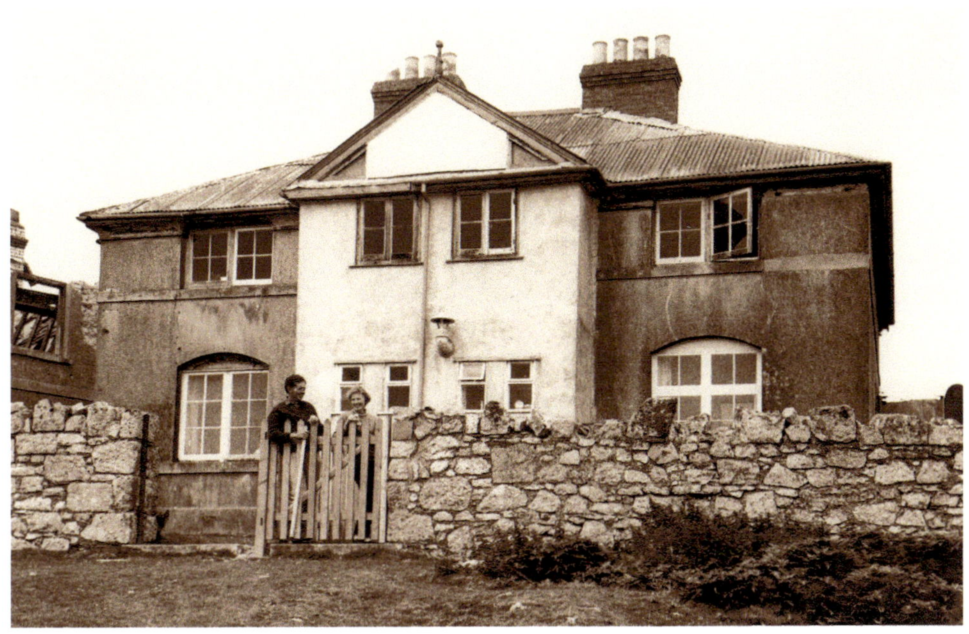

Signal Cottages

Above, John and Joan Dyke are pictured outside their island home at Signal Cottages in the mid-1970s. These houses have long since gone, along with the derelict coastguard cottages that can just be seen to the left, demolished about the time of the refurbishment of the nearby castle for holidaymakers. John was the island artist and his work has become much sought-after. The modern photograph (*below*) pictures the castle from the South Light, and shows how the castle now stands as a solitary sentinel above the landing bay, where it occupied a position with its near-neighbour the Signal Cottages.

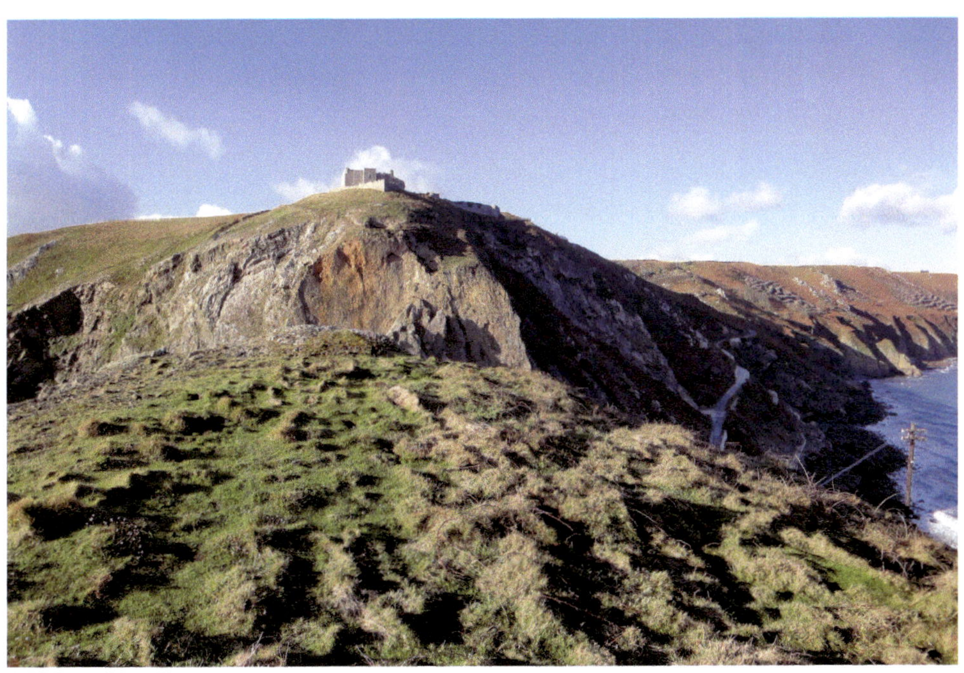

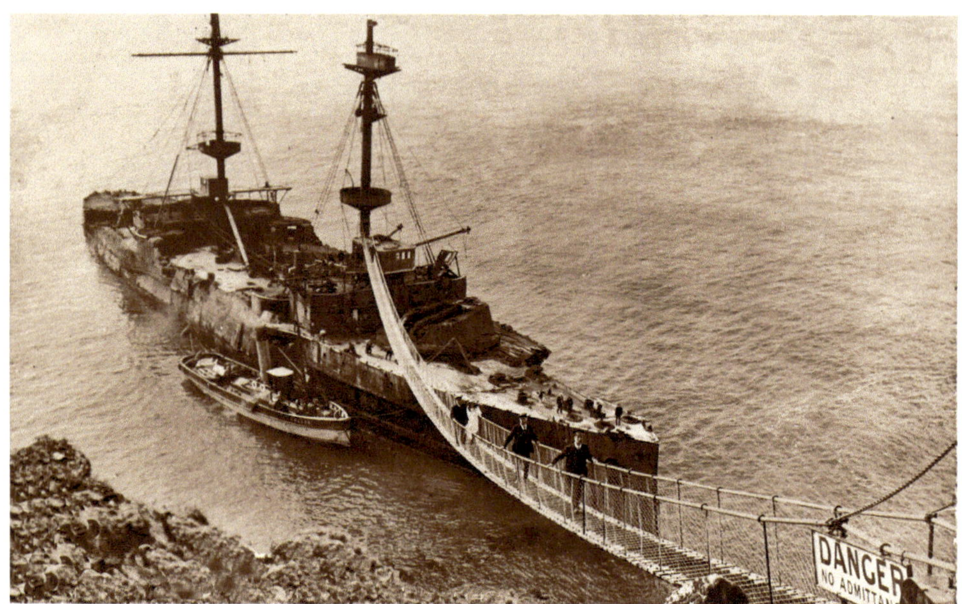

The Wreck of HMS *Montagu*

In 1906, a very new battleship of the naval fleet was engaged in manoeuvres in the Bristol Channel in thick fog. The captain, upon hearing the fog signal of the South Light, mistook it as being the signal from Hartland Point lighthouse. Thus he steered north and collided with Shutter Rock on the south-west tip of Lundy. It took some significant persuading to have him believe he was on Lundy and not on the North Devon coast! The ship lay wrecked for over a decade, whilst as much as possible was salvaged, before it slipped off into the depths. All that remains are the somewhat flimsy-looking stakes on the cliff top, as well as rusting cables, which once held the suspension footbridge that crossed from the island to the ship.

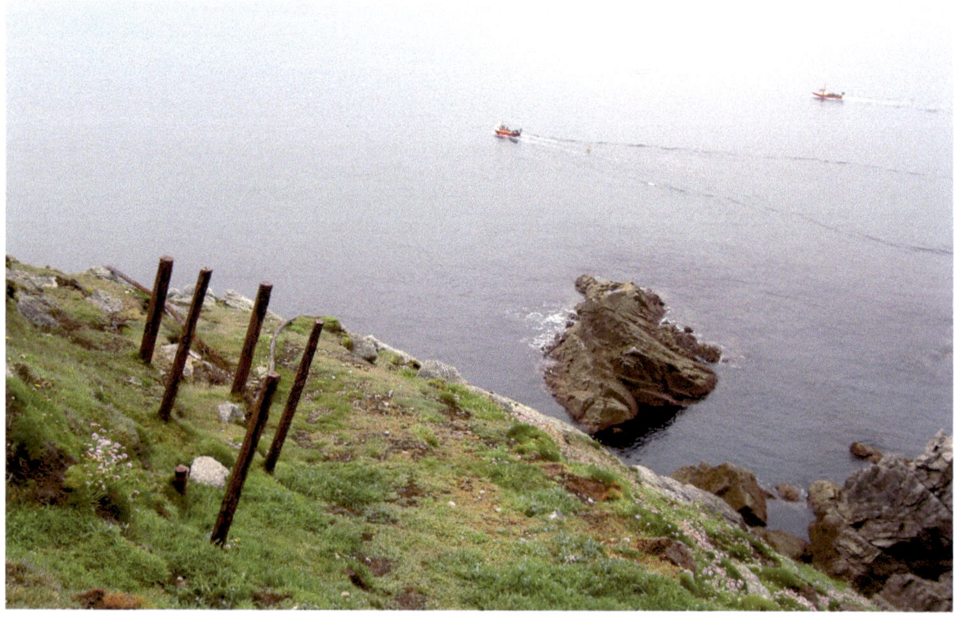

The Montagu Steps

Not actually associated with the wreck of HMS *Montagu*, a series of steps and an iron ladder were constructed near to the site of the wrecking of the *Montagu*. These were built when the island was in the ownership of the Christie family in the early 1920s and were intended as a west-side landing, during periods of easterly gales. The steep granite steps and some of the railings still remain, as can be seen below, but coastal erosion has made the path down to the Montagu Steps a challenging and vertiginous experience not recommended for anyone other than the most sure-footed mountain goat!

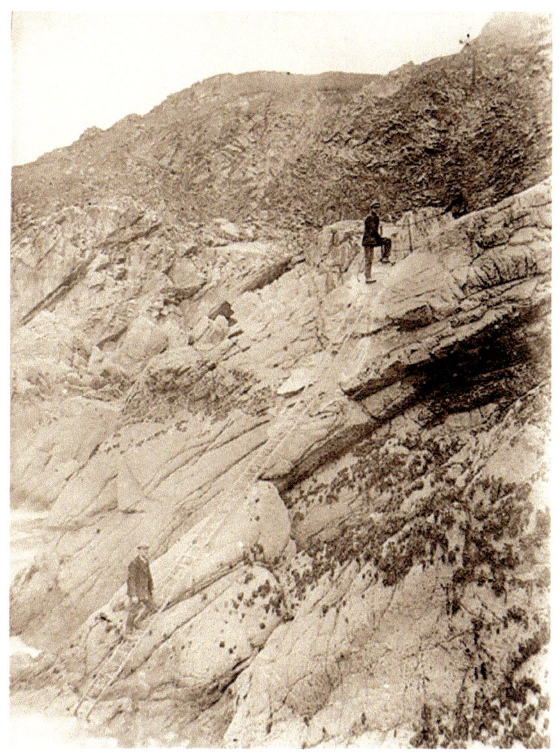

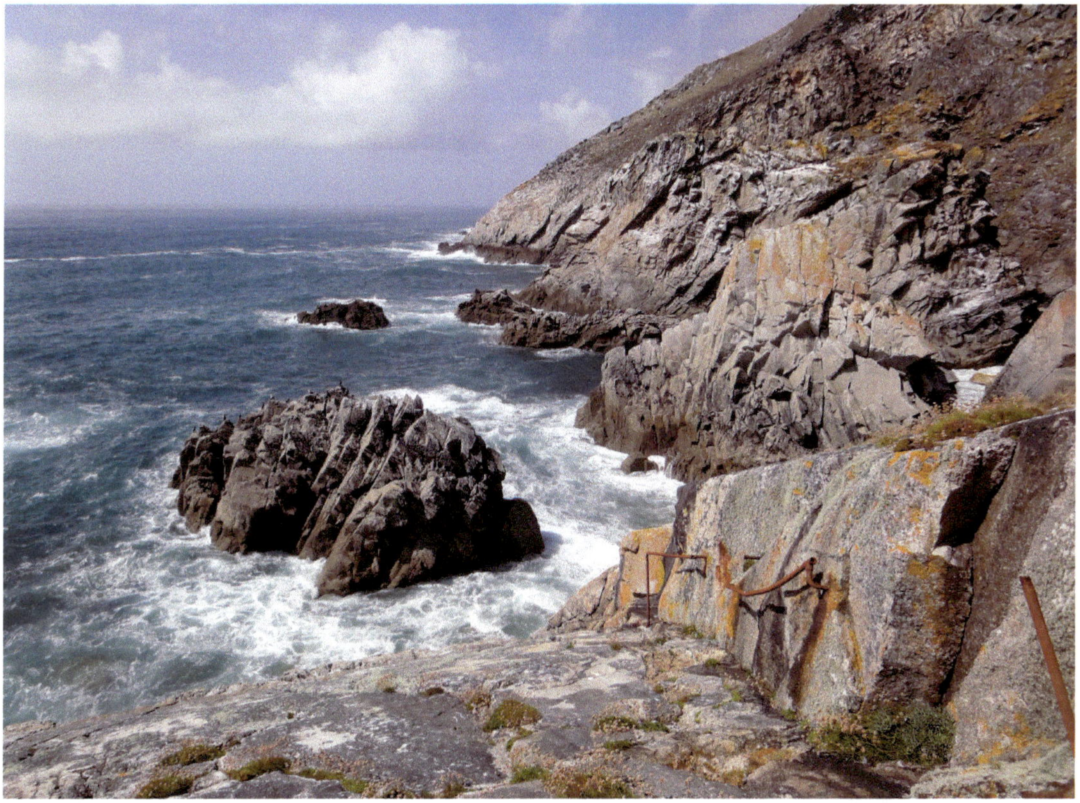

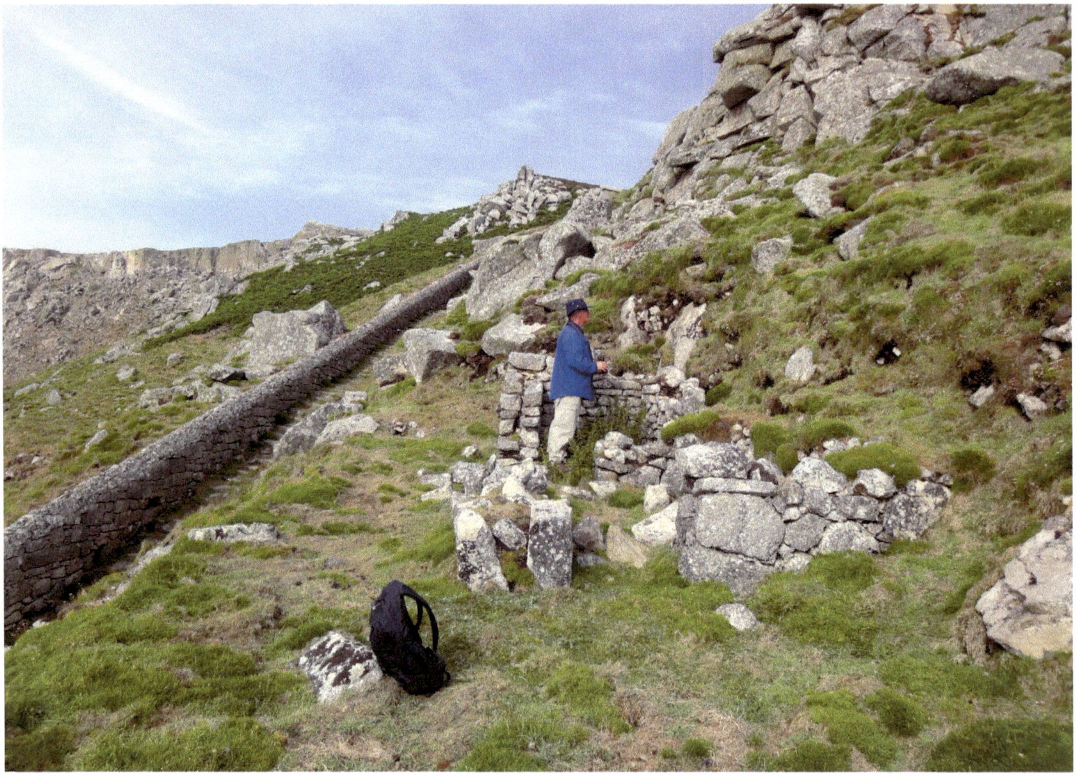

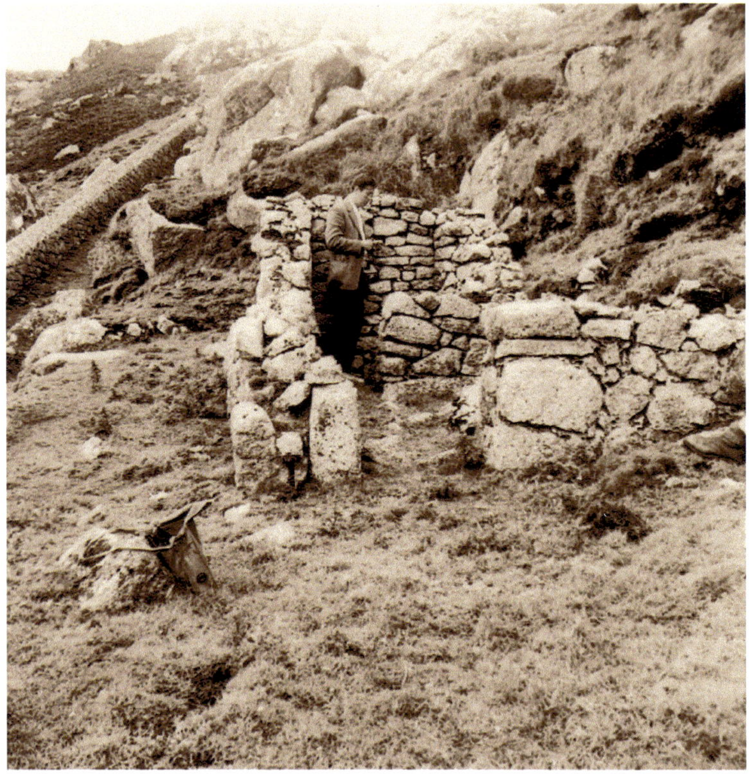

Lying just above the isolated cottages of the fog signal station is a ruin of a small building, probably a pigsty associated with the signal station keepers during the last half of the nineteenth century. The steep and exhausting steps that lead down to the fog signal station can be seen passing by on the left.

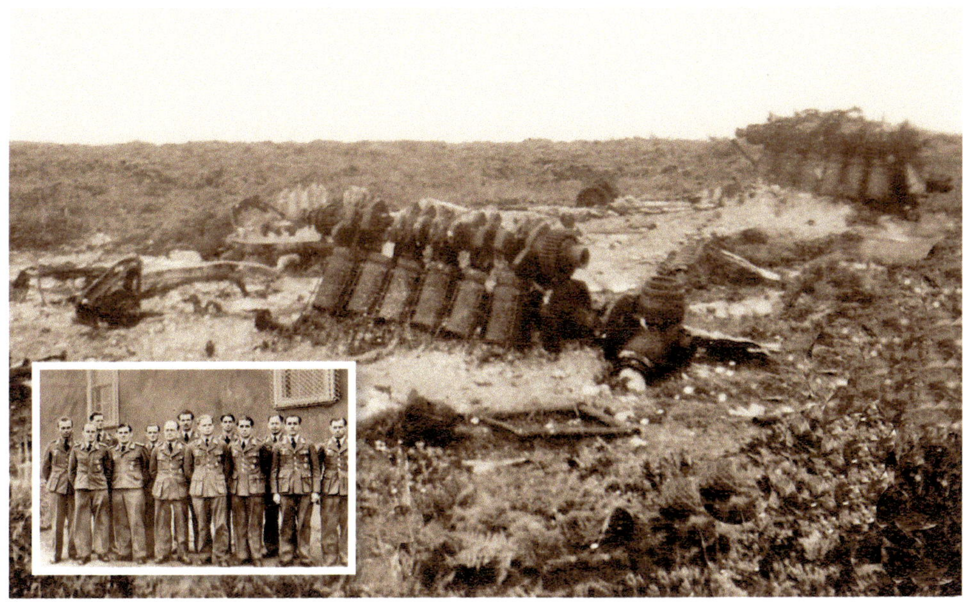

The Crashed Heinkel Bomber

The remains of a Heinkel III German bomber that crashed on Lundy Island, near to the halfway wall, on 3 March 1941. Fortunately, the crew all survived and surrendered themselves to a passing lighthouse keeper! Unfortunately, he was so worried that he gave them back their weapons and went for help, giving them time to destroy their aircraft by fire. Mr Gade and his island Home Guard took the crew into custody (some of whom are pictured in the insert), and they remained in a prisoner of war camp in Canada. Very little is left of the aircraft as can be seen in a recent photograph (*below*).

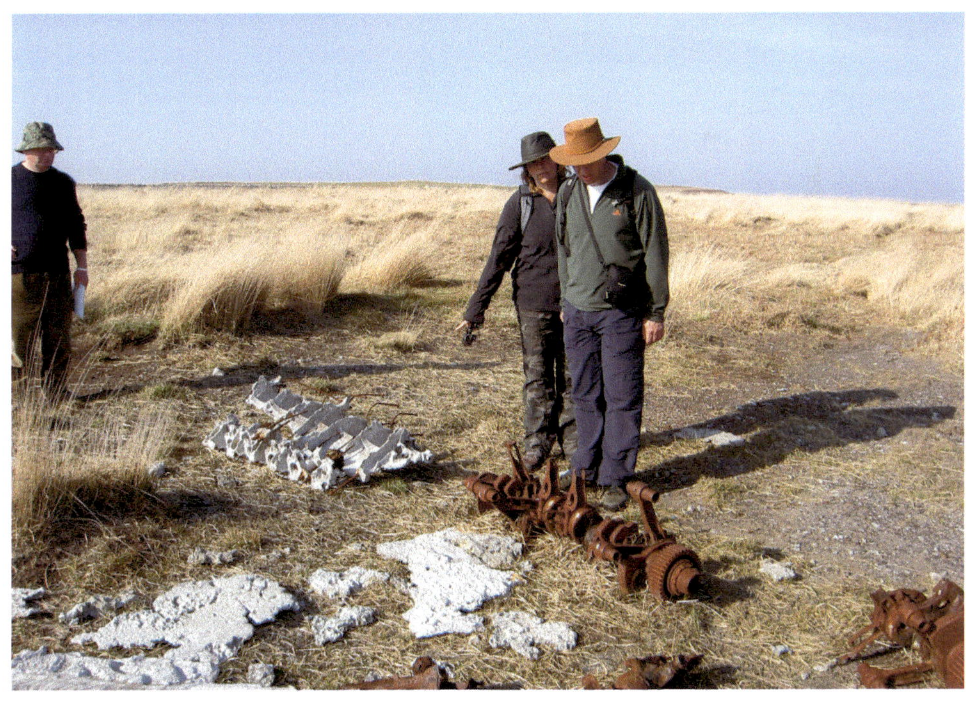

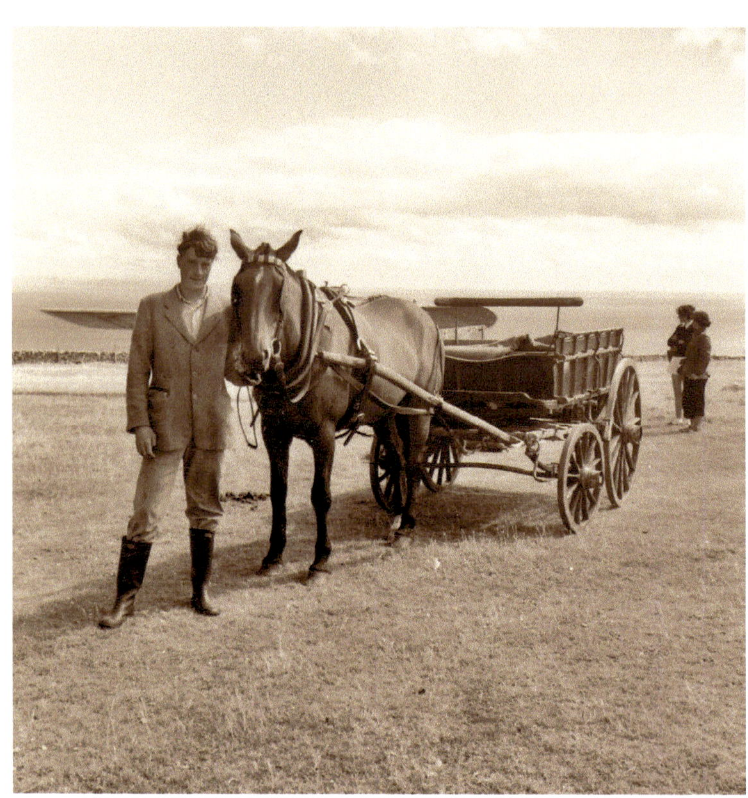

Transportation of Luggage for Visitors
The photograph to the left, from the 1950s, shows John Vicary and his horse 'Gayboy' collecting luggage from an aircraft that landed on the airstrip up by the Old Light. John used to hire himself out to transport visitors and take their baggage to the island hotel. In contrast (*below*) all the luggage of visitors is quickly unloaded from the *Oldenburg* onto a trailer for transportation up to the village and to properties.

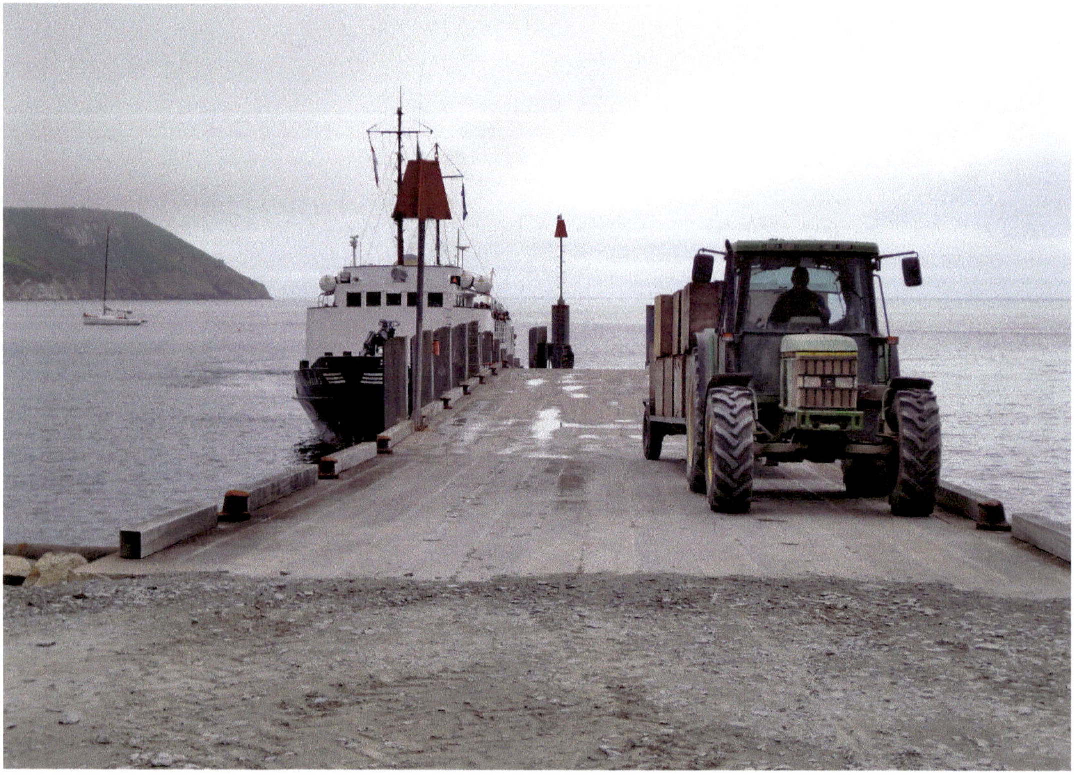

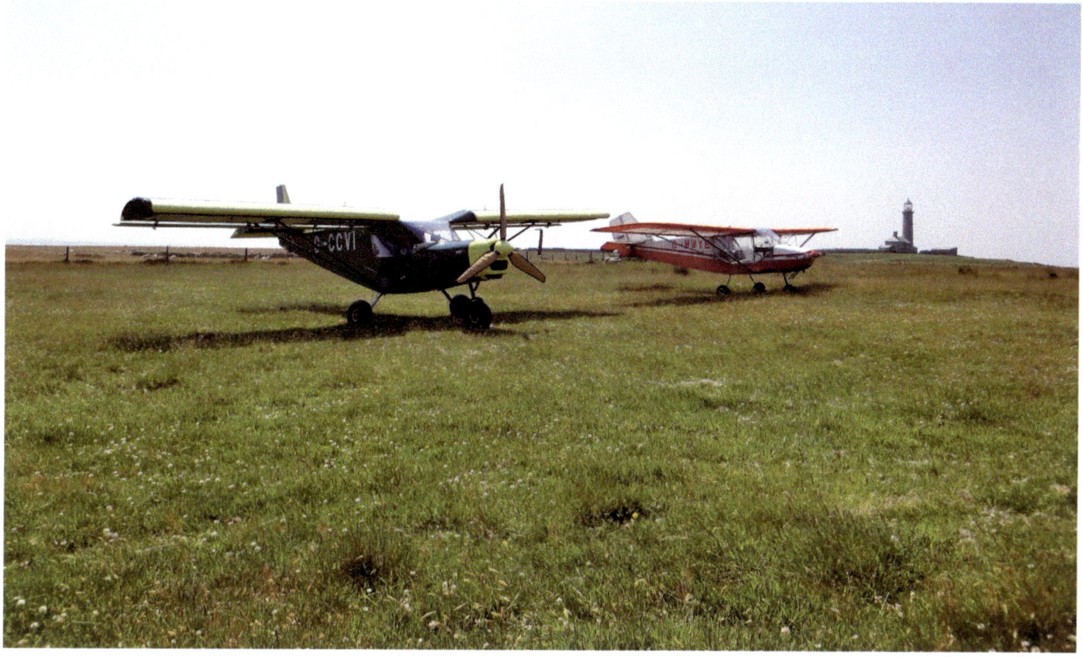

Aircraft on the Lundy Airstrip

Above, two small private aircraft are seen on the fixed-wing landing strip, which is situated on Acland's Moor to the north of the Old Light. Small aeroplanes are frequent visitors to the island. Mr Harman established the air service in 1934 using the aerodrome near Barnstaple, which is now known as Chivenor, the home to the RAF Search and Rescue Flight. Below is pictured one of those early aircraft, a de Havilland Dragon Rapide, delivering passengers and goods to Lundy.

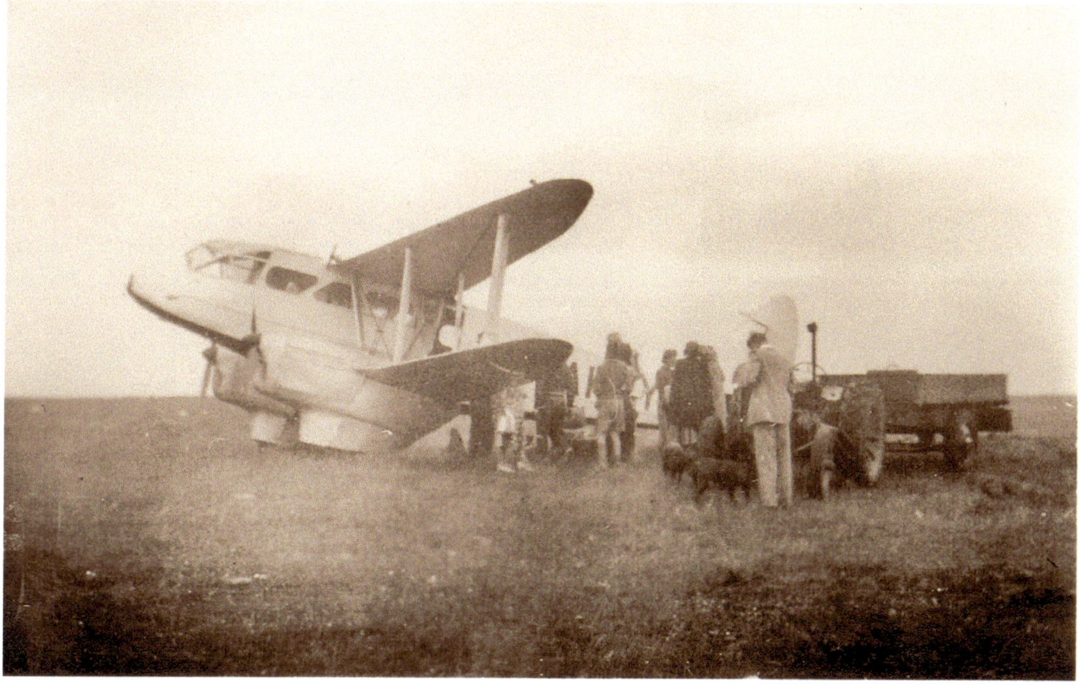

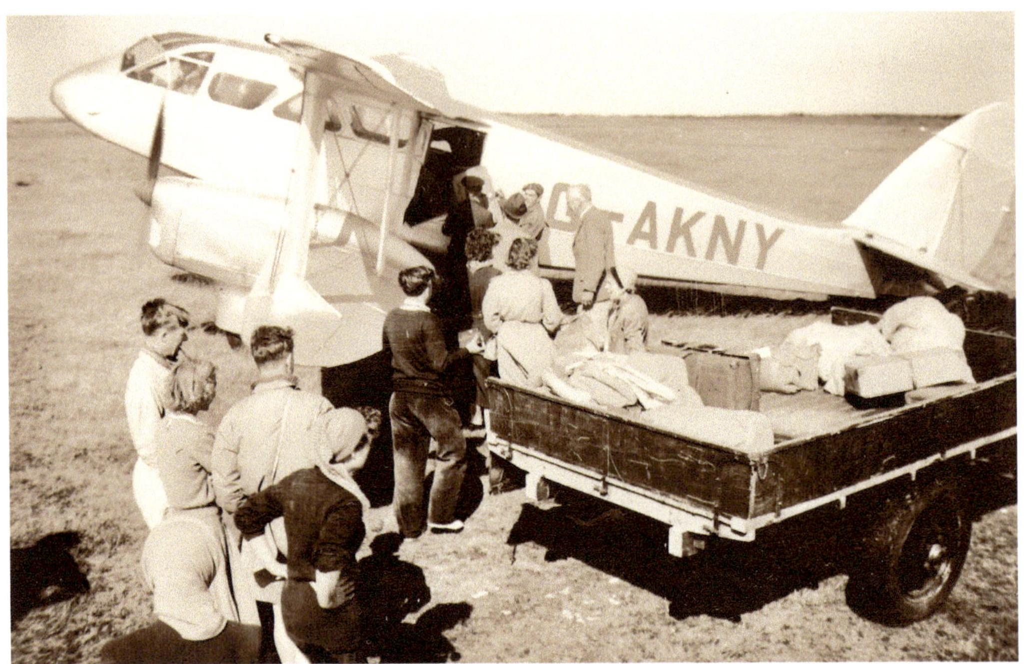

Lundy International Departure Flights!

Whilst the local flights in the mid-twentieth century were invariably from the local aerodrome, near Barnstaple, some aircraft came from further afield. Below, seen making a double circuit, is a private visitor from Somerset. The landing strip often has sheep on it, so a first fly-past is necessary to persuade the sheep to move out of the way to facilitate a landing, difficult enough with a large lighthouse in the way! Some things on Lundy simply never change – the winter flights by helicopter in the twenty-first century also involve a small trailer and tractor!

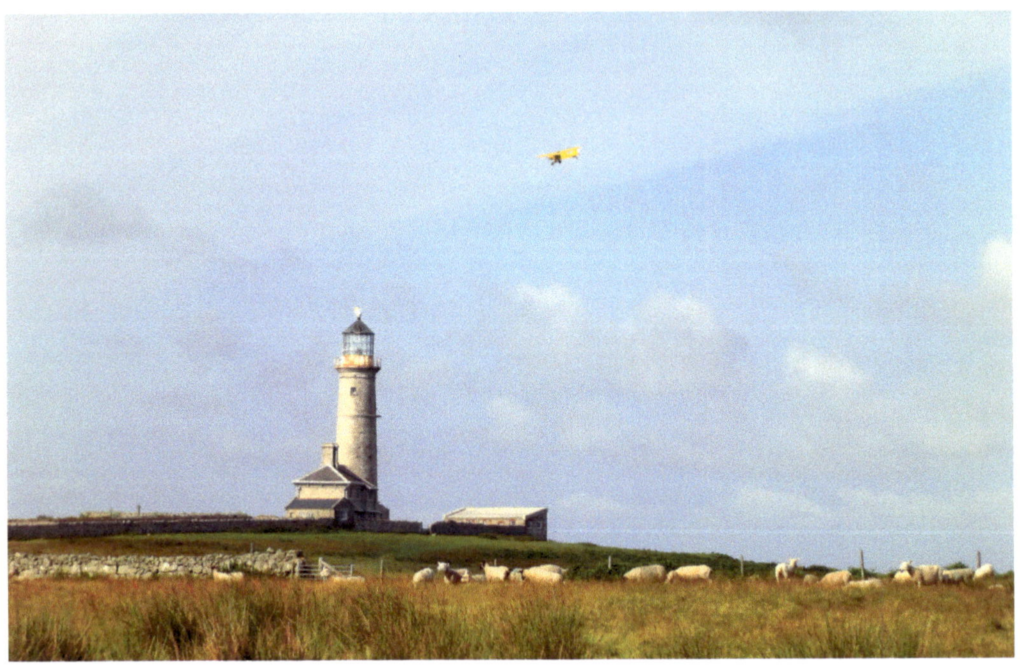

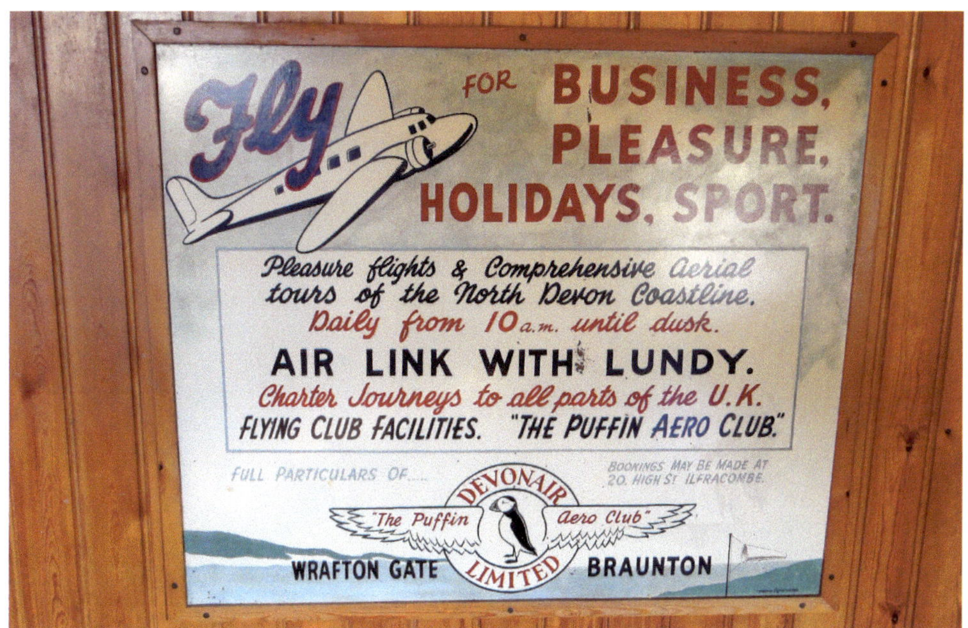

The Puffin Aero Club

If the Himalayan airport at Kathmandu can have a 'Yeti Airline' flight, so Lundy can have the 'Puffin Aero Club' flights! Above, a large advertising board promotes the flights from North Devon to Lundy Island. This board now adorns the lounge wall of the Barn accommodation in the village. A ticket from the 1950s (*below*) displays the price of a 17/6 return from the North Devon Aerodrome – if only prices remained the same!

TRAVEL BY AIR TO
LUNDY ISLAND

(THE ISLAND YOU WILL VISIT AGAIN AND AGAIN).

Your Holiday will be incomplete without a Visit to this Historic and Beautiful Isle.

Excursions by Air 17/6 return

COMFORTABLE TRAVEL.
FREQUENT SERVICES.
MANY HOURS ON ISLAND.

BOOKINGS MAY BE MADE HERE

OR AT THE AERODROME.

LUNDY AND ATLANTIC COASTS AIR LINES, LTD.,

NORTH DEVON AERODROME.

TEL. BRAUNTON 121.

HEANTON COURT, BARNSTAPLE.

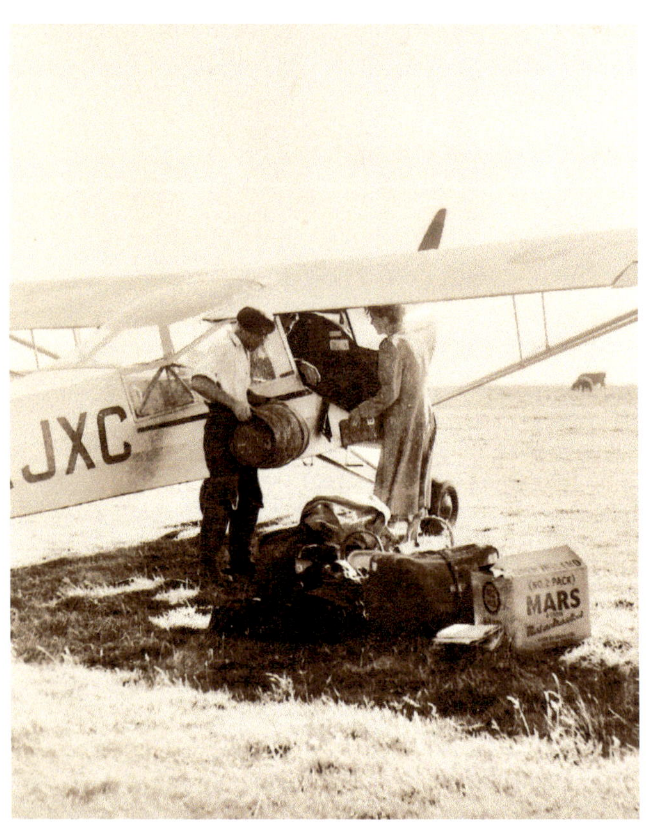

Private Flights to Lundy

The older photograph (*left*) shows a small privately owned aircraft being loaded on the airstrip. Once Mr Harman had opened up the island to flights after the 1930s, those rich enough to own an aircraft were able to make weekend visits. In modern times, private flights are also made from numerous airfields on the coast. Frequent visitors in their bright-yellow aeroplane are Dave Berger and his son Max (*below*). The large whitewashed boulders to the right of the photograph mark the landing strip, and they can be mistaken for sheep from the air, hence the fly-past before landing to move the sheep away!

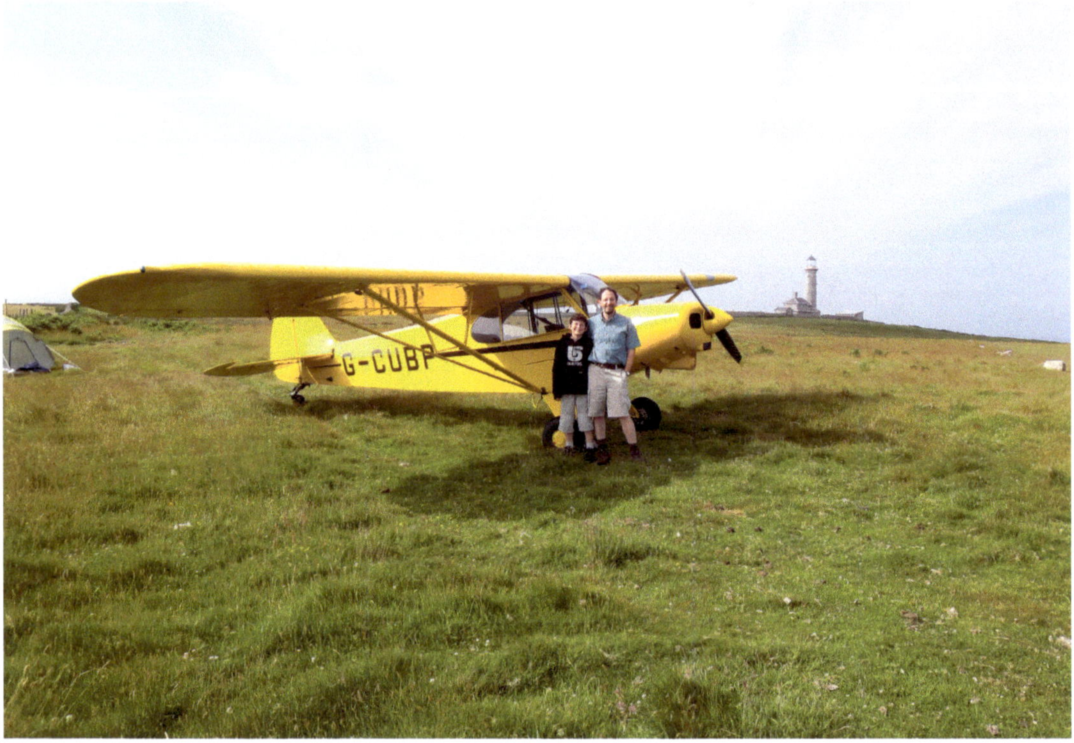

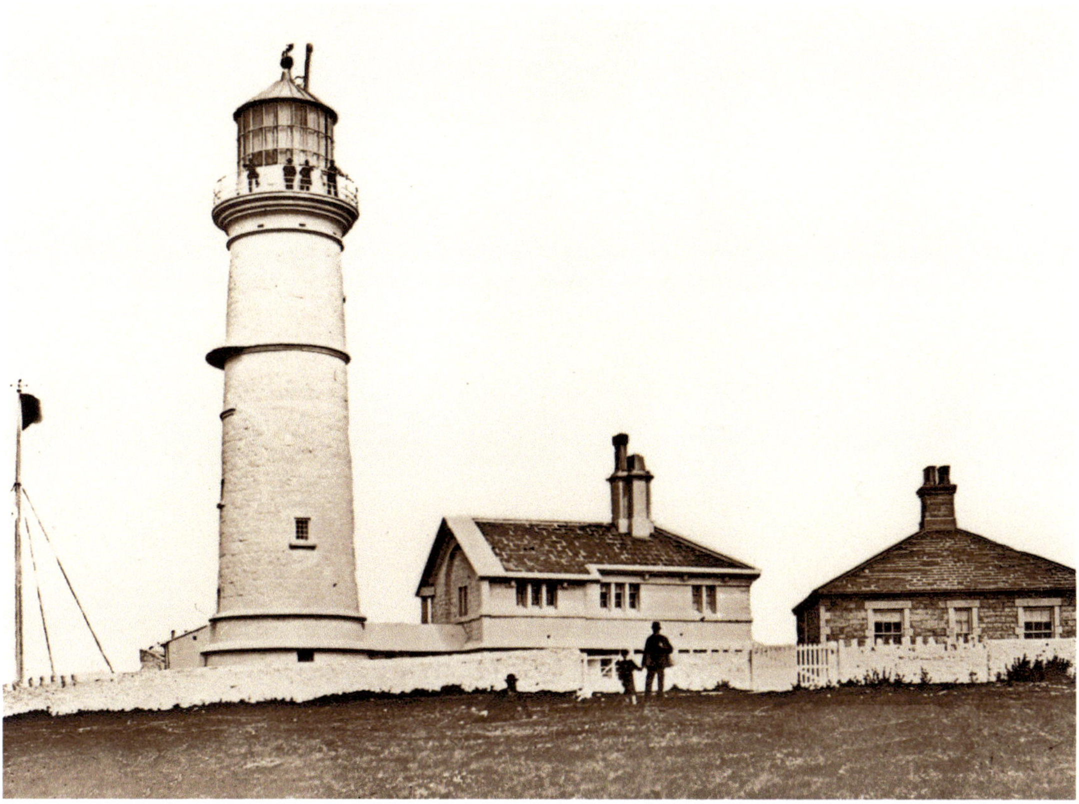

The Old Light on Beacon Hill

When the engineers of Trinity House came to the island, in 1819, they decided that the best place to construct their new lighthouse was on the highest point of the island. The architect was Daniel Alexander, who, ten years previously, had built Dartmoor Prison. Unfortunately, no sooner had the light been illuminated it was realised that, being the highest lantern in Trinity House at over 500 feet above sea level, it was constantly in the clouds and obscured. The Old Light comprised of an upper and lower flat for the Assistant Keepers, plus a detached house for the Principal Keeper. The photograph above shows the lantern curtains, closed to avoid the dangers of the sun's rays being focused inwards. The more modern photograph, taken from the adjacent cemetery, shows that the detached house has long since been demolished, but the Old Light remains, available for rent for holidays in the upper and lower flats.

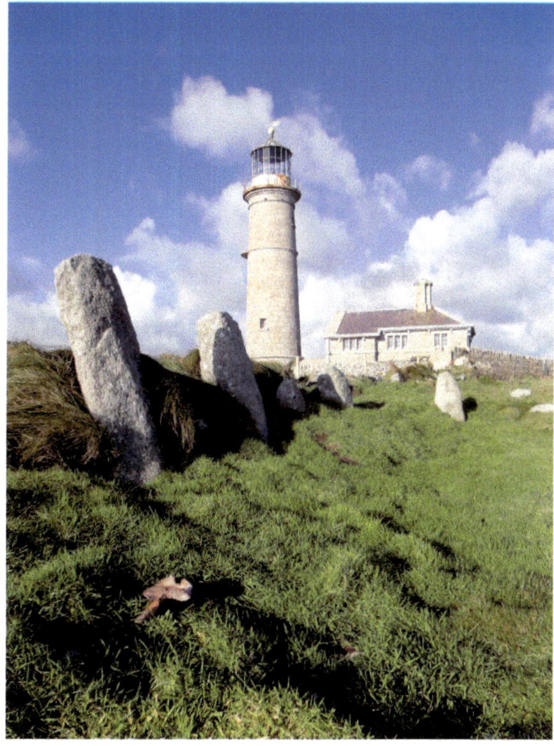

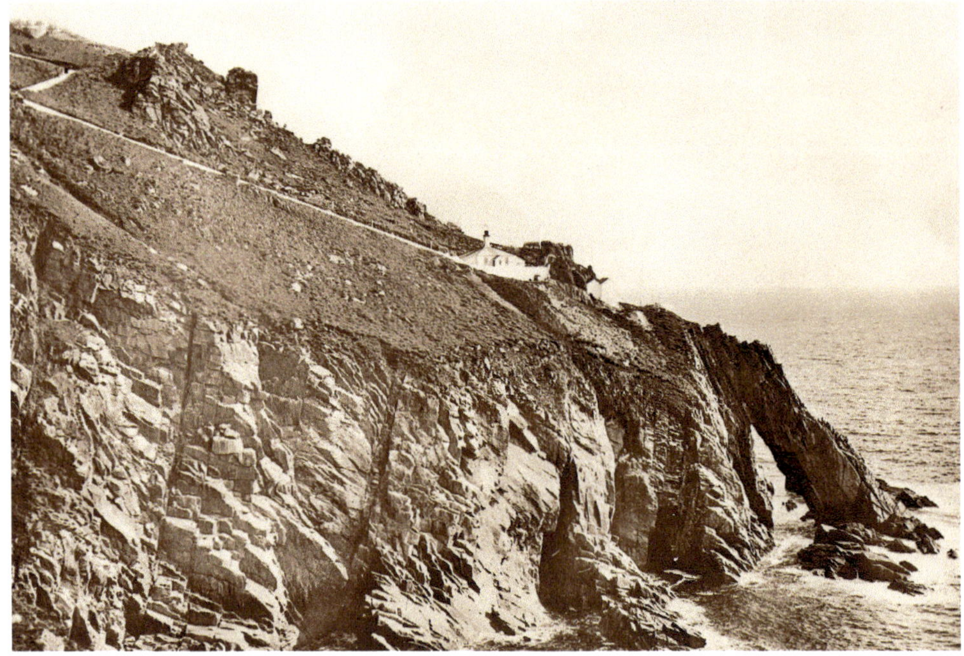

The Fog Signal Battery Station

Once the problem of the Old Light lantern being in the cloud was discovered, it was decided that a fog signal station was needed. In 1862, two cottages and a battery station were constructed low down on the west side of the island, to the north of the Old Light. Two Georgian cannons were mounted, which fired a blank shot every ten minutes in time of fog. Signal rockets replaced the cannon in 1878, and the site was eventually abandoned in 1896 when the new North and South Lights were constructed to replace the Old Light. The cottages lie as abandoned relics of the past.

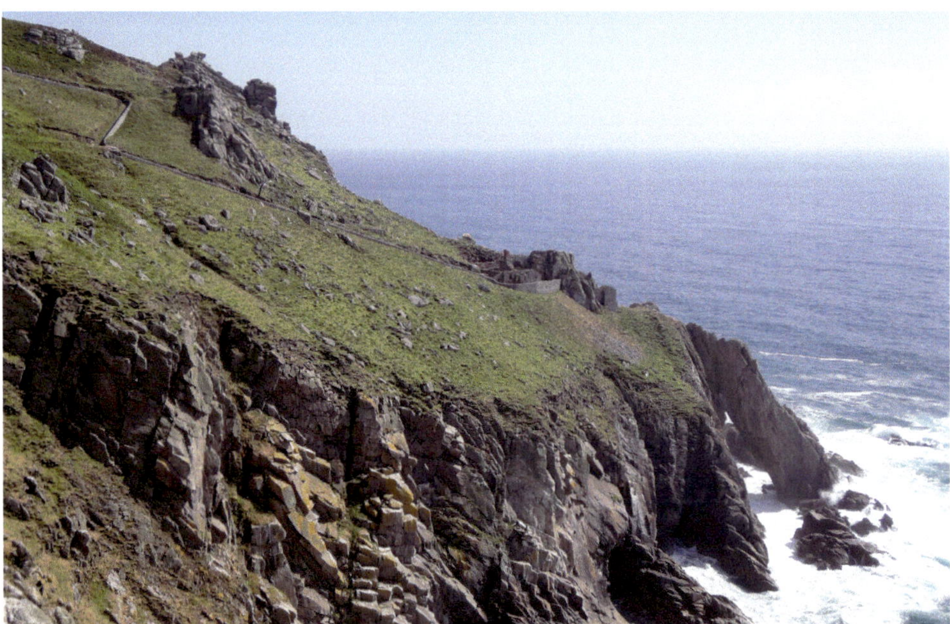

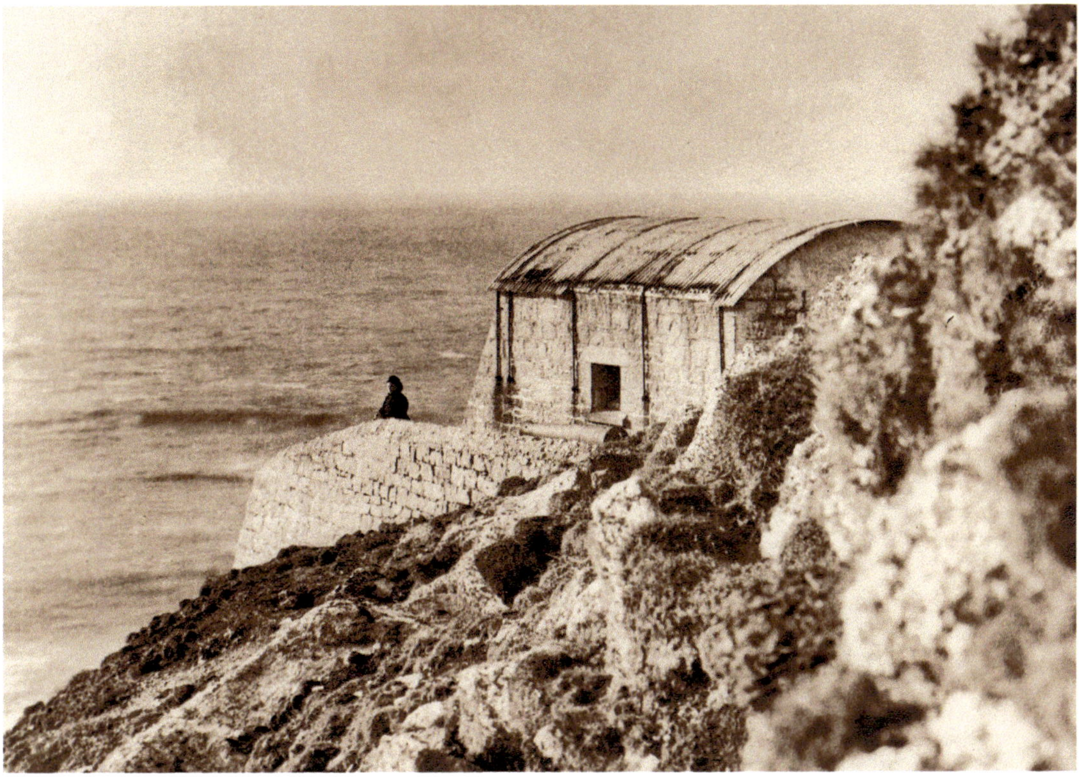

The Cannon Building at the Battery

The substantial granite building that housed the cannon had thick walls and a flimsy roof. This was to prevent any explosion destroying the building, simply blowing the roof off instead. The two cannon still remain as artefacts from the nineteenth century. Unfortunately, erosion prevents an exact copy of the black and white photograph being taken as the nearby cliff has fallen away. Because of the dangers of the location, fog signal battery station crew were forbidden to have any more than two children at the site – although it is reputed that two families lived here with ten children.

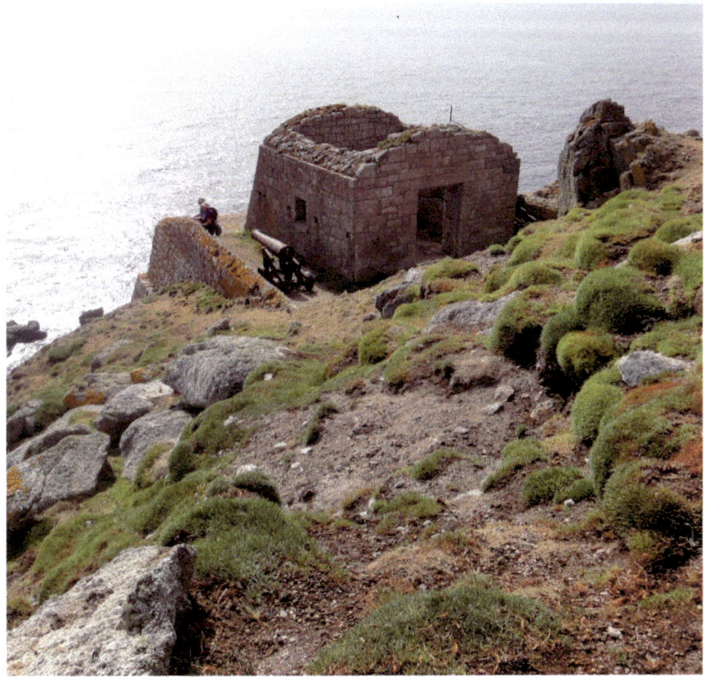

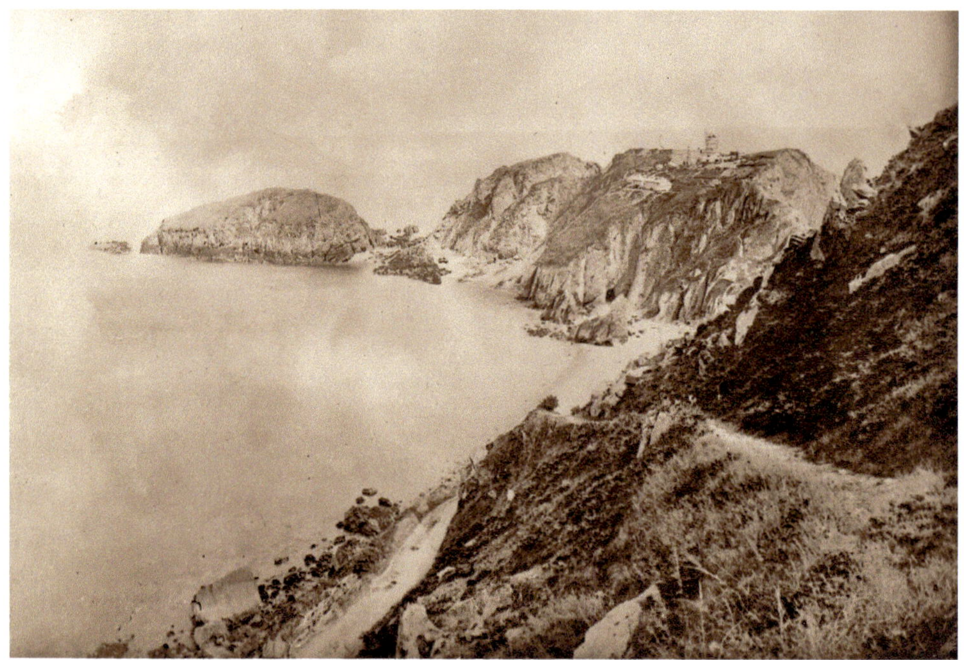

The New South Light above the Landing Bay

In 1896, Trinity House built new lighthouses at the south and north ends of the island, much lower than the Old Light, to avoid an obscured signal in low cloud. The older photograph (*above*) shows the terrace of cottages that the construction workers lived in whilst building the lighthouse. This row of houses has since disappeared and only a narrow ledge remains where they once stood. These two photographs also show clearly the original old 'goat' track and the newer road leading up to the island plateau.

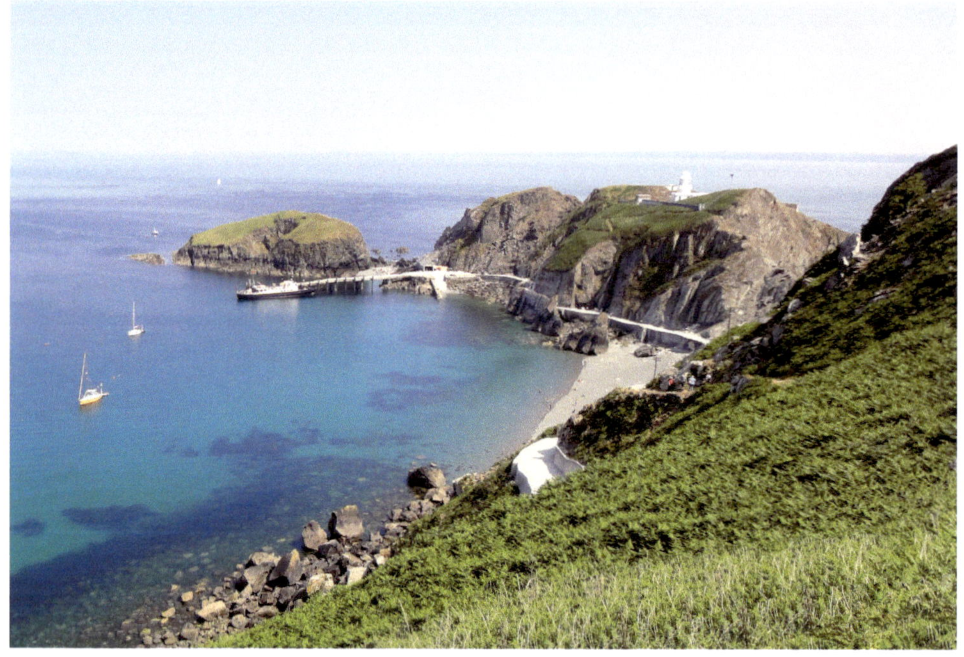

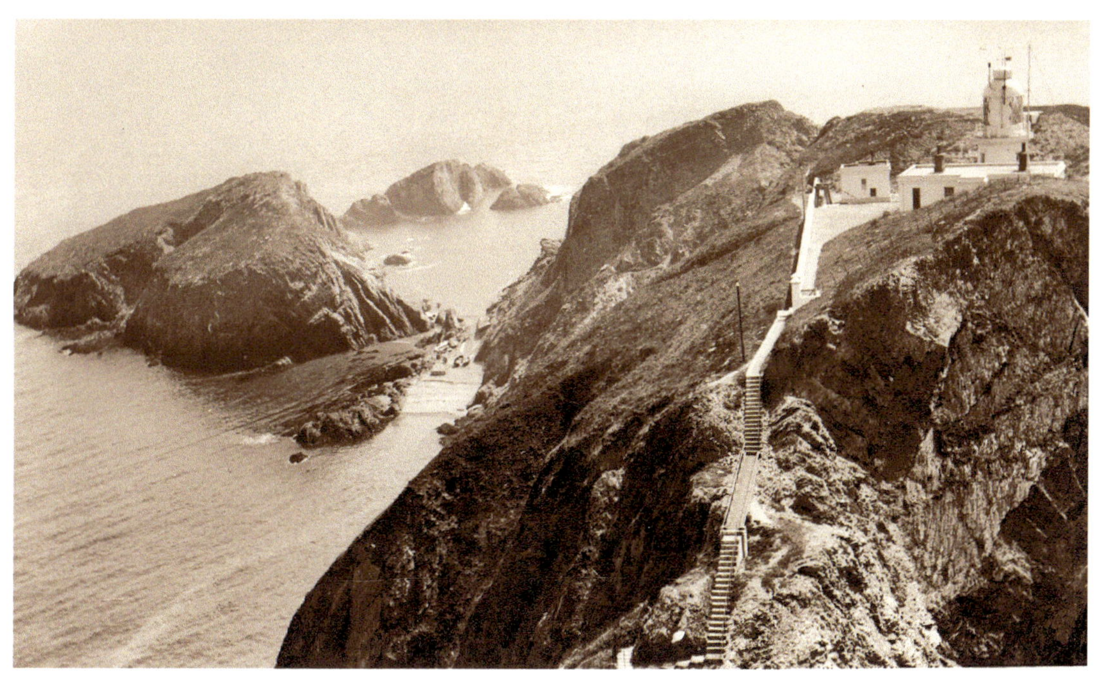

The South Light Steps, as seen from the Castle

Both photographs have been taken from near the castle, at the entrance to Benson's Cave. The older photograph clearly shows the former route for the lighthouse keepers to climb the steps up from the landing bay below. The newer photograph shows that since the late 1980s the shape of this area has changed dramatically, following the construction of the new road to the divers' shed. Steps have been constructed to access the South Light from a point just out of view, near the top of the landing jetty. The 1920s Christie's Quay is also shown clearly in the newer photograph, thus dating the older picture to before 1924.

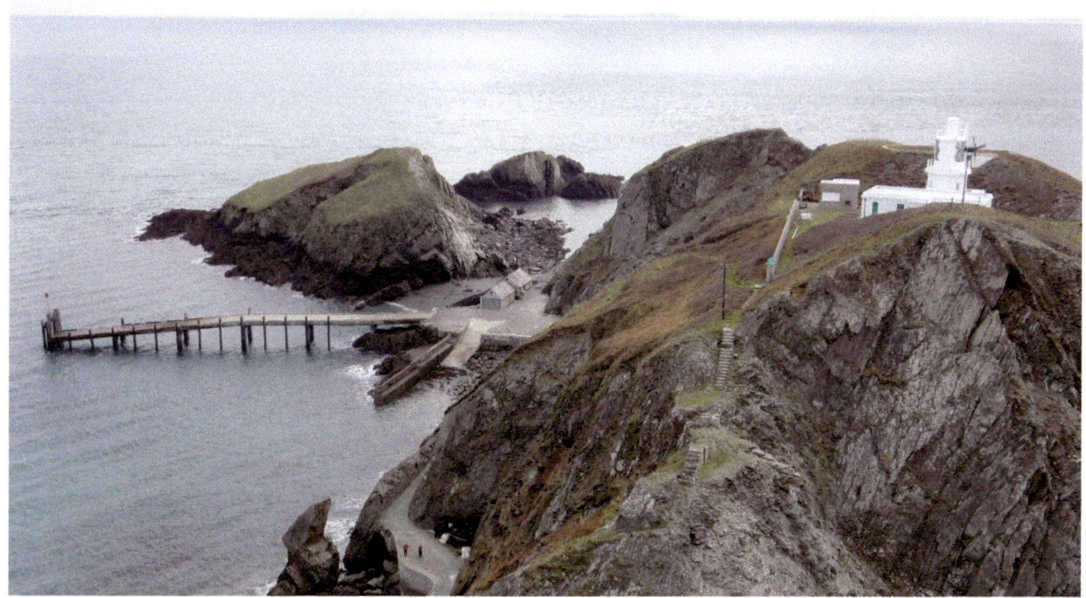

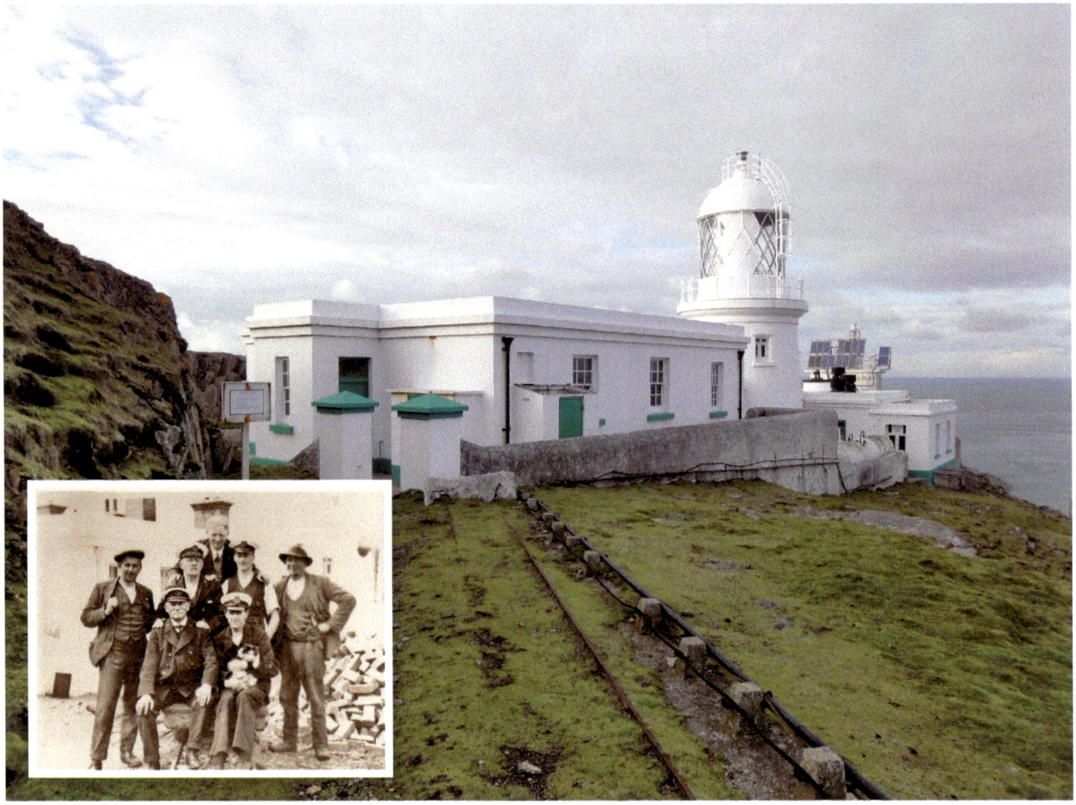

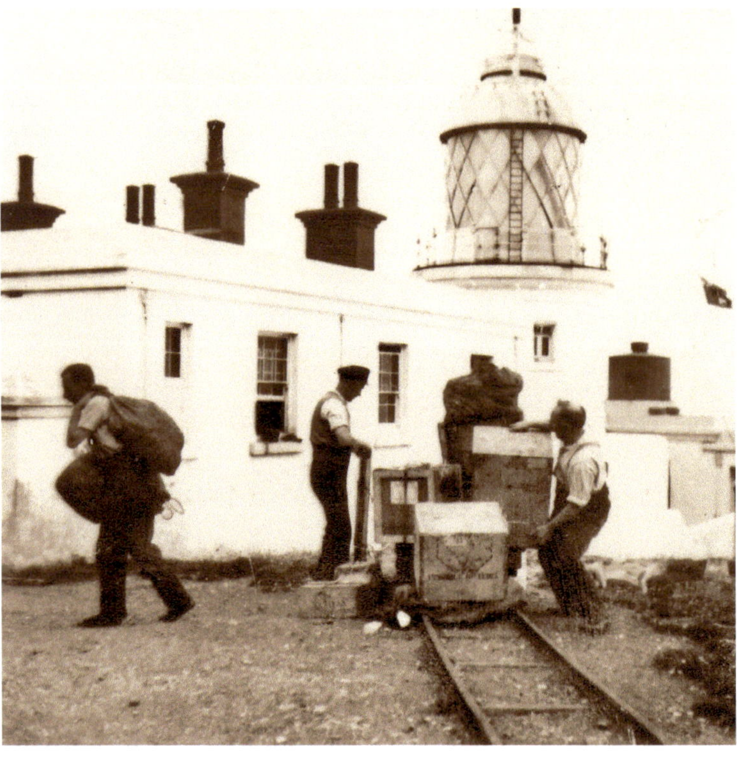

The North Light

The North Light was constructed in 1896 at the same time as the South Light. There was a tramway with rails leading from the lighthouse to a landing stage winch, where stores were hauled up a great height from sea level. The goods were then placed on man-hauled carts and transported to the light down a slight gradient to ease the work.

The insert shows the North Light keepers, including Bob 'Daddy' Hall – the Principal Keeper – pictured standing second from the left in the Trinity House cap.

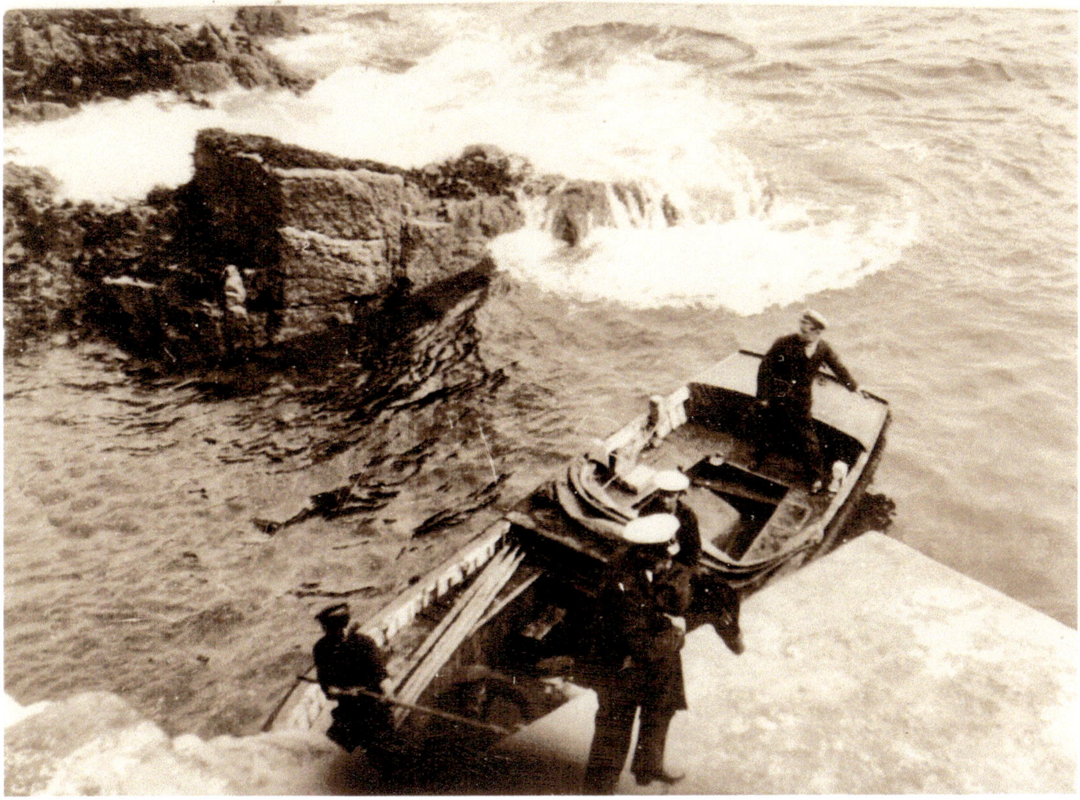

The North Light Landing Stage

Access to the North Light was by small
tender boat, which brought the keepers
to a concrete platform at sea level.
There were a number of platforms to
allow for a landing at various stages
of the tide. The keeper then had a
tortuously long flight of steps to climb
his way up the cliffside to the tramway
winch high above. The steps still exist,
but much of the railings have rusted
away, making the descent and ascent
a nervous experience for some! The
more modern photograph shows how
the swell could easily make a landing
very difficult down below. The isolated
landing stage is now well populated
with seals.

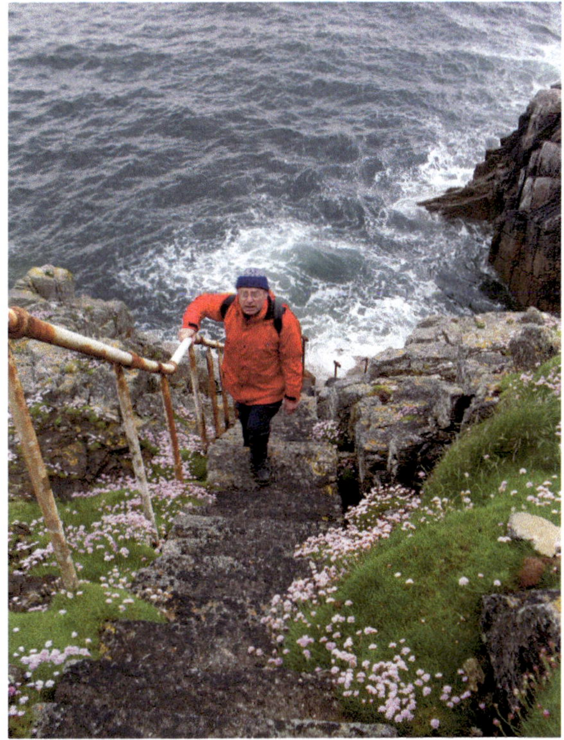

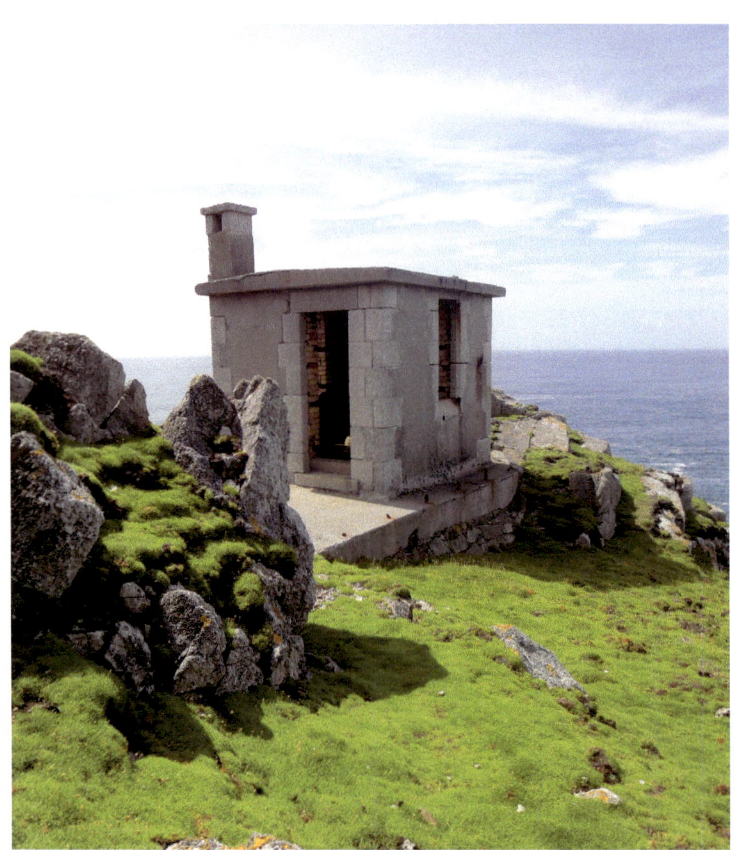

Admiralty North Lookout

The old Admiralty lookout is located on the seaward side of the North Light, right on the very north end of Lundy, at the top of the high cliffs. It was built after the North Light and was used as a lookout for the Admiralty crew, with far-reaching views all the way north to the coast of Wales. The building still stands abandoned and makes a good vantage point to observe the seals in the bay below the lighthouse. This small building had been abandoned before the construction of the Admiralty Station at Tibbets to the south.

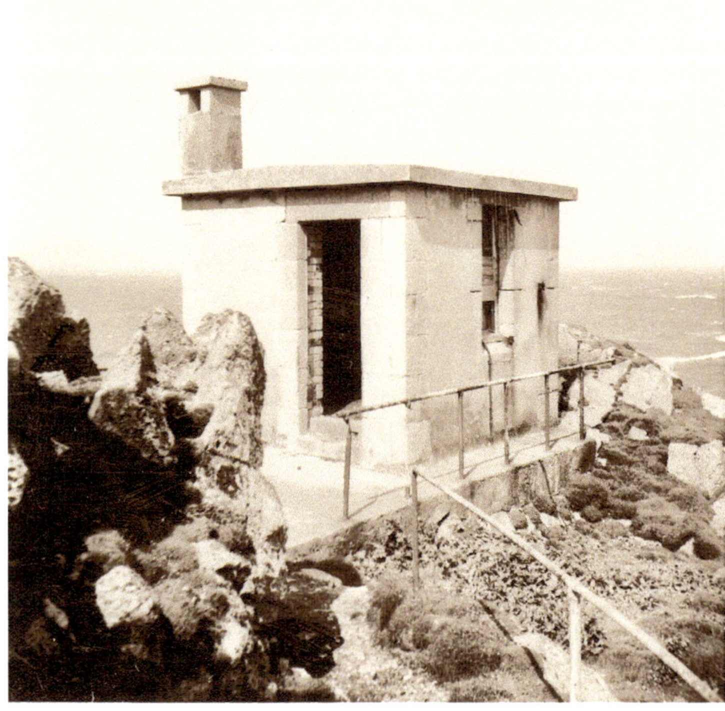

Virgin's Spring

At the very north end of the island, below the North Light tramway, is a sea cave known as Virgin's Spring. It is accessible only from the sea and goes a considerable way into the island, below the area of the North Light. It is called the Virgin's Spring because this is where fresh water reputedly bubbles up from the seabed. When looking at the area of the north end in the modern photograph, you can clearly see the North Light and horizontal line of the tramway to its left. The flight of concrete steps from the landing stage is also pictured. Virgin's Spring is the cave to the right of the landing stage area.

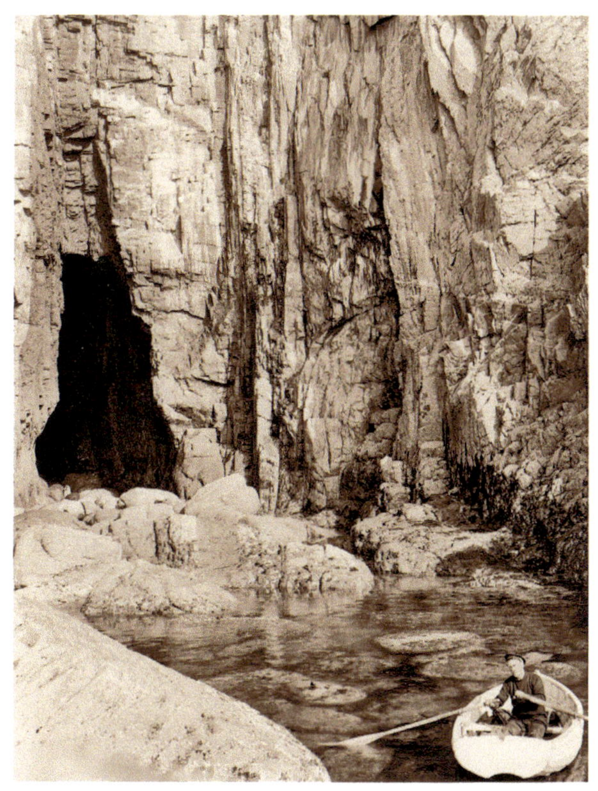

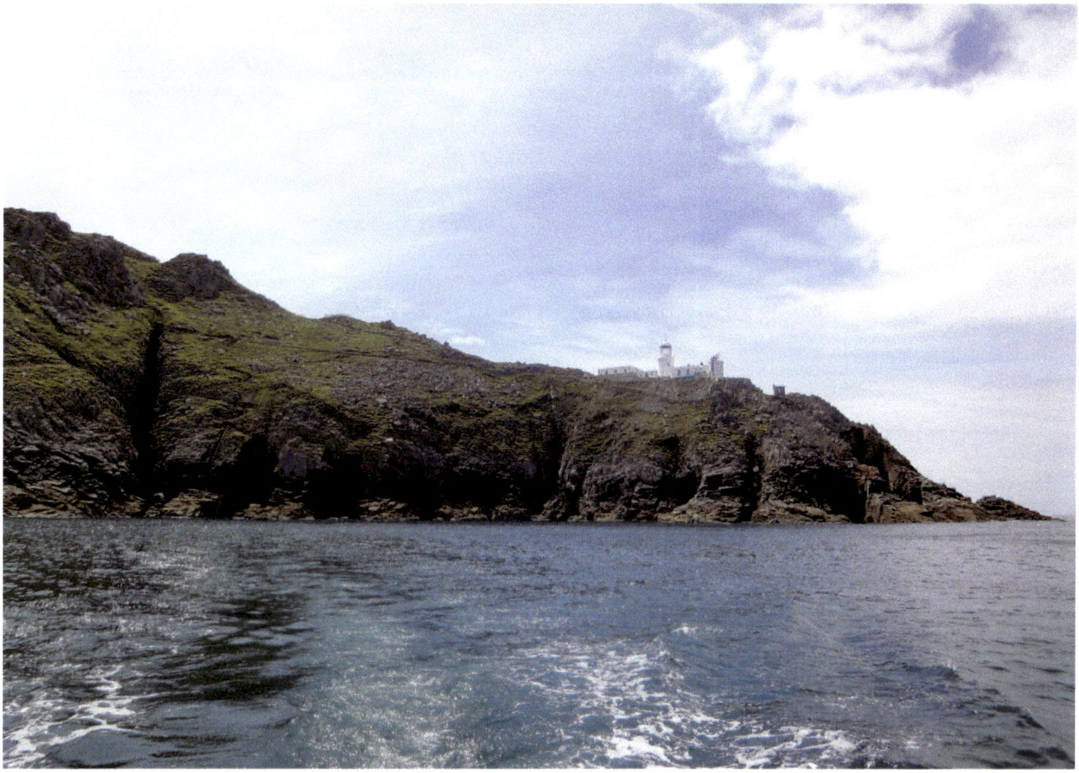

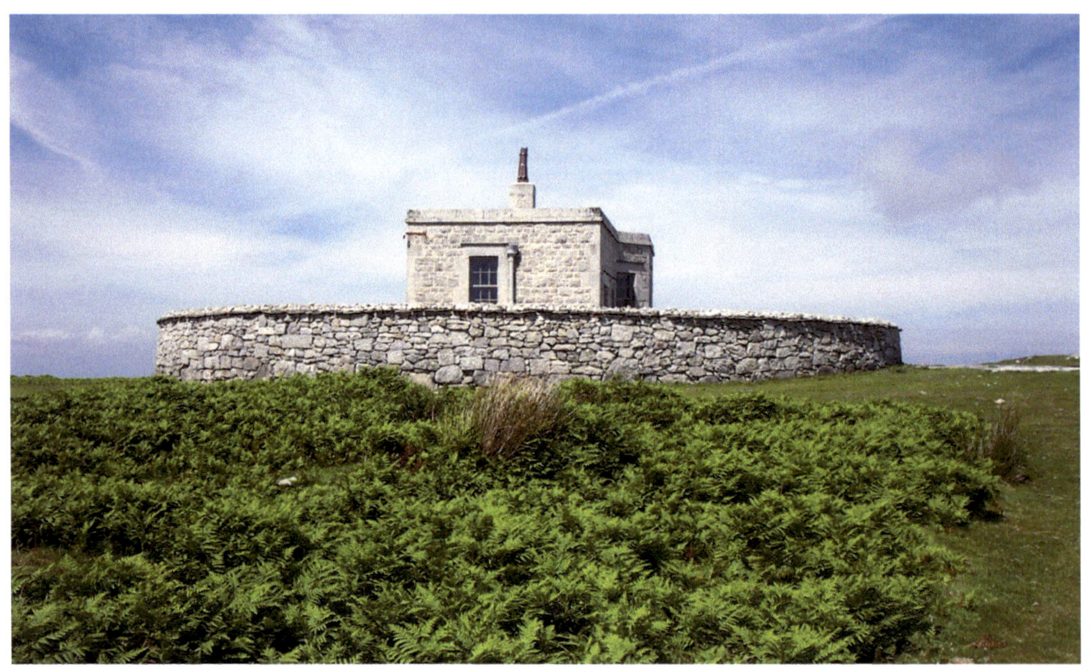

Admiralty 'Tibbets' Lookout

The Admiralty built this signal and watch station in 1911, and it was in use until 1928, simply known as Tibbets. There was a watch room on the roof, until it was removed in 1971, with an outside iron ladder, from which it was said fourteen lighthouses could be seen on a clear night. The Harmans converted Tibbets into the first Lundy holiday cottage. A visiting stonemason constructed the perimeter wall in 1989 to prevent livestock using the building as a shelter in stormy weather. It is the most isolated holiday cottage on the island with no mains electricity connected.

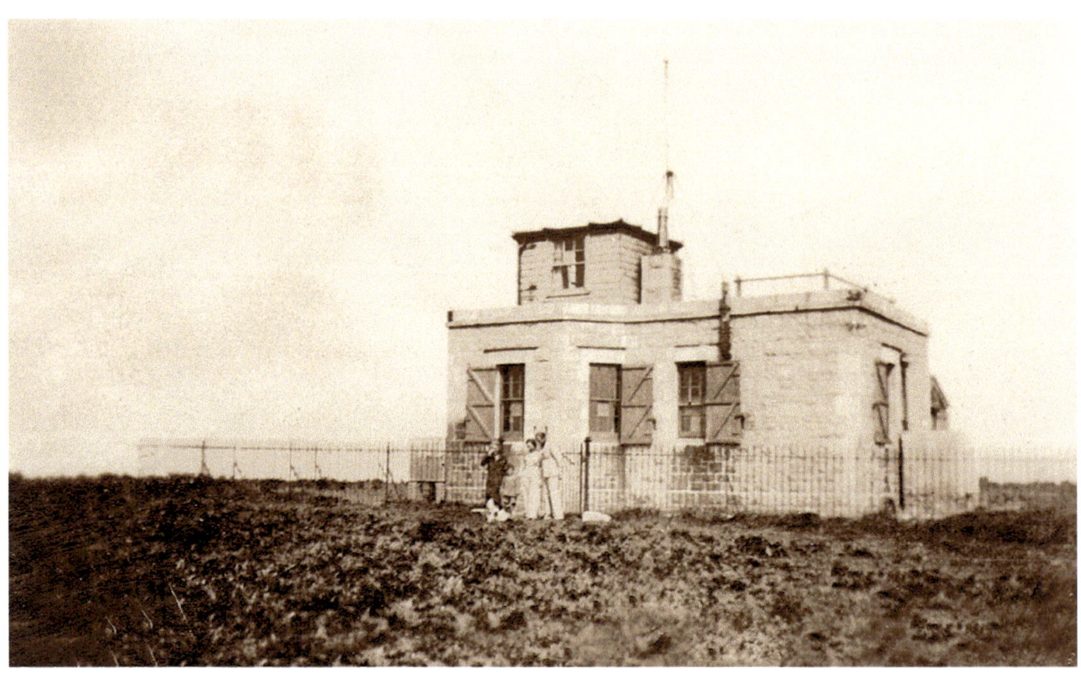

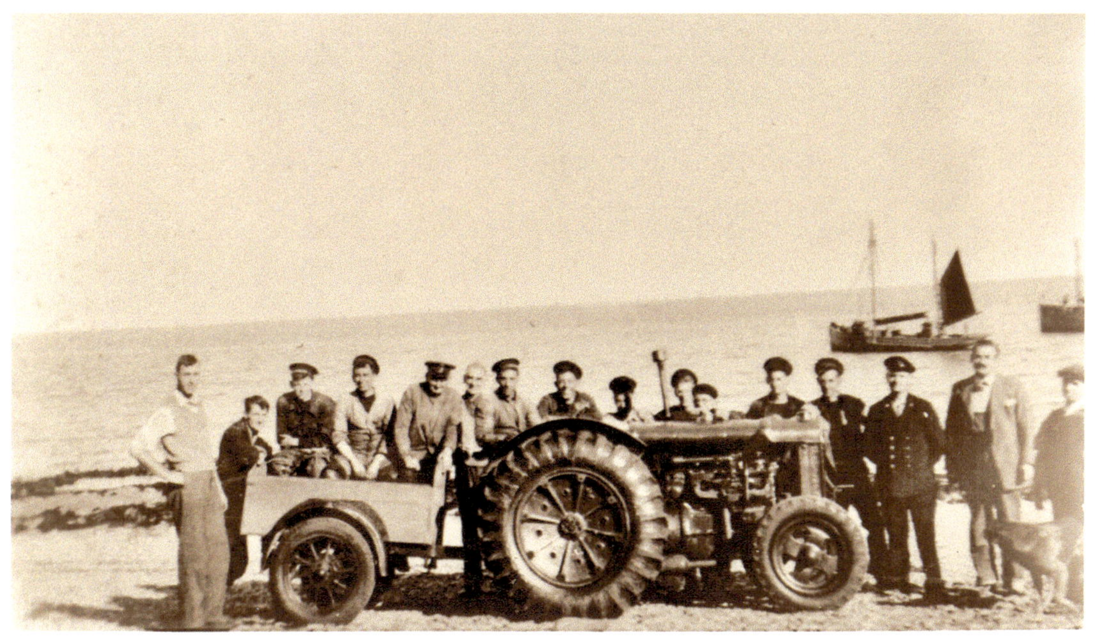

Tractor Transportation

A new Fordson Tractor arrived on the island in 1941 and is pictured above on the landing beach. Tractors are still greatly used on the island, and although much bigger nowadays, they still manage to negotiate the narrow beach roads with large loads and stores, as can be seen below. The newly constructed slipway can also be seen along with the beach road, which has become a lifeline to the economy of the island.

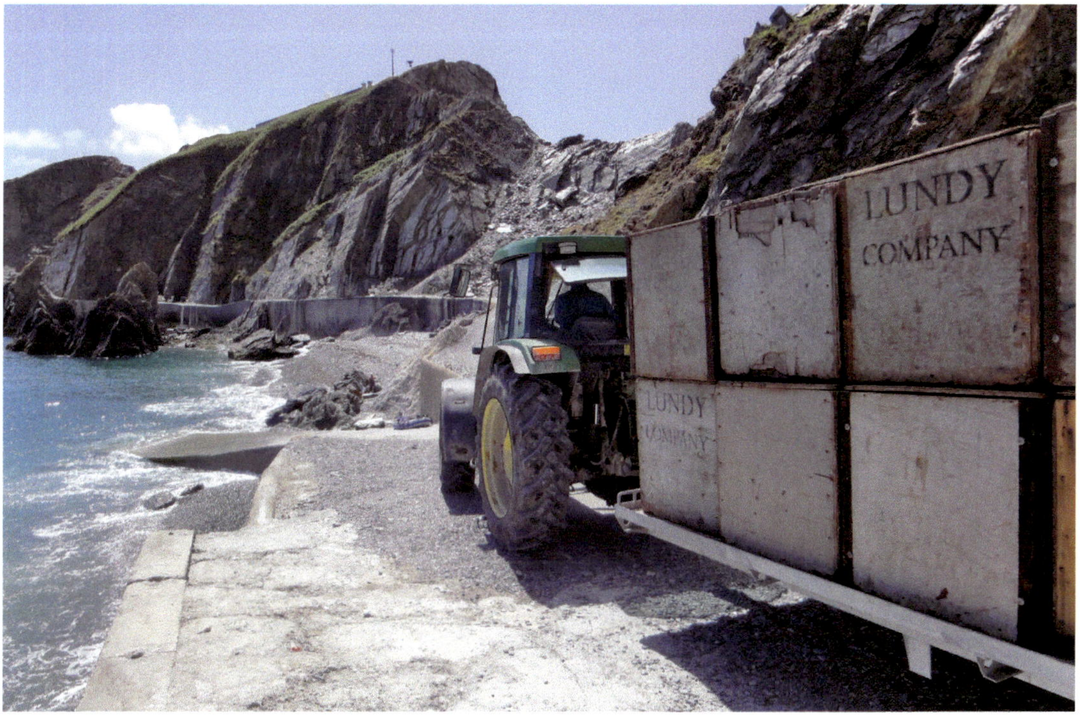

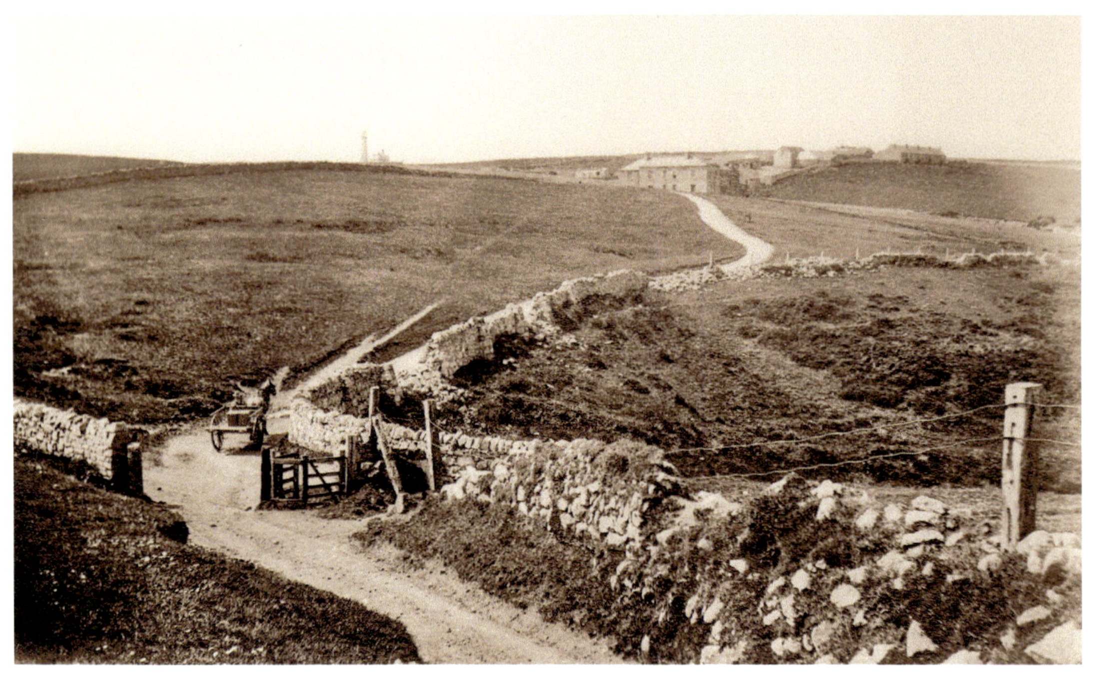

St John's Valley and the Village

The older photograph (*above*), taken before 1896, shows a horse and cart making its way up the main road towards the village, prior to the construction of the new church. The newer colour photograph, taken from the same viewpoint, shows a similar image of a quad bike and trailer doing exactly the same thing a hundred years or more later! This time the photograph includes St Helen's church and the slightly altered village buildings.

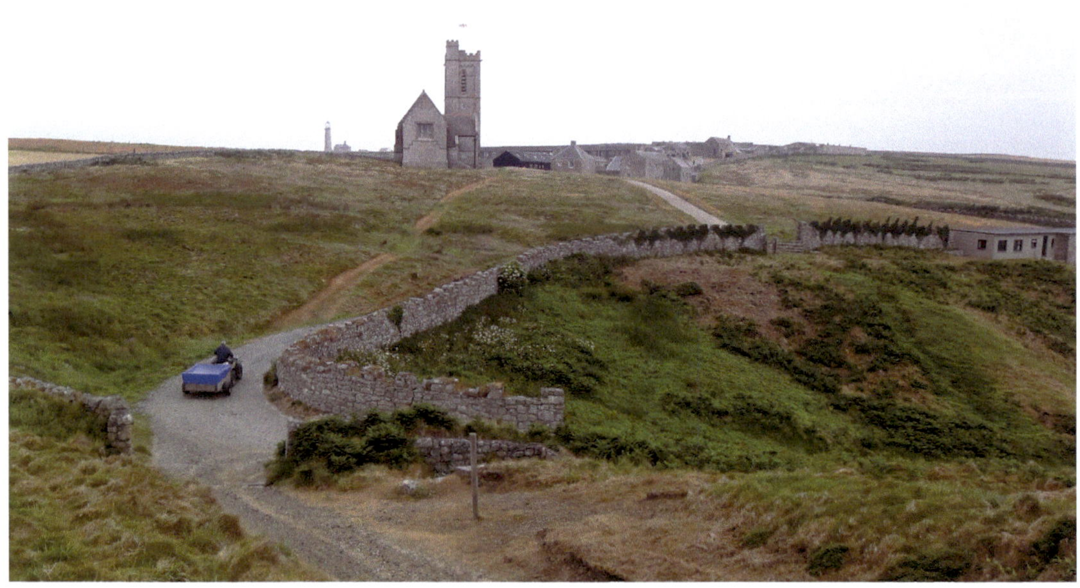

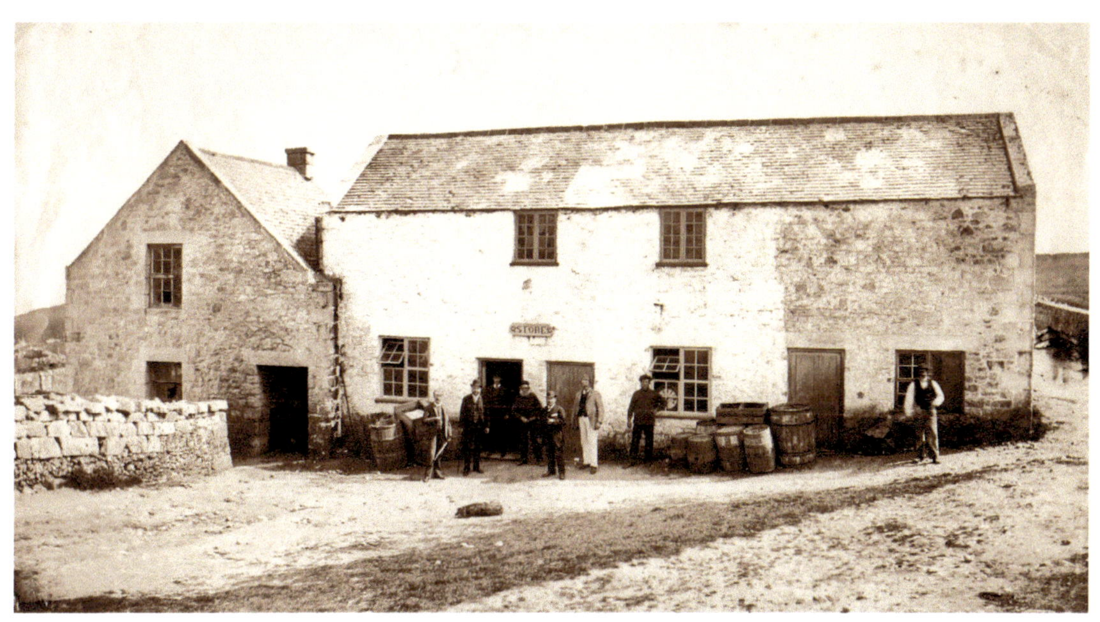

The Marisco Tavern

The Marisco Tavern is situated in the village centre, and is understandably the centre of village social life. In the older photograph (*above*) it was simply the store for the island and is pictured in 1885 when Mr Frederick Wards was the storekeeper. The store had in fact been established in the time of the Lundy Granite Company, in the mid-1860s, as a provisions shop for the employees. The photograph to the right, taken on a moonlit night, shows the building today with the moon reflecting off the still waters in Bideford Bay beyond. The name Marisco Tavern was introduced in the twentieth century.

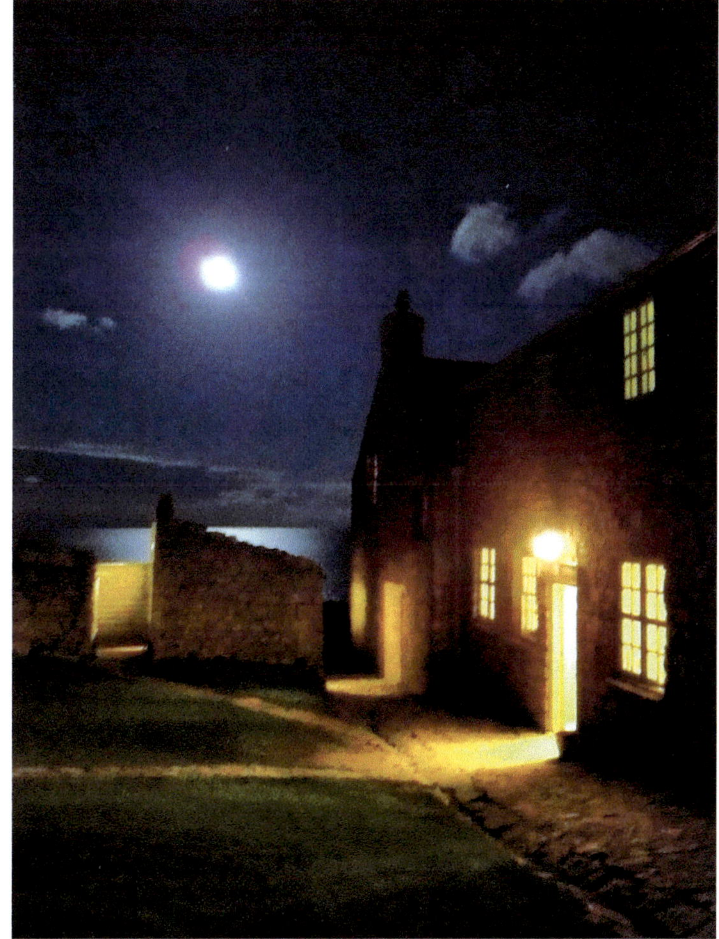

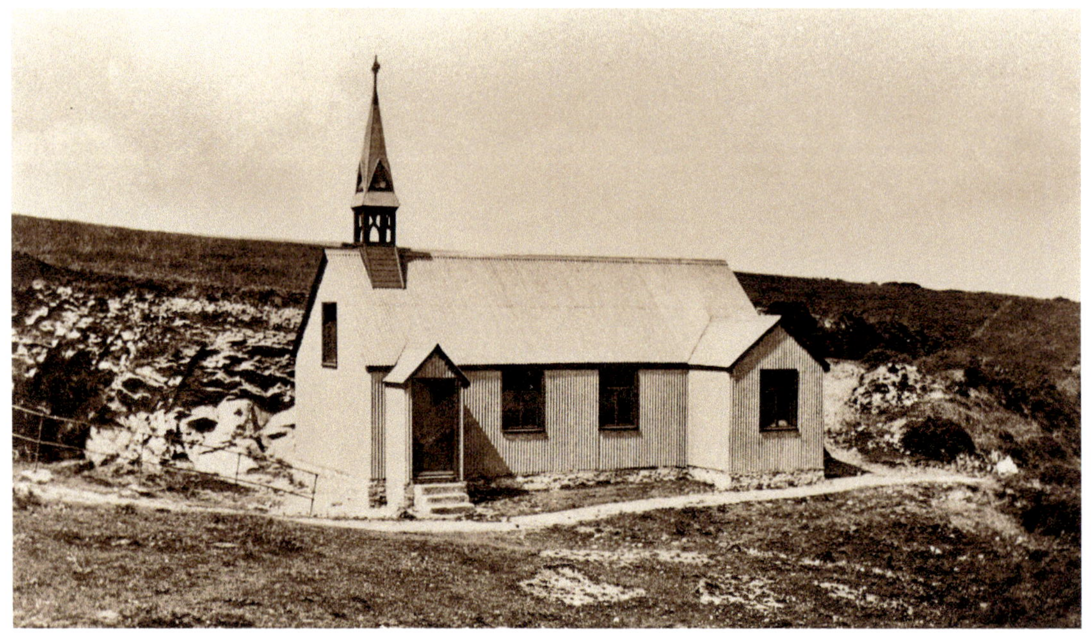

The Island Churches

Mr William Hudson Heaven purchased Lundy in the early part of the nineteenth century. His son, The Revd Mr Hudson Heaven, built a little iron church dedicated by the Bishop of Exeter in 1885. This small church, which had only taken eight days to construct, was superseded by the existing church in 1897. From thenceforth, the island became known as 'The Kingdom of Heaven'. The old iron church, which stood at the rear of the area of the modern-day Government House, then became 'the Mission Hall' but has since been demolished. At the time of writing, the future of the existing church is a matter of great discussion due to the fragility of the structure.

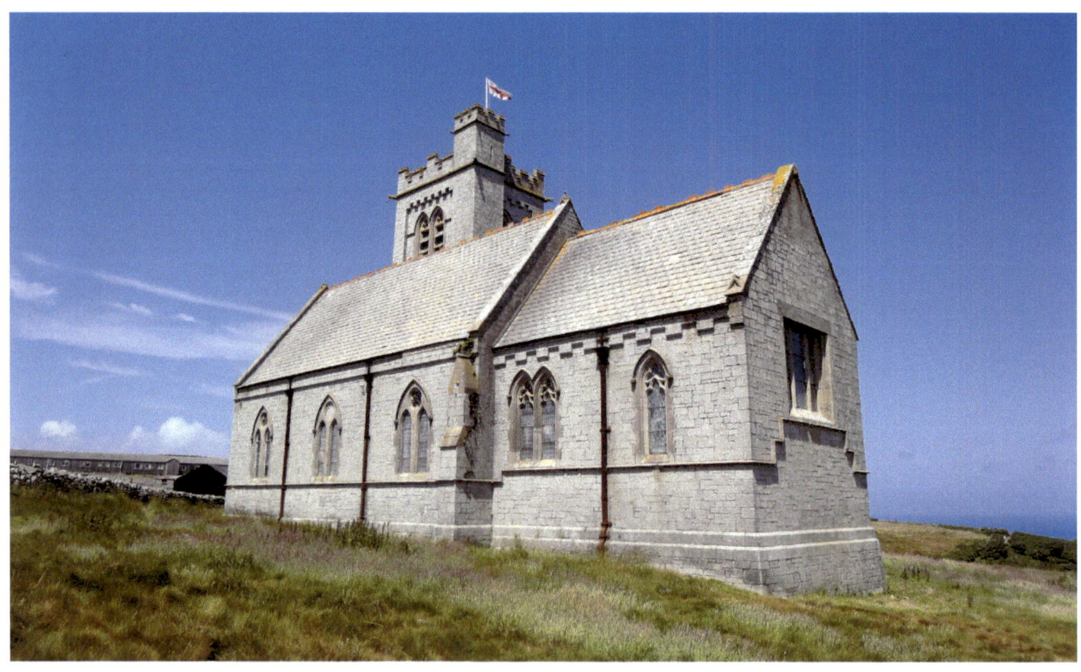

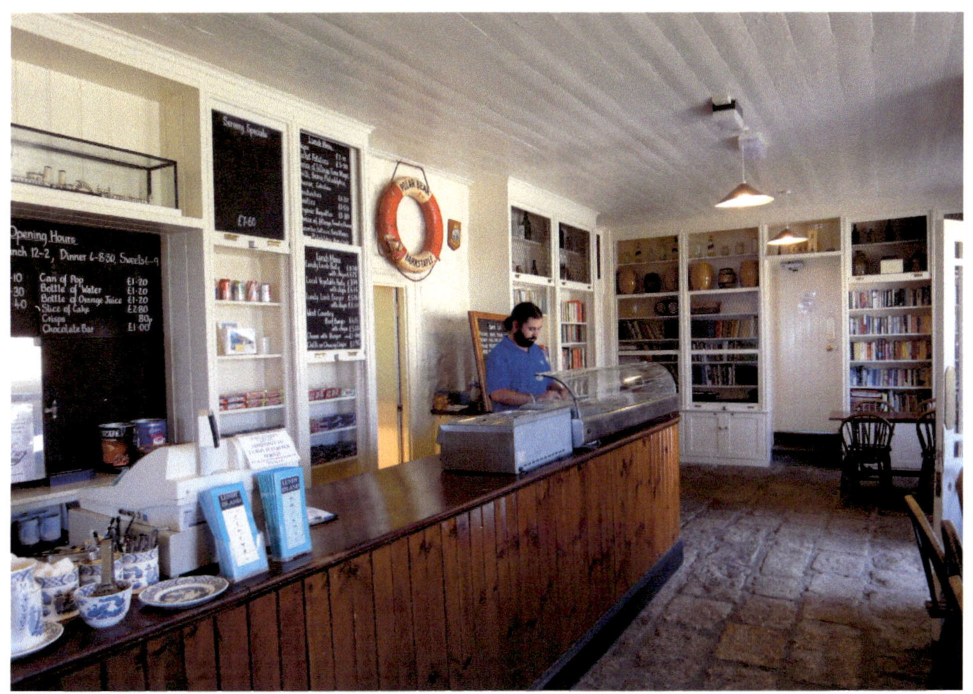

The Tavern Interior

The black-and-white photograph shows the interior of the store in July 1906, with the storekeeper Mr Pennington at the bar. A description of the premises at that time makes it clear that the store was also the island pub. The more modern photograph (*above*) with Ceri Stafford, is taken at exactly the same angle and shows that the Marisco Tavern is not only a pub but is the library, café and general hub of the island.

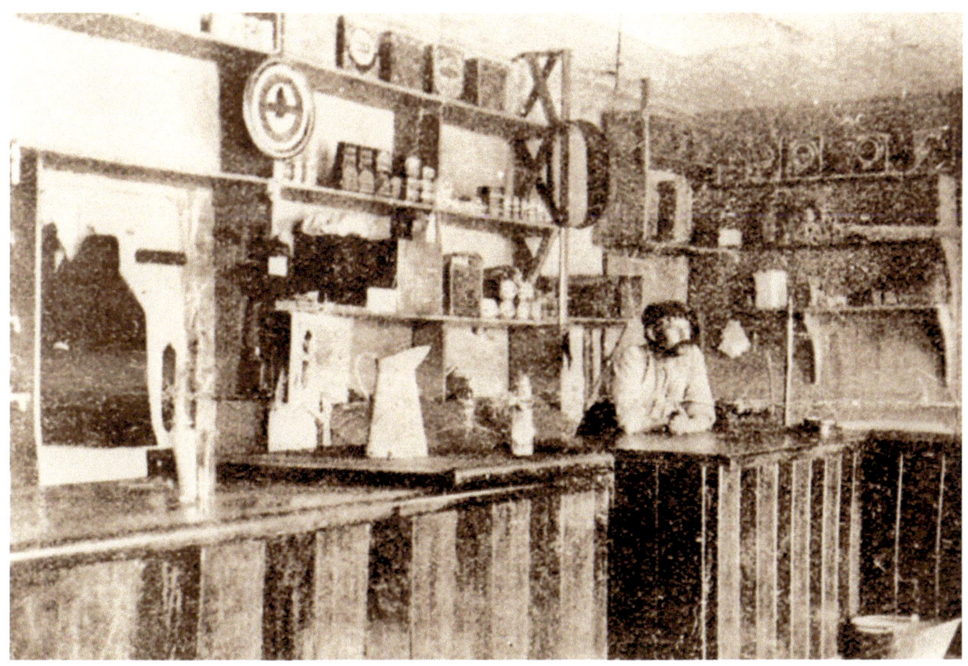

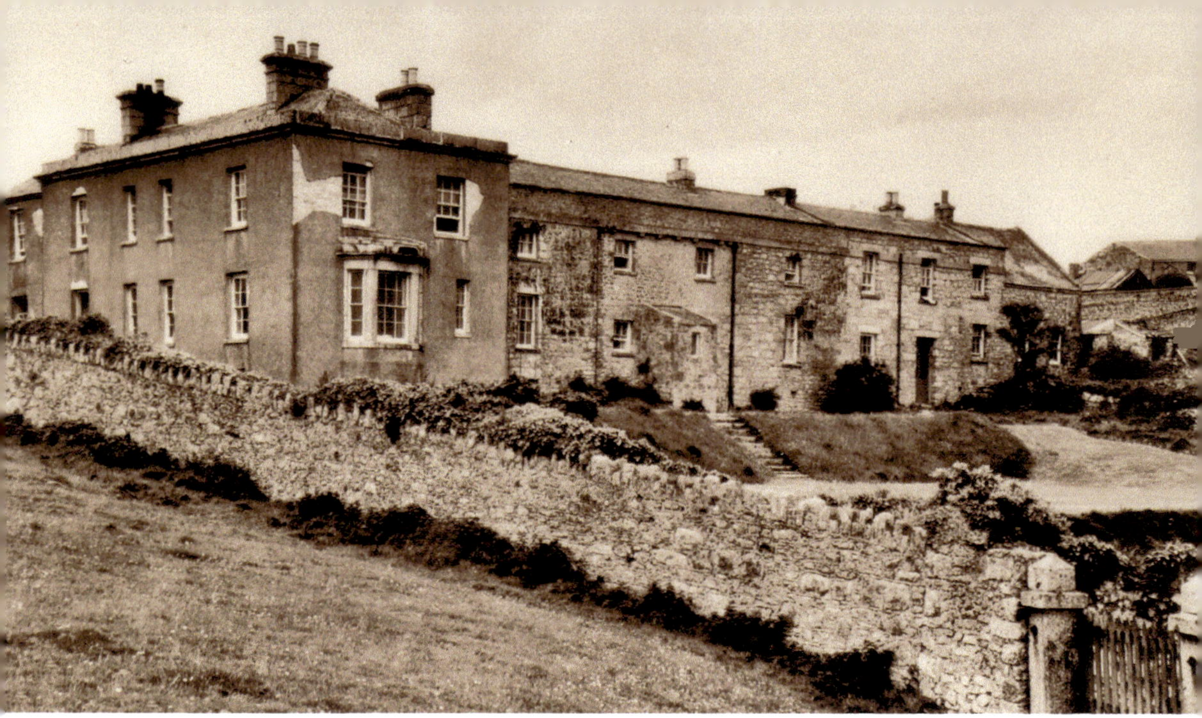

One of the buildings that has altered almost beyond recognition is the former Manor Hotel, which survived up until the Landmark Trust took over the island in the late 1960s. Much was demolished and rebuilt, and today the whole complex at the centre of the village comprises several separate buildings, as can be seen in the lower photograph, taken from a similar viewpoint.

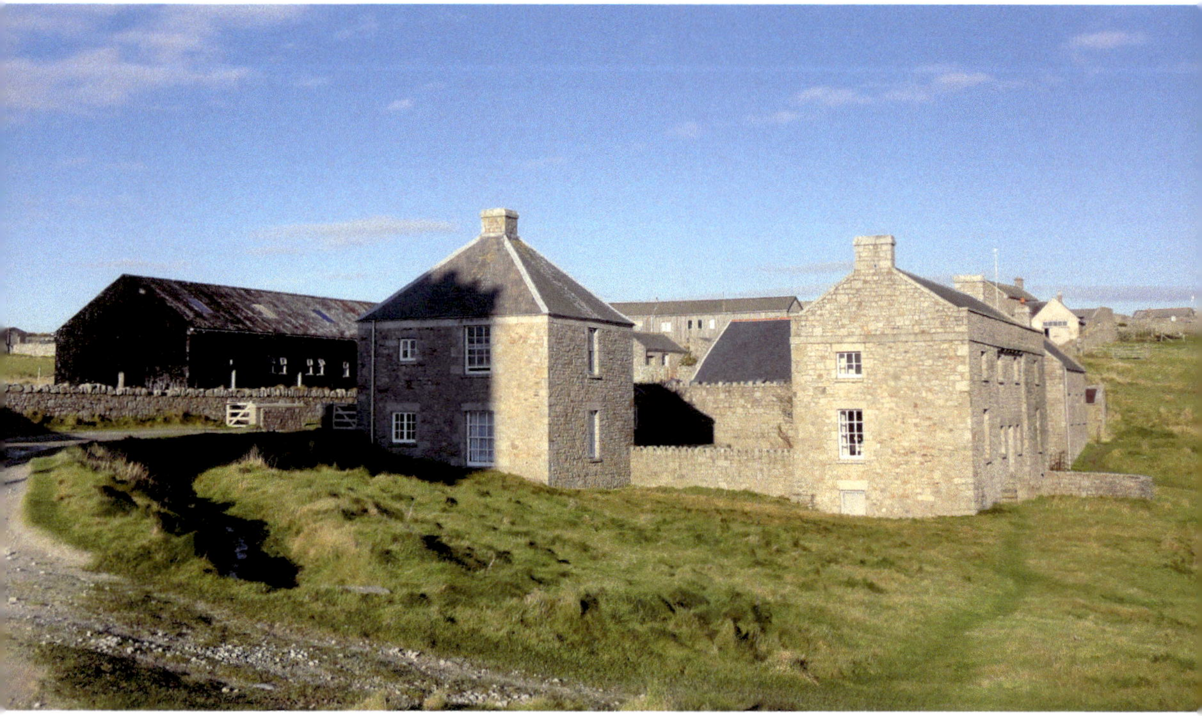

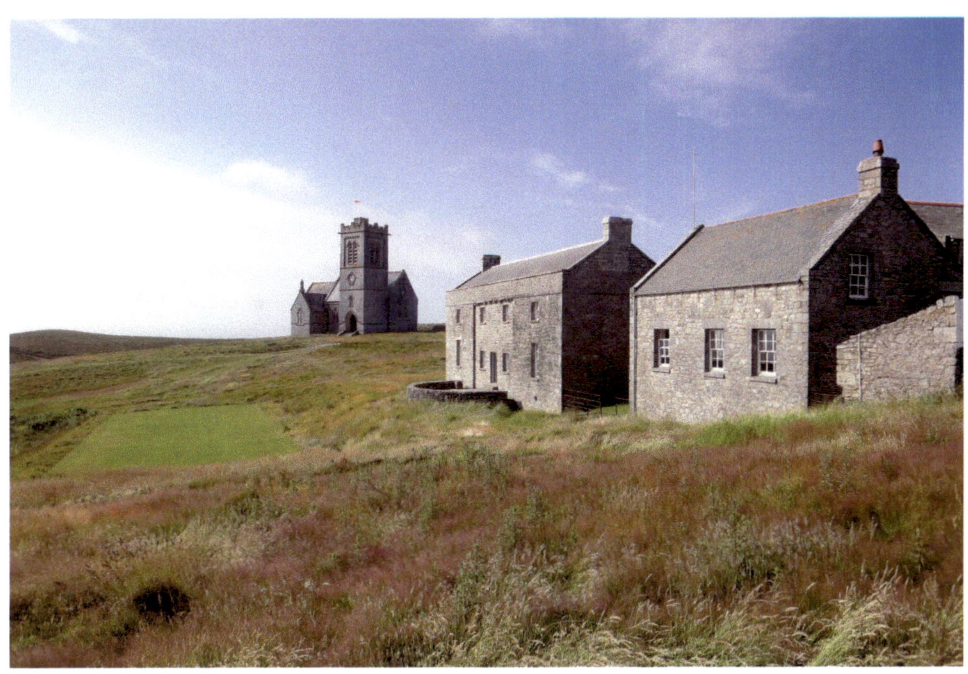

The Manor Hotel and Church

These two photographs, taken from an identical location, show just how much the main buildings in the centre of the village have changed. The older photograph includes St Helen's church, constructed in 1897, along with a wall, long since demolished, which surrounded the tennis court at the rear of the hotel. The more modern photograph shows the flat area, formerly the court, but now shows that the modern accommodation is separate from the Marisco Tavern, which is the right-hand building in the picture.

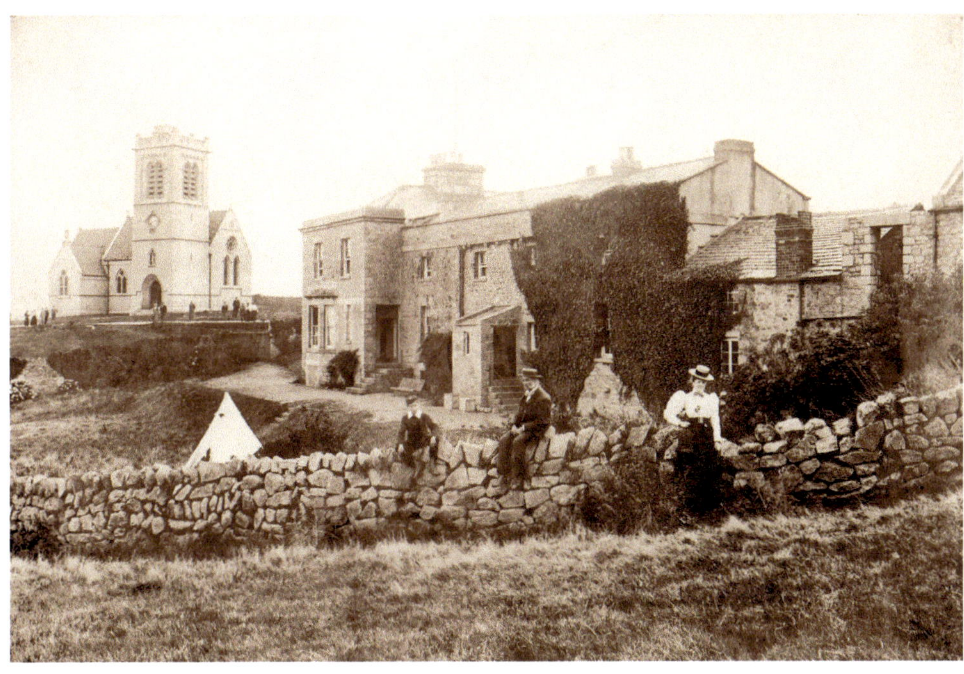

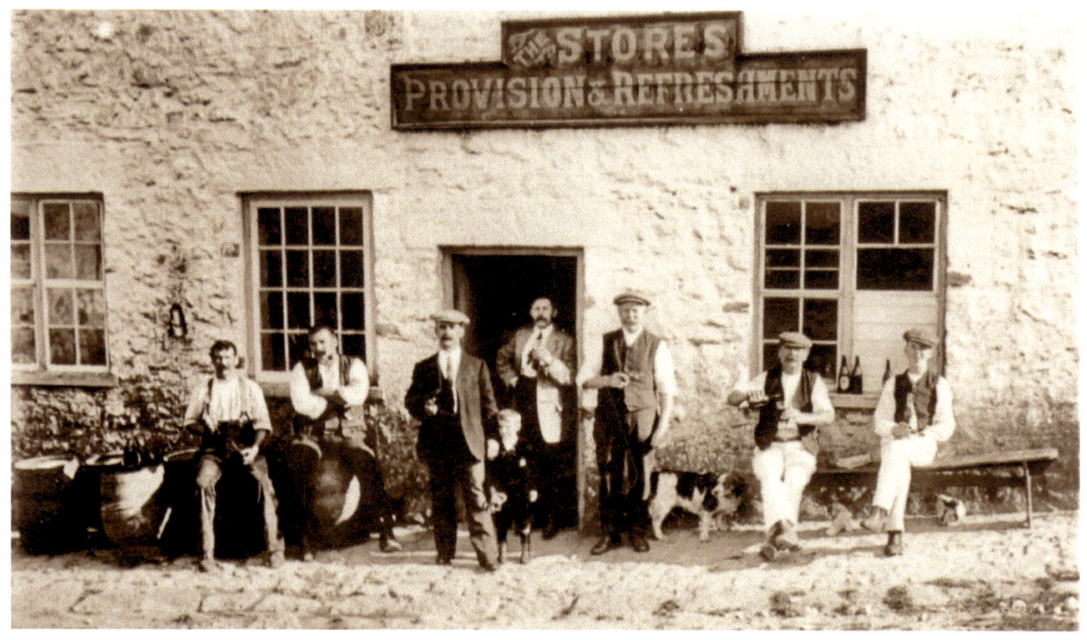

'Stores, Provisions and Refreshments'

The Tavern, pictured in about 1906, with Mr William Pennington standing in the doorway, glass in hand. It was just prior to this phase in the life of the store that it was also extended to become an inn. It has remained as such ever since, and for much of its existence it did not require any liquor licence or need to adhere to mainland licensing hours! Progress, alas, has ensured that the Marisco Tavern now falls in line with mainland licensing legislation, as the visitors in the lower photograph would no doubt have discovered!

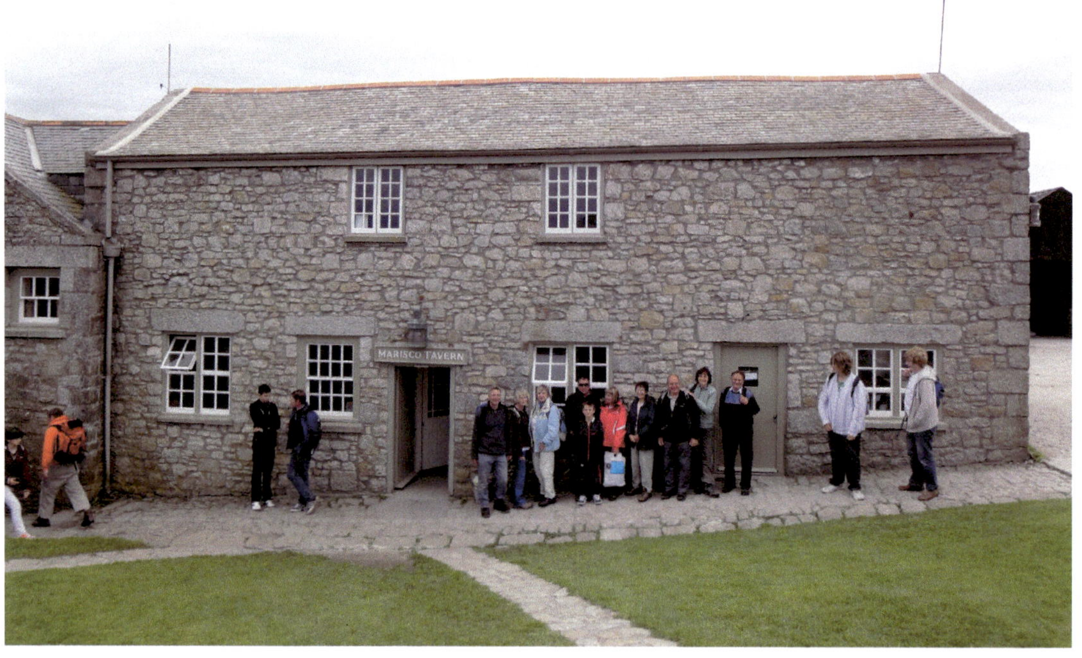

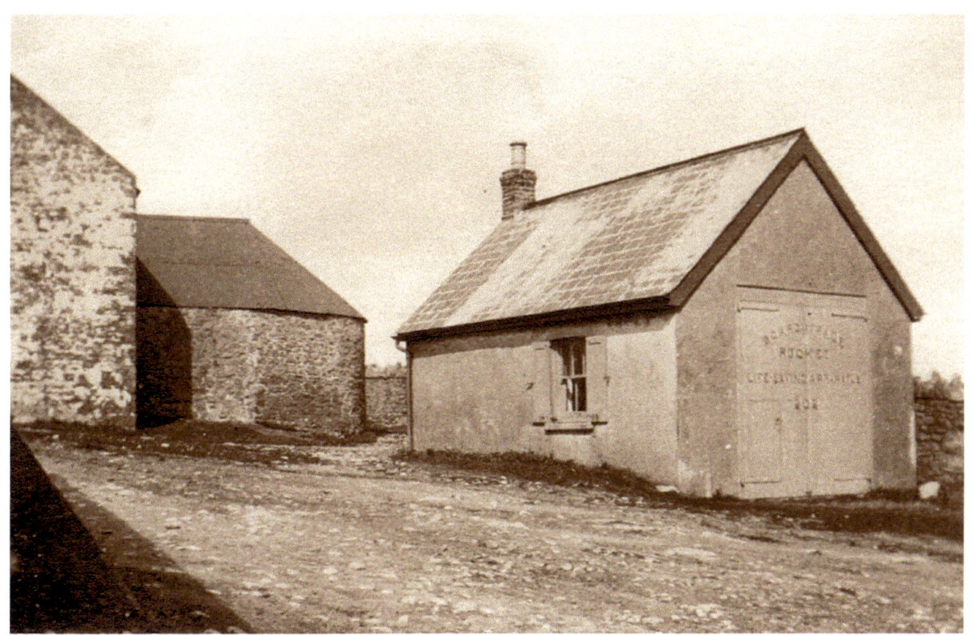

The Rescue Rocket Apparatus Shed

The Rocket Life-Saving Apparatus Shed (*above*) was constructed in 1893 to house the equipment used to rescue shipwrecked and stranded sailors. The Commander of the Coastguards at Ilfracombe supervised regular practice training days. The building today has been refurbished and converted into a very interesting exhibition and display centre, with interpretation boards around the walls. It also incorporates a museum display about the history of the island.

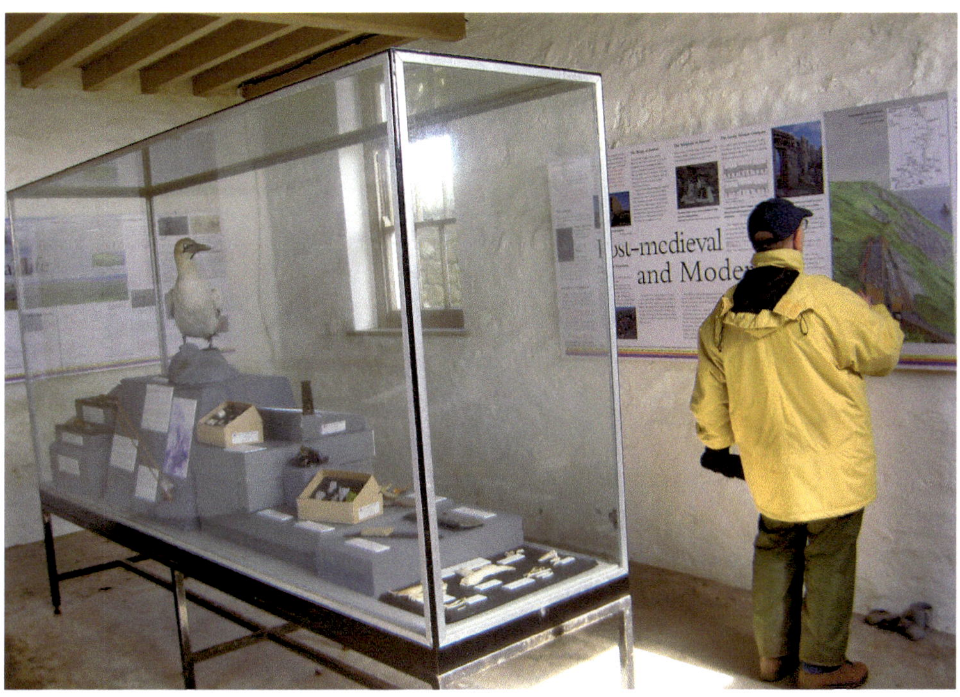

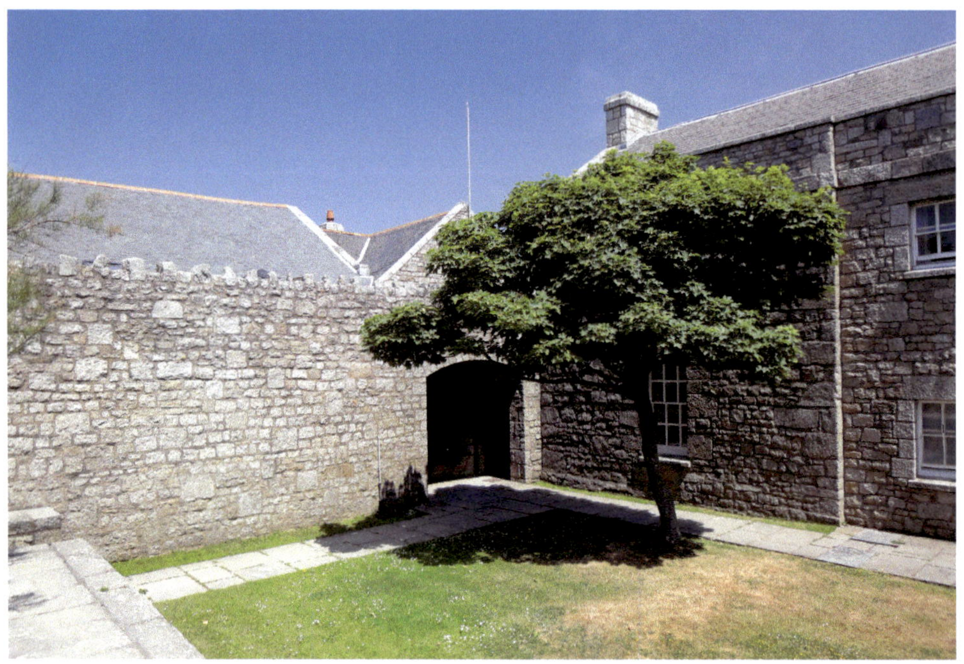

The Quadrangle at the Rear of the Manor Hotel

Today, the Old House North and Old House South (*above*) form a very sheltered grassy quadrangle at the rear of the tavern, bordered by the Radio Room and Square Cottage. Until the 1970s, this area was the backyard of the Manor Hotel, seen below on 'wash day'. It is probably this complex of buildings that has altered the most since the Landmark Trust took over the lease on the island in the late 1960s, transformed into various well-appointed holiday cottages for rent.

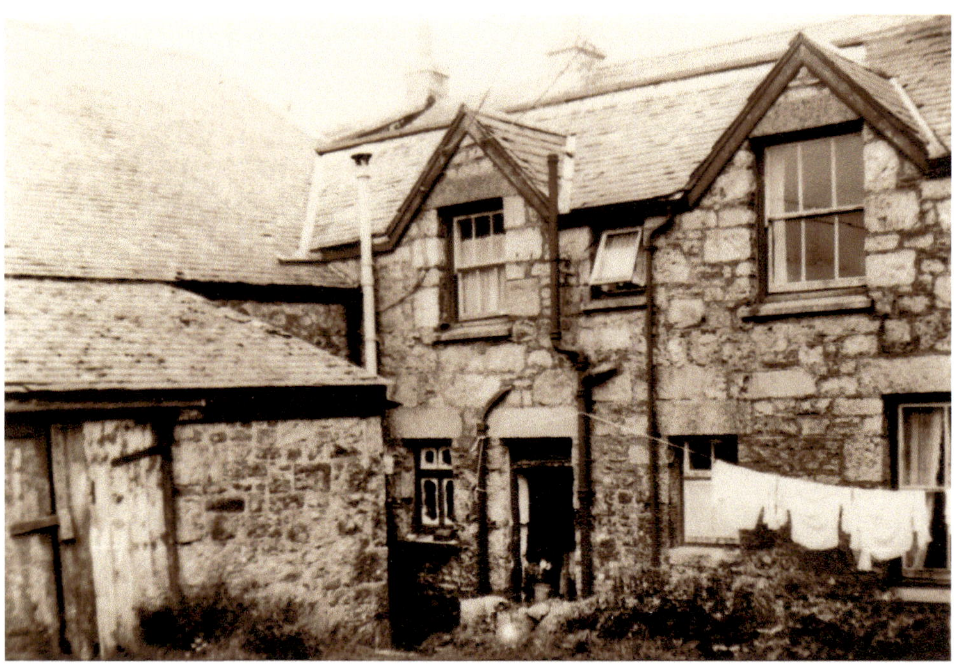

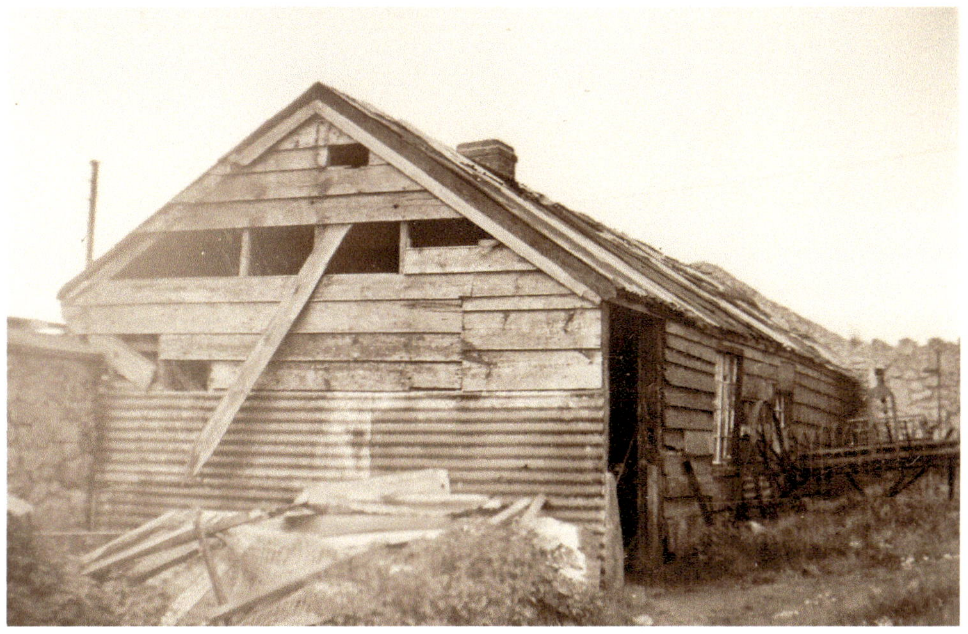

The Smithy

The old, black smithy shed is situated between the tavern and the island shop. A farrier, Mr Padget from Fremington near Barnstaple, who used to visit Lundy to tend to the needs of the working horses, used it within living memory. Until recently, it lay abandoned and was simply used as a store shed. It has now been cleared out by Mark Penrose, a volunteer blacksmith, who came to work on Lundy in 2010. Mark has now managed to restore the forge significantly and is able to use it to produce handmade metalwork.

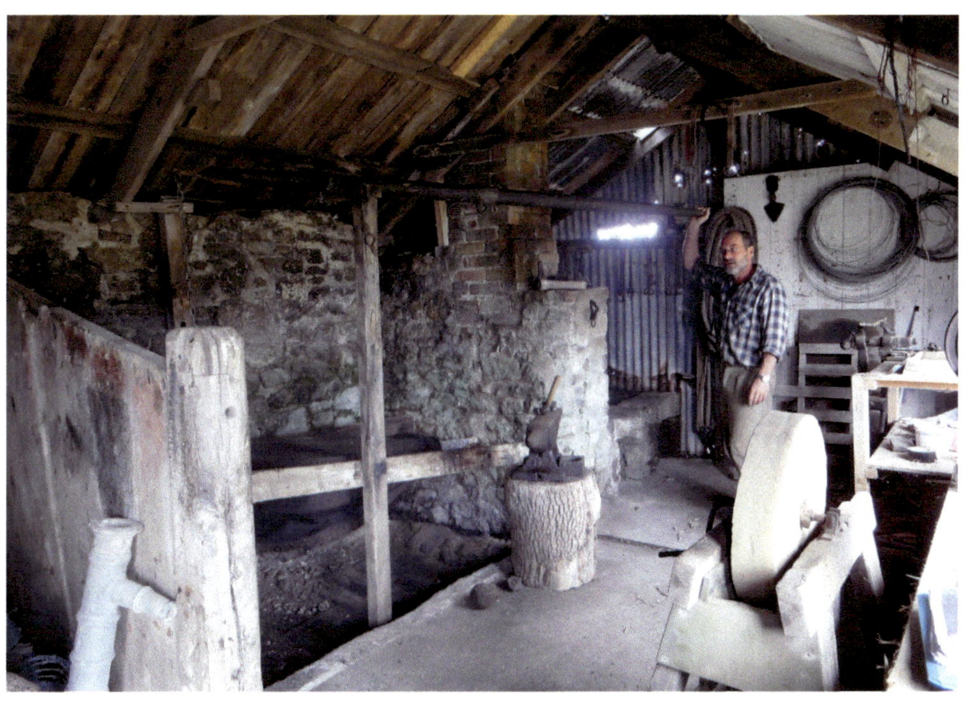

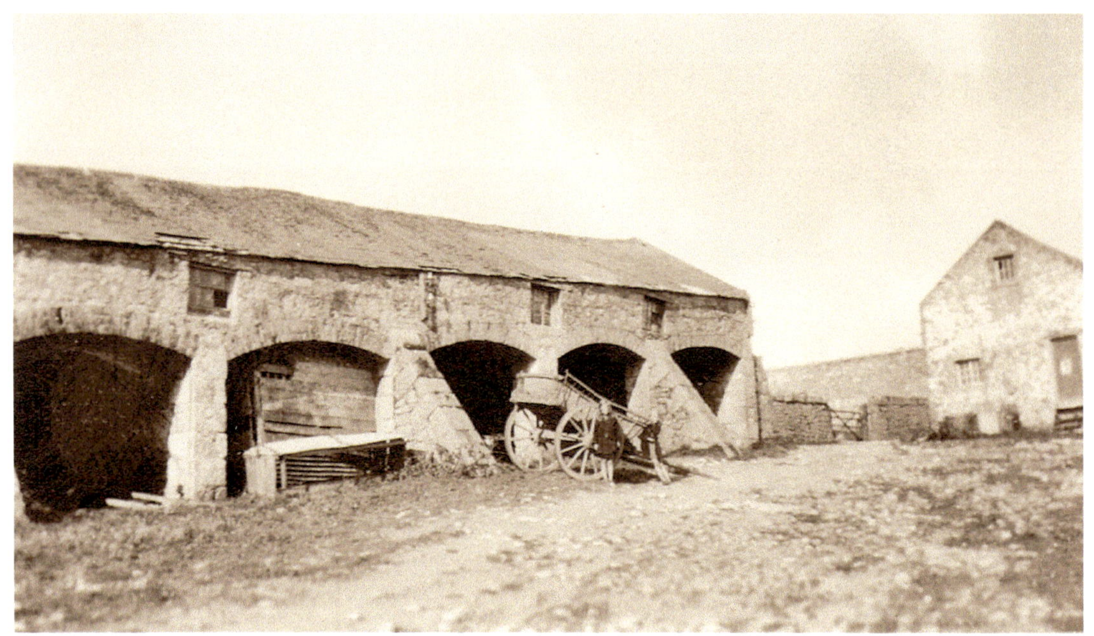

The Linhay

This building looks much the same outside as it has always done. The young children of the early twentieth century, in the photograph above, are leaning on a cart, which is situated outside the present-day shop. In the older photograph, the building on the right is the barn, which is used as hostel accommodation for visiting school groups. The cart was the mode of transport of the period, but in the colour photograph the modern-day mode of transport around the island can also be seen.

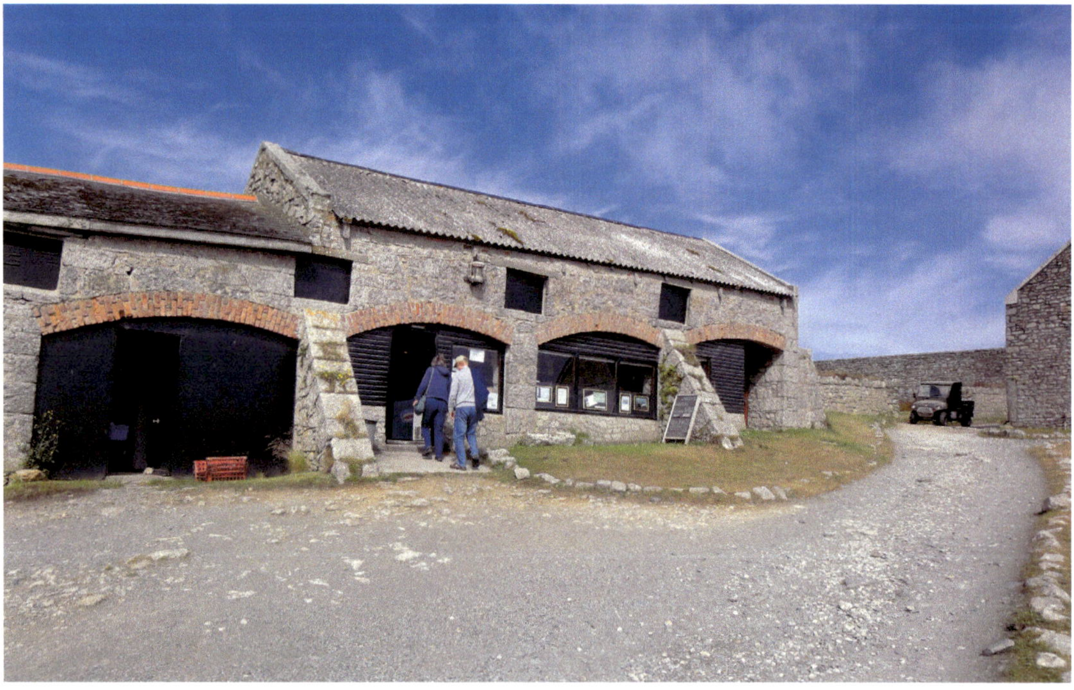

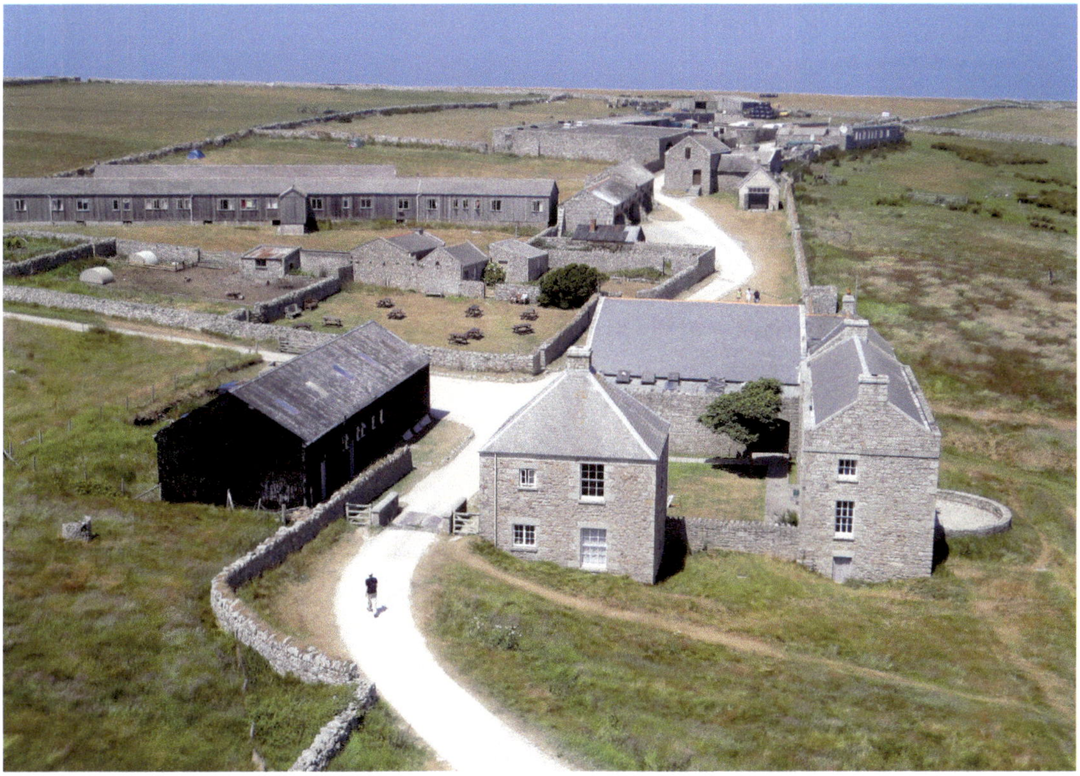

Aerial View of the Village

Taken from the top of the church tower, these two images certainly well describe the various changes that have taken place over a period of almost a century. As was seen in the photographs on pages 54 and 55, the Manor Hotel building directly in front of the camera had been altered beyond all description since the 1970s.

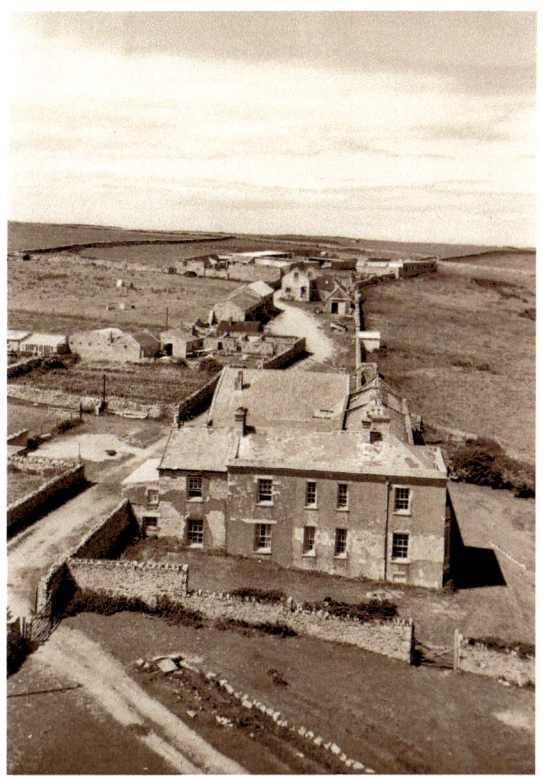

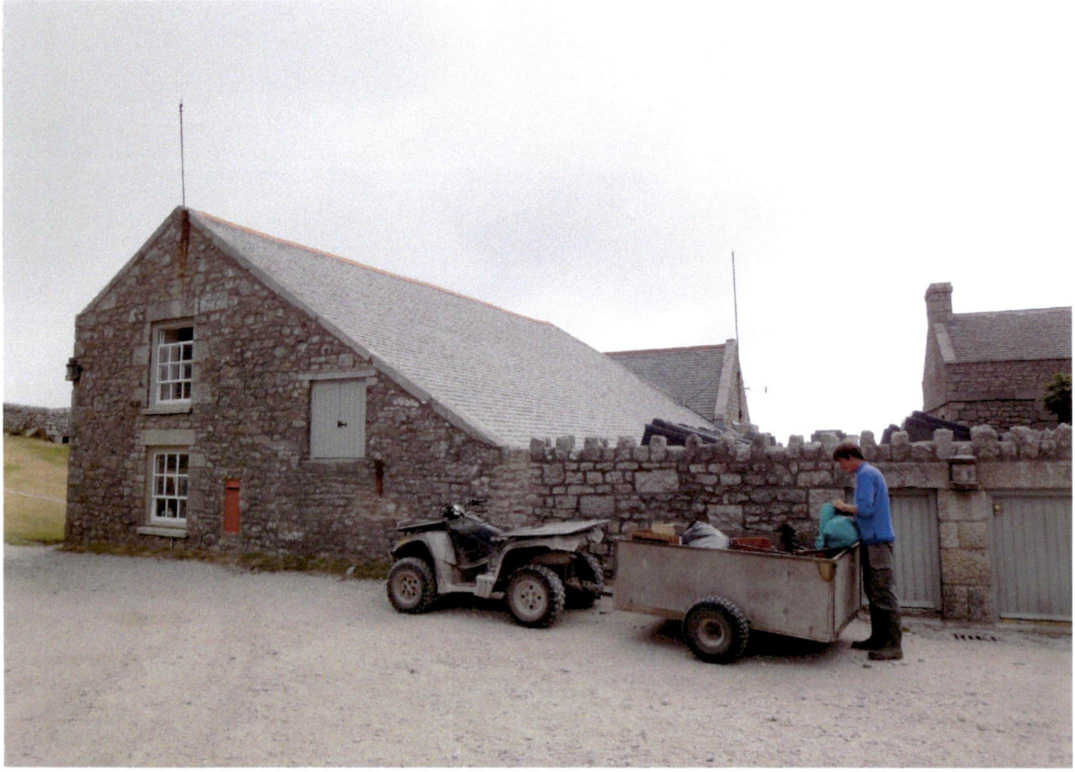

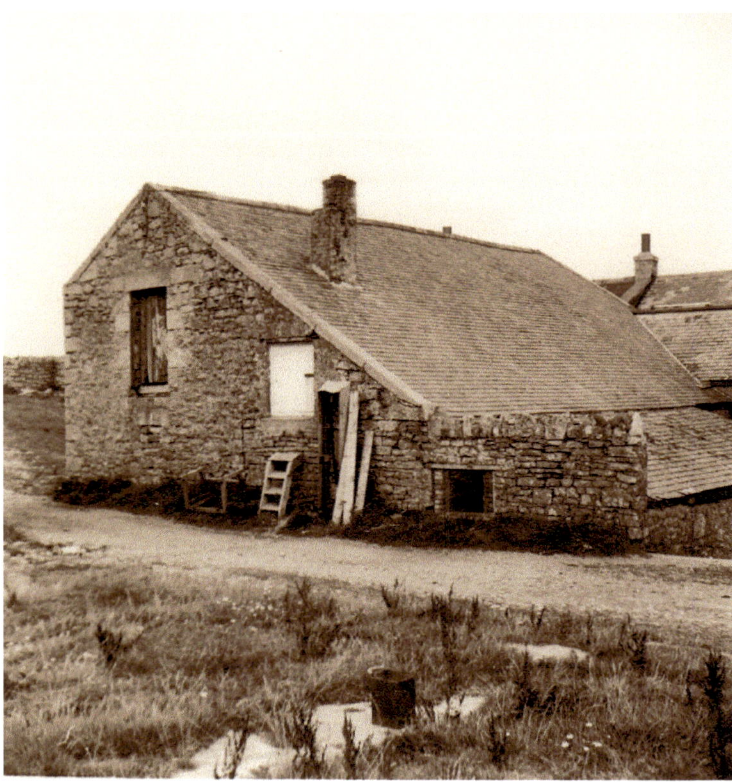

The Island Office

The Island Office (*above*) has changed very little on the outside since the older photograph was taken, in the early part of the twentieth century. It now has the Lundy mail box in its wall and is open on sailing days as a reception for those staying on the island. In the upper photograph, taken from the same viewpoint, you can see Chris Flower, the Ranger, loading up his quad bike and trailer.

Lundy Island 'Moves with the Times'

The old photograph shows the Fordson Tractor, which arrived on the island in 1941, when Land Girls were posted to Lundy. The view shows Vince Squire at the wheel of the tractor with Frank Cannon behind and Sammy Johns from Hartland in the trailer. The modern photograph, taken on the same spot, pictures Derek Green, the Island General Manager, talking with Rob Cheetham at the controls, with Keith Ward, the island decorator in the trailer. The advertisement describes the arrival of the Fordson and the demise of the horse.

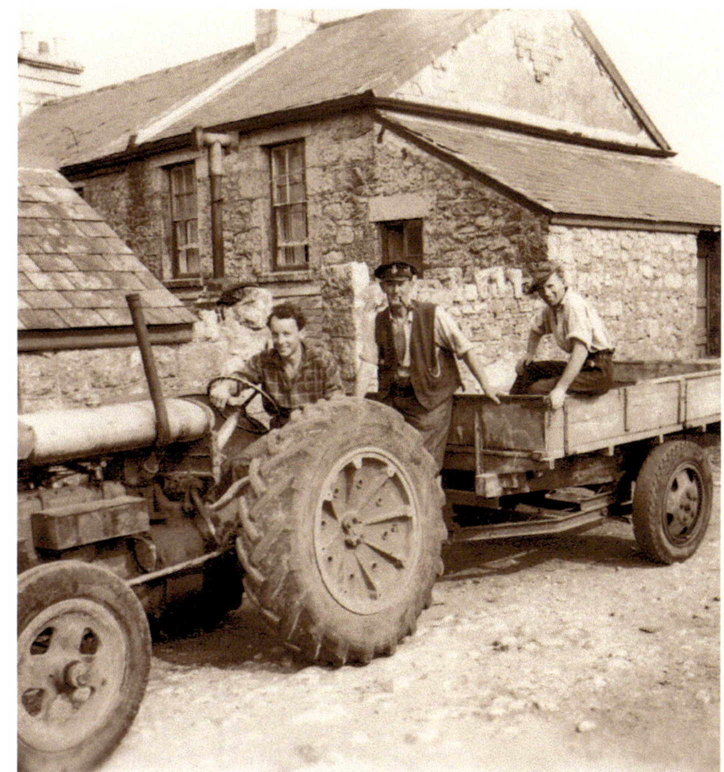

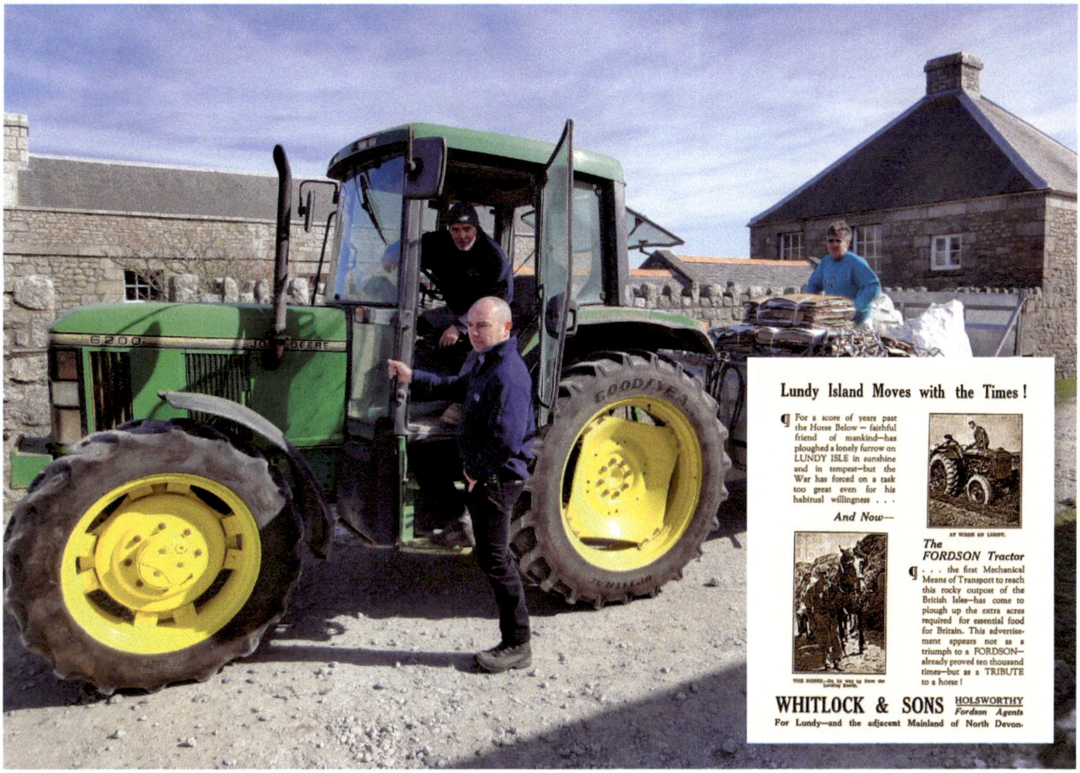

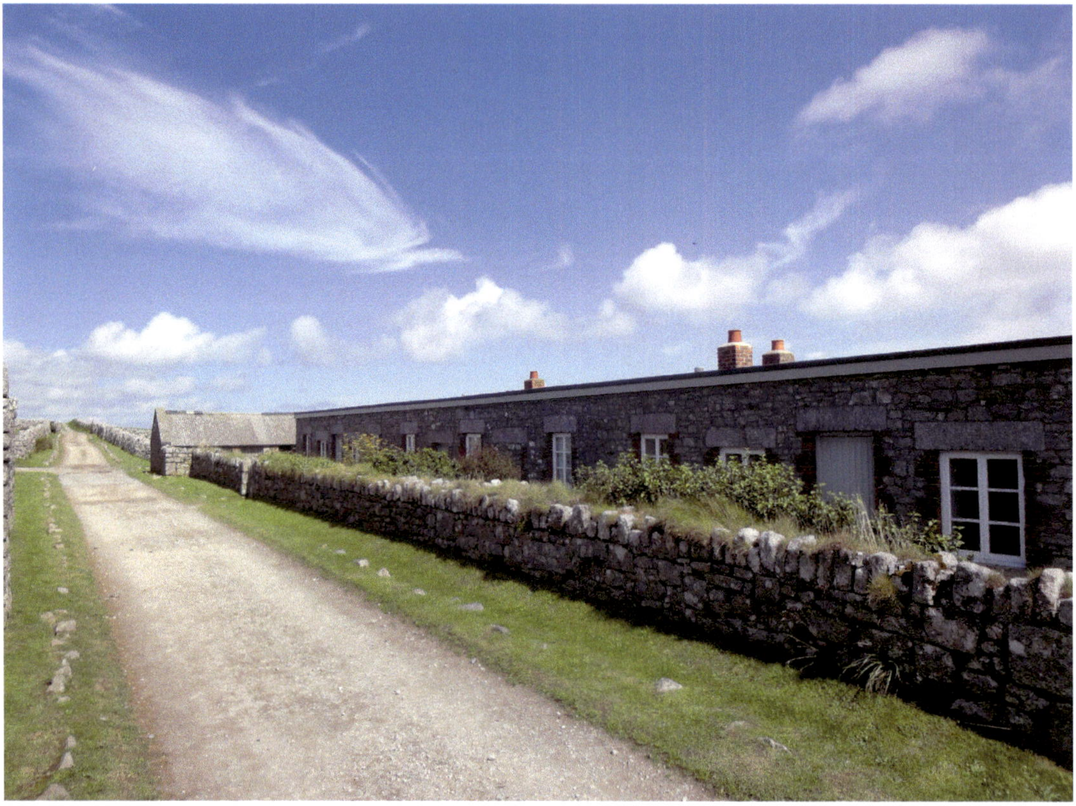

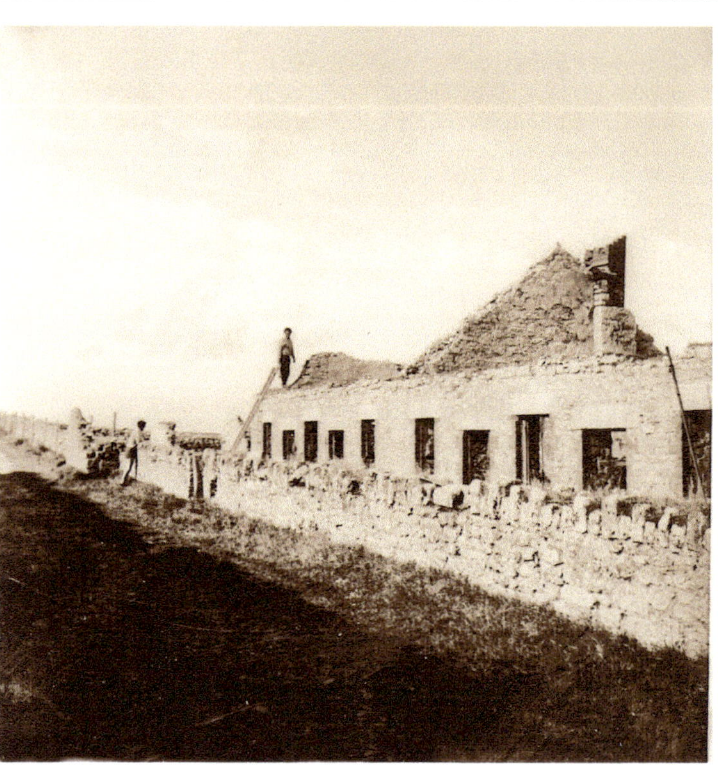

Barton Cottages, the High Street

Barton Cottages had originally been used for the staff working at the quarries in the 1860s. The buildings had pitched roofs in their early days but since they were renovated, after Landmark took over the island, their roofs have been flat. They now comprise small cottages to accommodate island staff. The lower photograph shows work being carried out in the early 1960s.

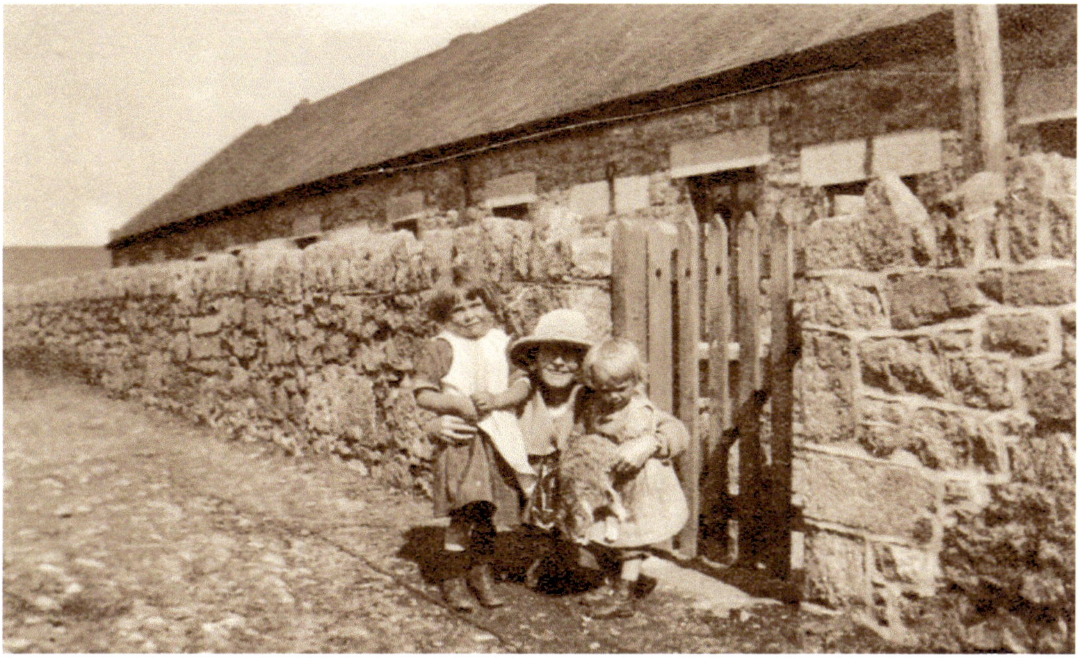

Barton Cottages and Children

The older photograph (*above*) shows Mrs Blackwell of Instow with some of the island children, outside of Barton Cottages. In almost identical circumstances outside of the same cottage gate (*below*) are Dawn Wilson-North and her two children Emily and Harriet from Exmoor on a day-trip.

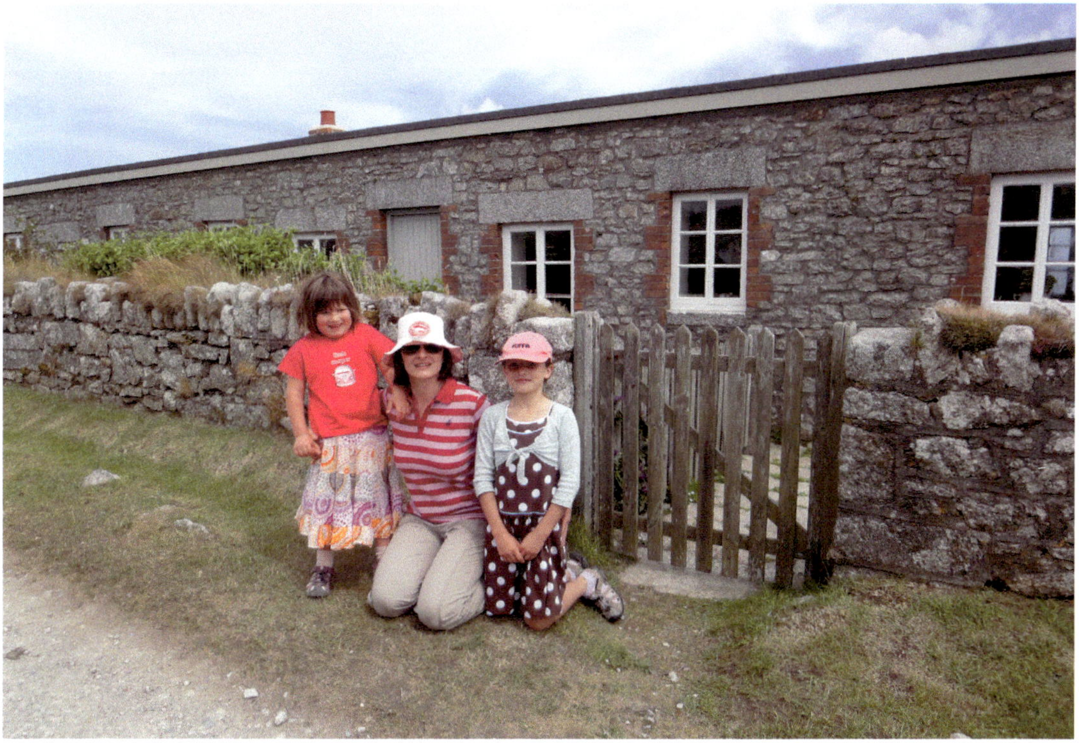

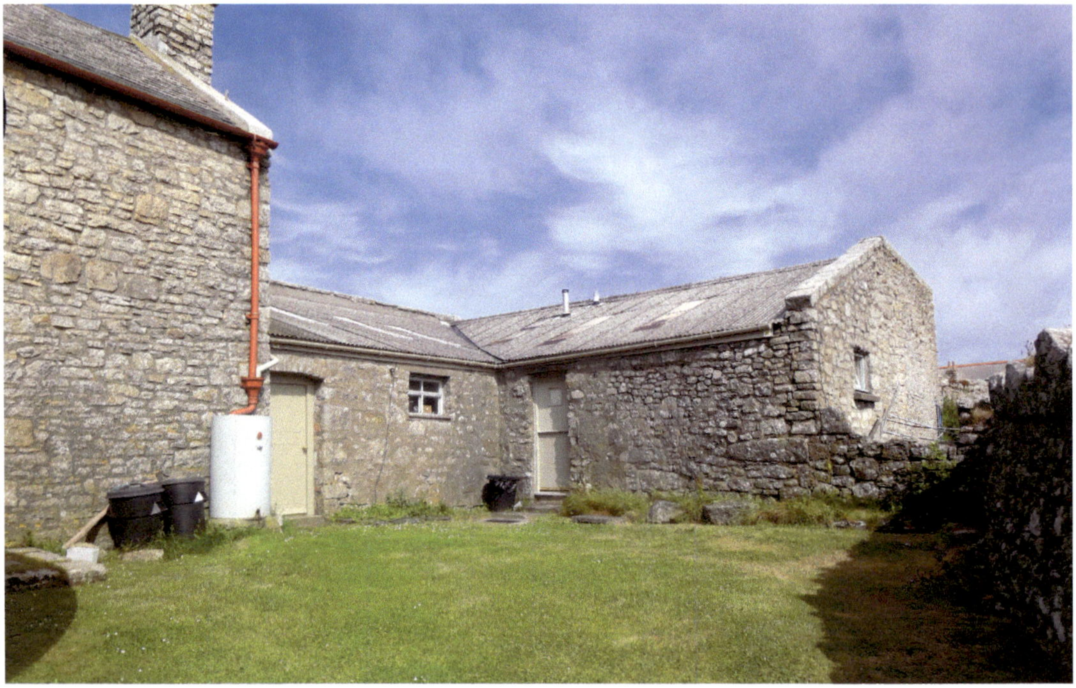

The Old Stables

At the rear of the barn in the village, tucked away behind the Exhibition Shed, is what used to be the stables for the island. The building was renovated significantly in the 1970s and now provides a small cottage for a member of staff.

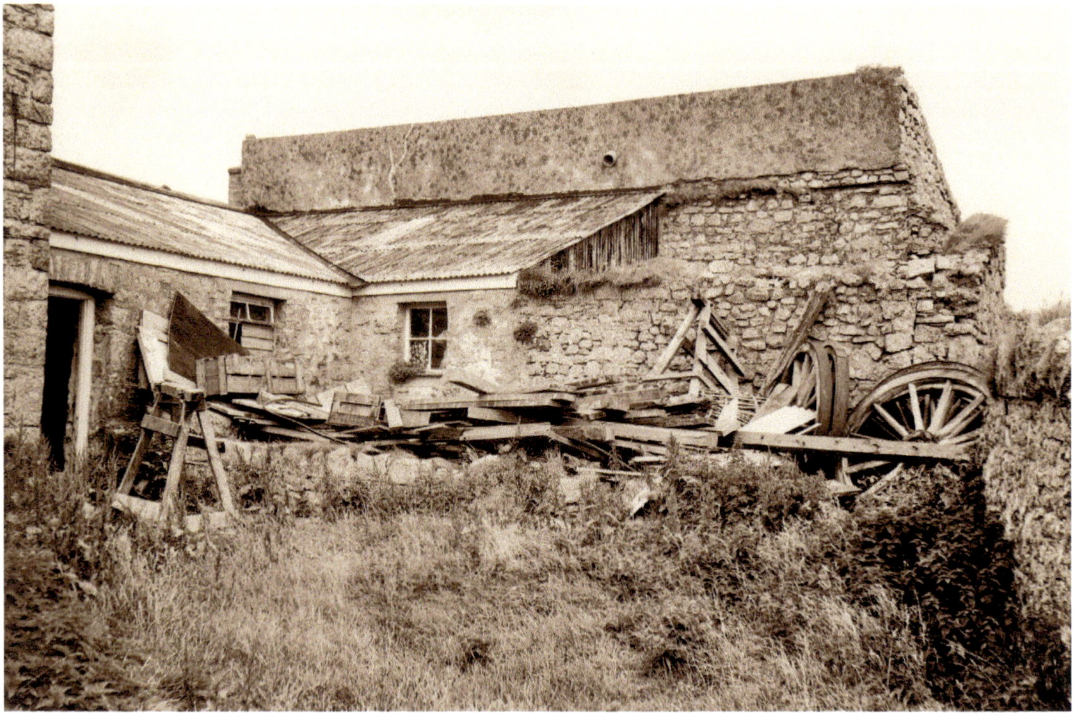

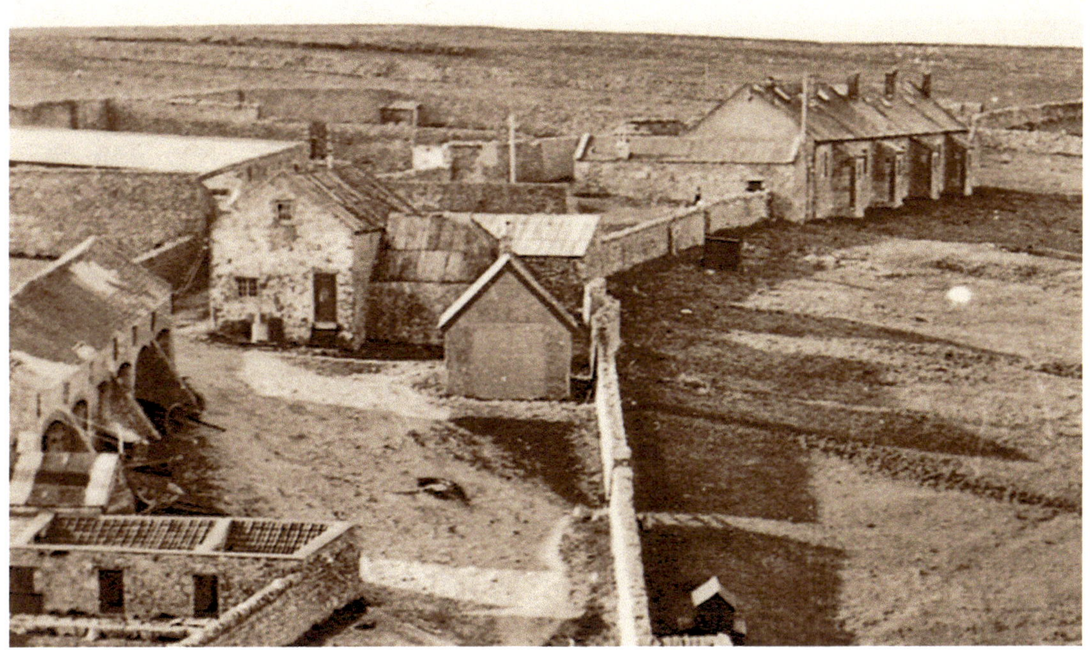

The High Street

The flat-roofed Barton Cottages in the High Street (*below*) originally had pitched roofs, as seen at the top of the above image taken before the 1950s. They have now been renovated as accommodation for staff. Other than the removal of the pitched roofs, it is quite easy to identify the current-day Barton Cottages from the old High Street buildings.

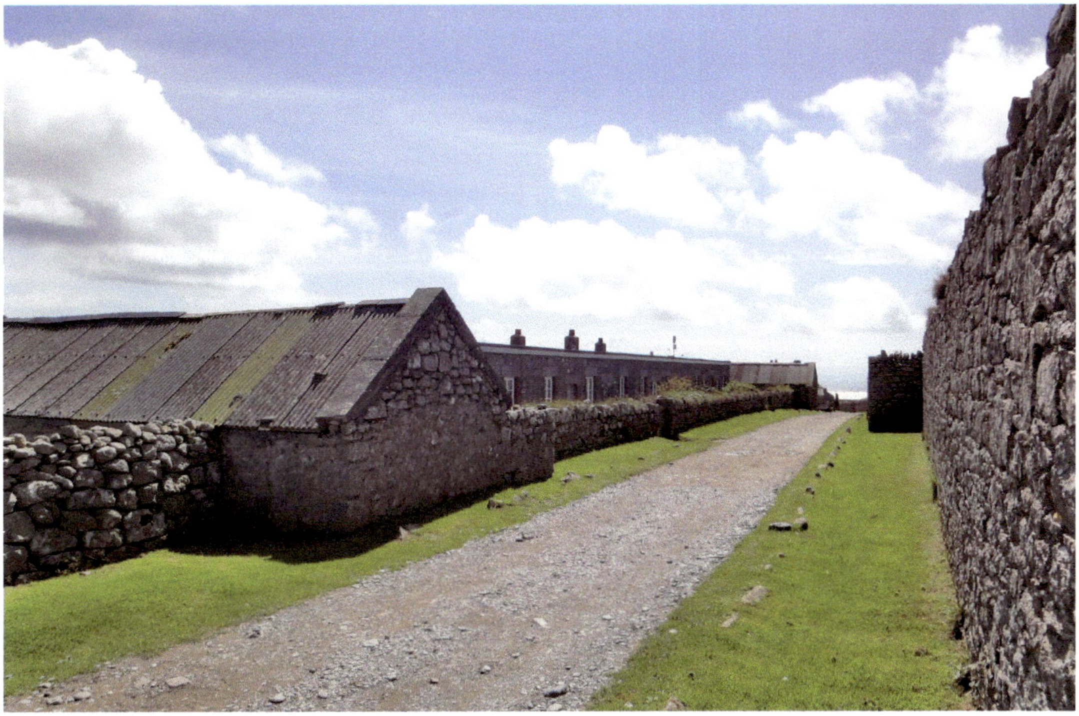

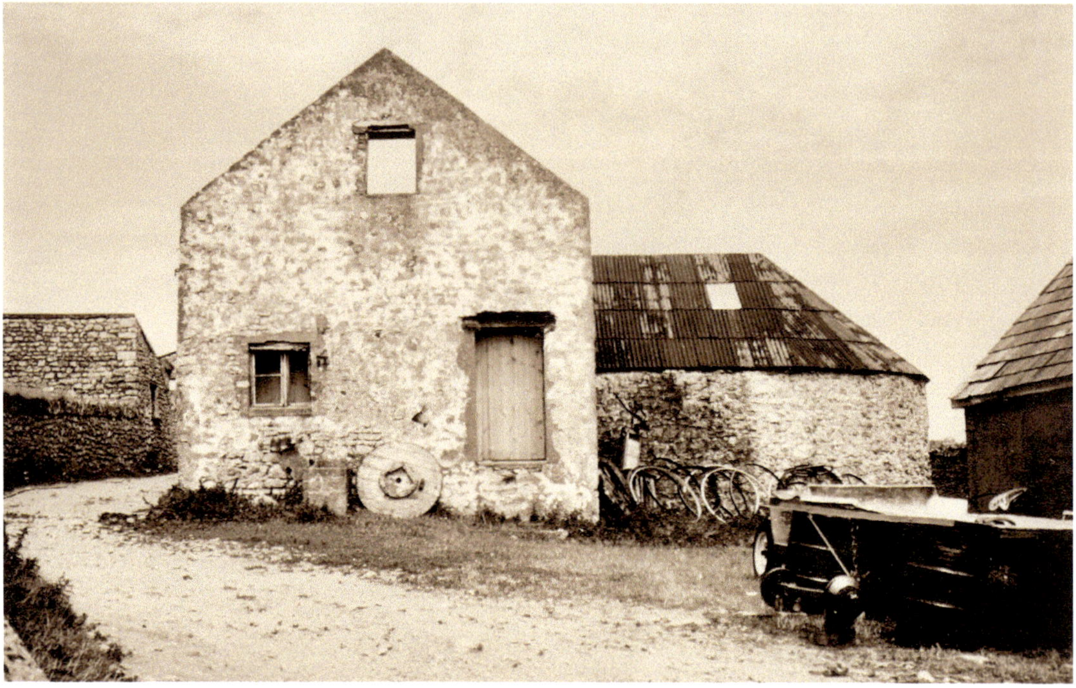

The Old Barn

Providing the largest accommodation on the island, the old barn was a complete shell in 1969, at the time the Landmark Trust took over Lundy. It was converted into bunkhouse hostel accommodation for groups and school parties who frequently visit the island.

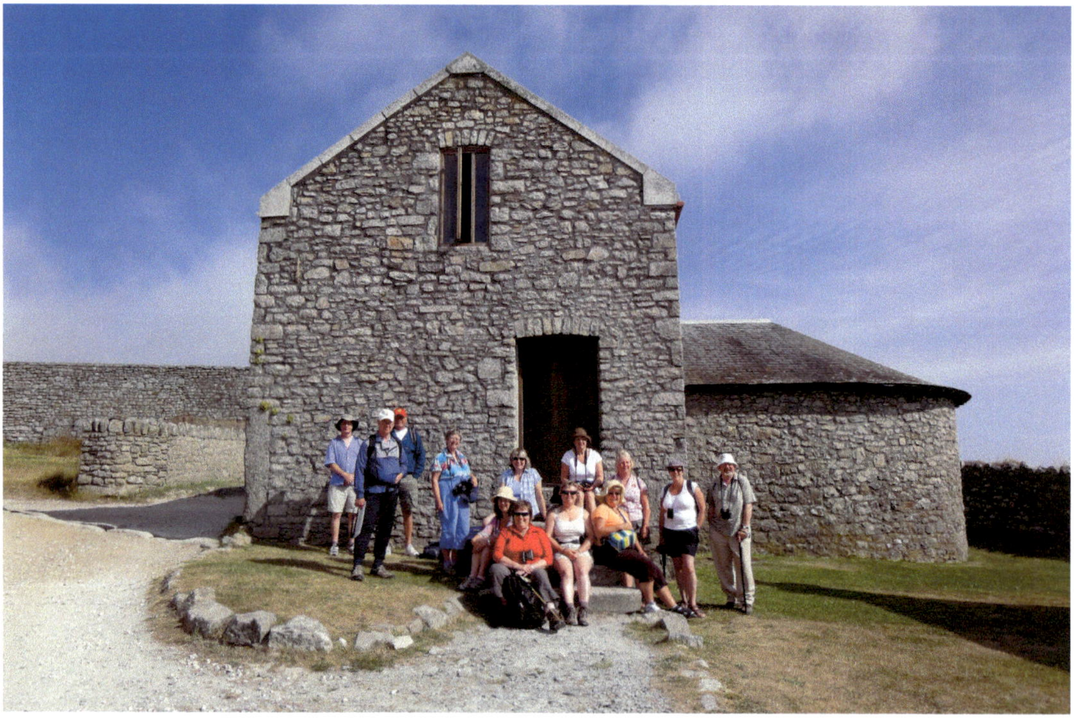

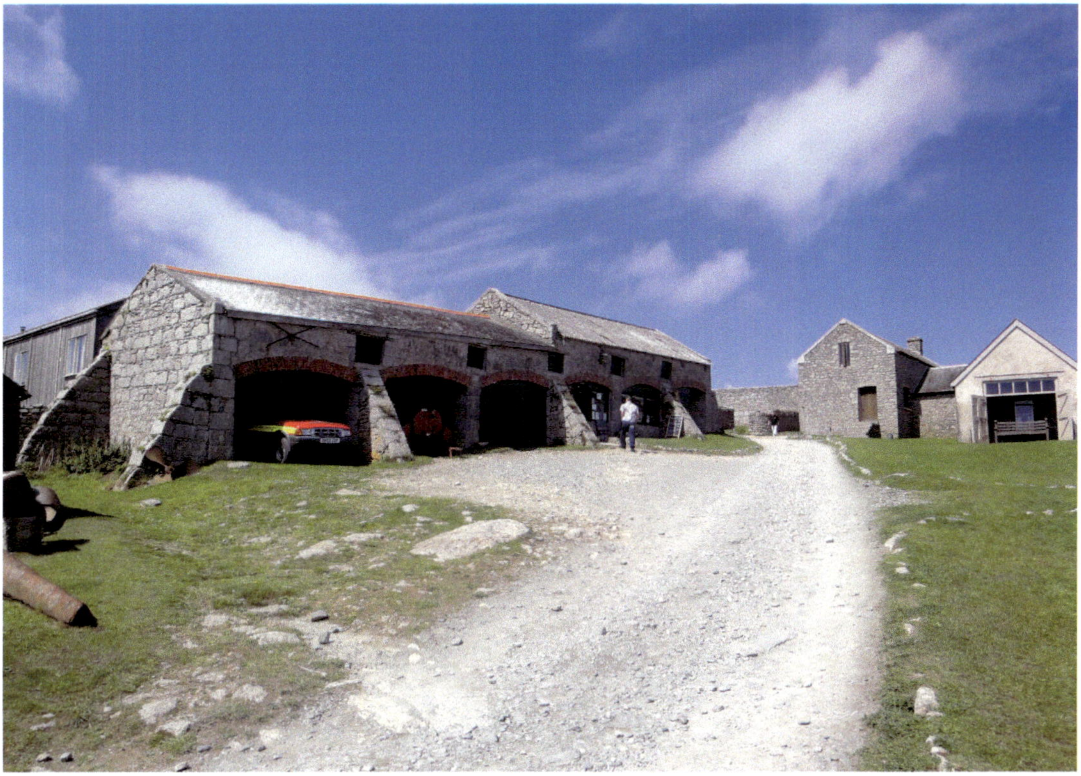

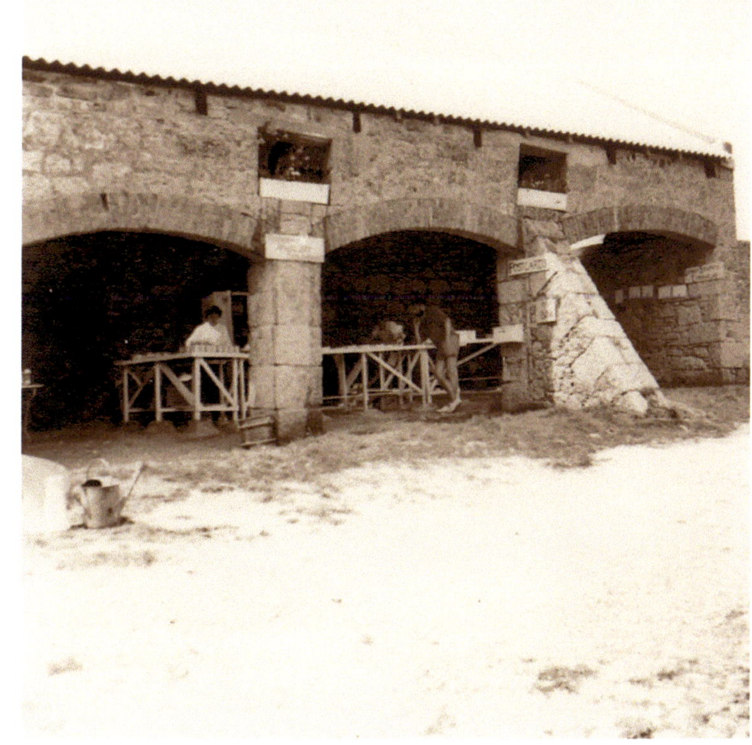

The Island Shop

The island shop is now located in the Linhay buildings. The original store was in the building now occupied by the tavern. In the 1960s, with the arrival of a large Campbell's steamer, many visitors came ashore and wanted to buy souvenirs. In the early days of the shop, a few volunteers set up a trestle table to sell postcards and gifts to the trippers. The modern photograph (*above*) shows the fire station on the left side.

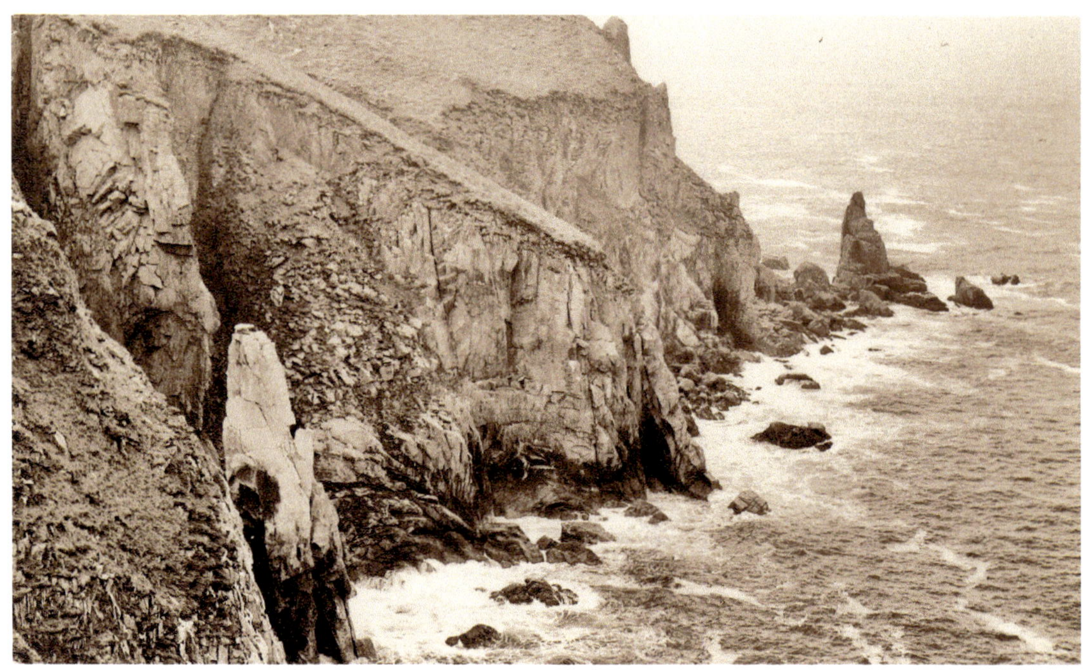

Needle Rock and Jenny's Cove

Throughout all the variety of photographs in this book, this is the only landscape image. It is inserted to show without doubt that the island has changed very little at the hand of nature and weather conditions over the past one hundred years. The hand of man has changed so much but the elements are much kinder. This photograph shows the location of some of the puffin nests. In the newer photograph (*below*) look closely for the two people standing on top of the ancient Mangonel Platform, where a medieval catapult once stood to guard the landing spot below.

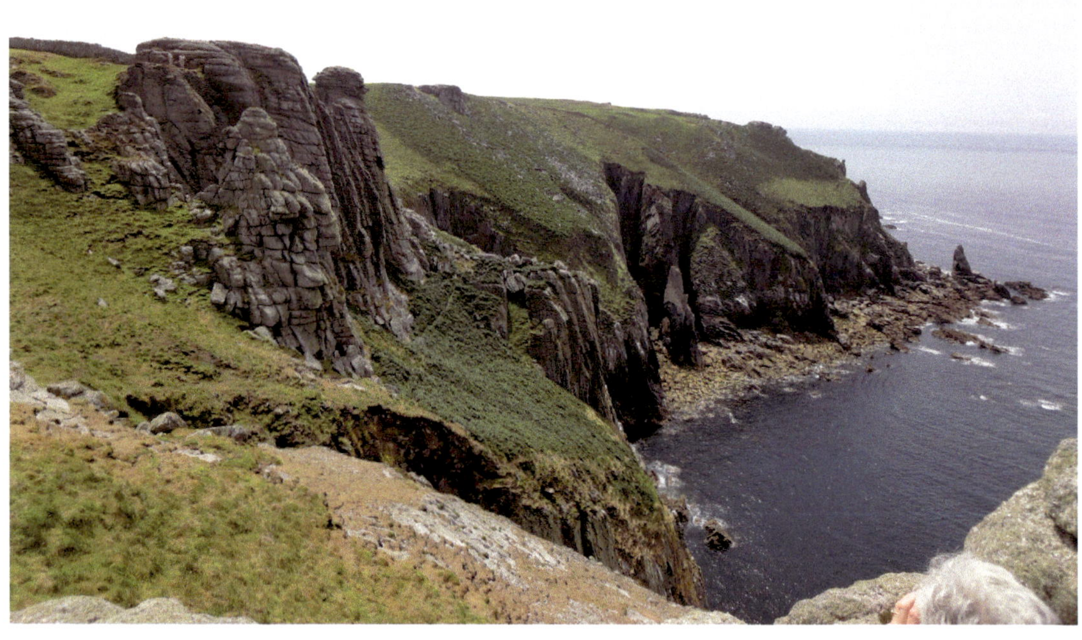

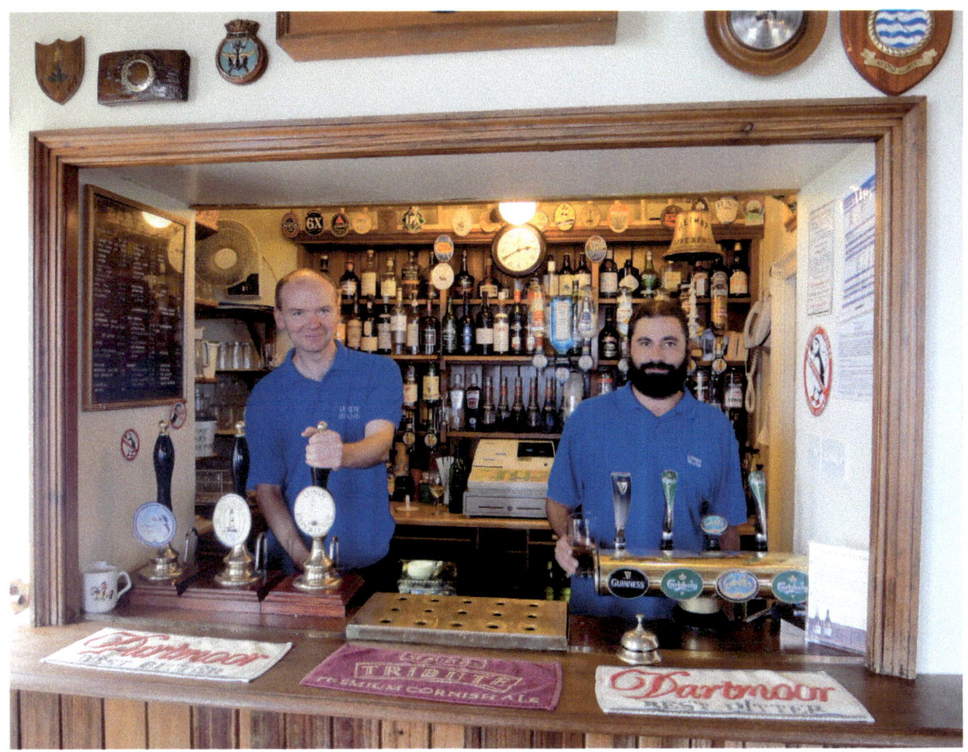

The Tavern Bar

Above, Barman Grant Sherman pulls a pint in the tavern bar, ably assisted by Ceri Stafford. The older image (*below*) shows the barman Jim Prouse in the early 1950s in a crowded bar-room. A couple of lighthouse keepers from the South Light are also enjoying a pint in their off-duty hours.

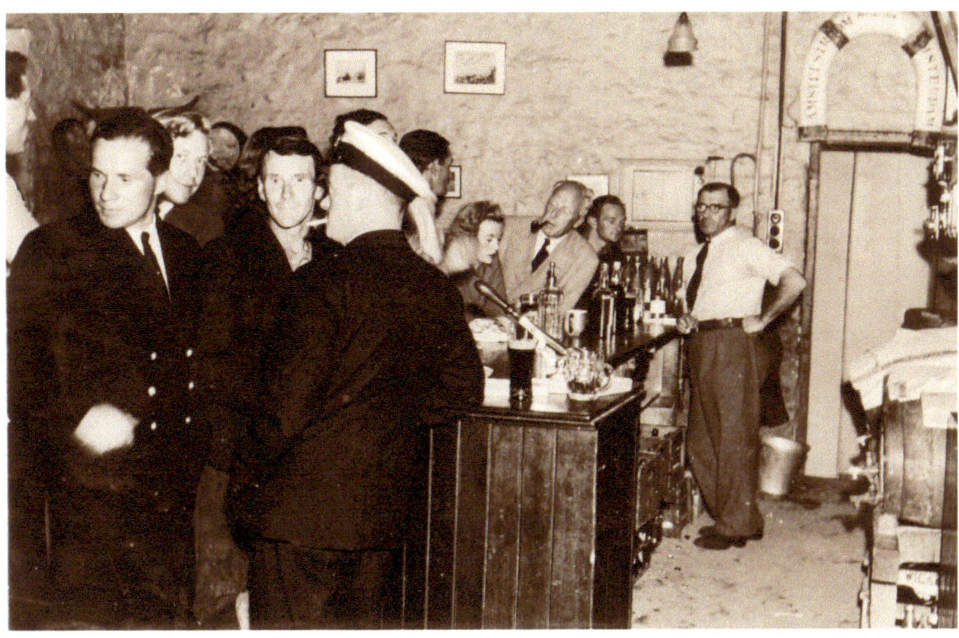

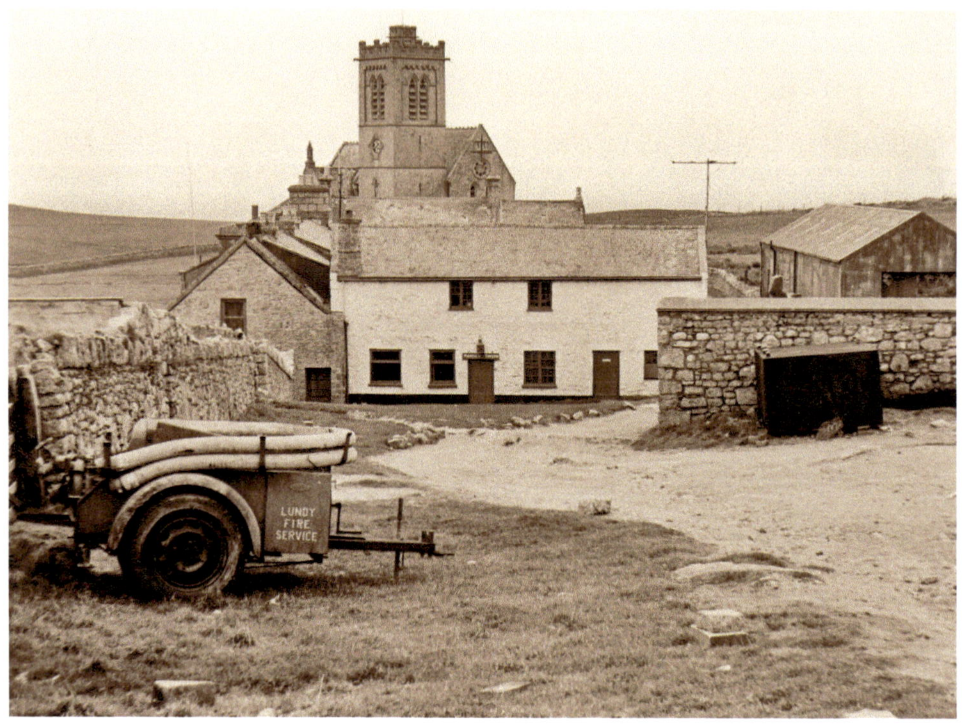

The Lundy Fire Service

How things have changed! Above stands the Lundy Fire Service portable pump, used for fighting fires. This used to be pulled along by the island tractor. In contrast, the newly presented fire appliance, for the use of the island firefighters, is seen with the whole crew of the Lundy detachment of the Devon & Somerset Fire & Rescue Service. Regular training days are held, run by the fire service trainers from Barnstaple and North Devon.

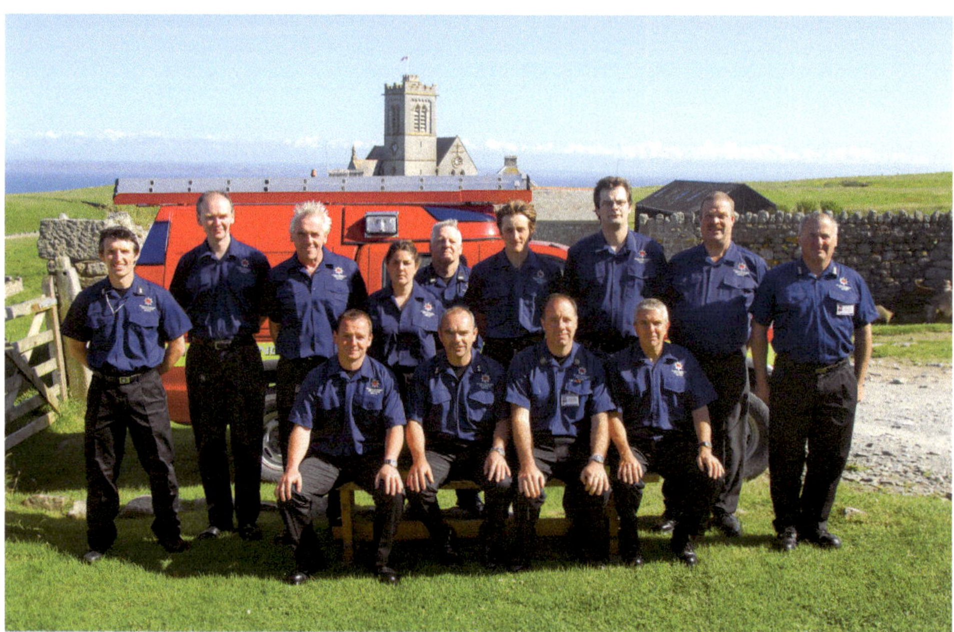

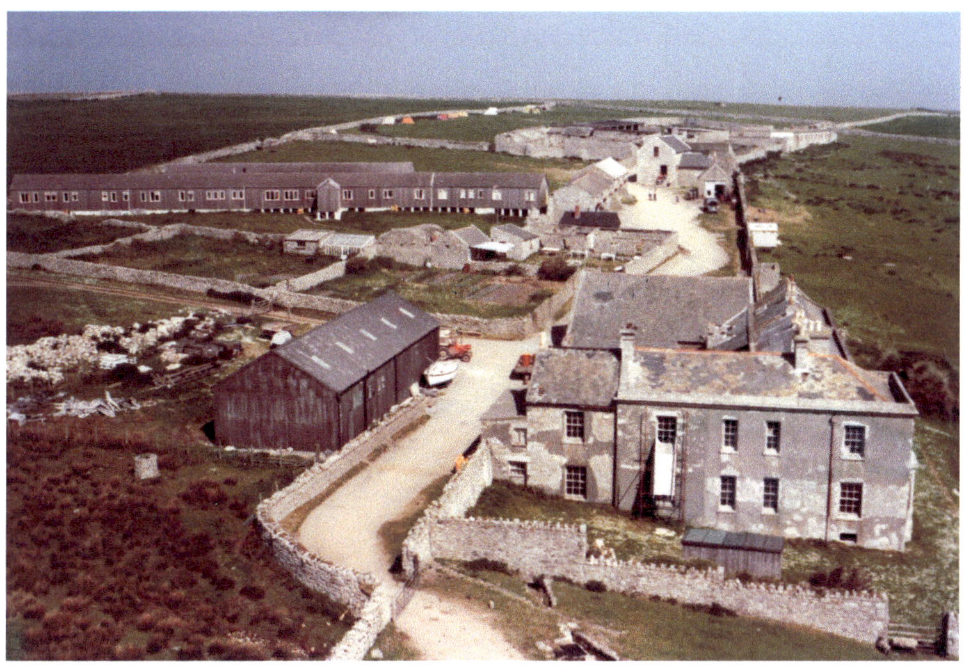

The Development of the Village

This view of the renovation work, started in 1978, is taken from the top of the church tower, and the contrast clearly shows what changes have occurred since then. The lower photograph shows the modern-day scene following the restoration and creation of new buildings from the site of the old Manor Hotel. It is interesting to see the tents in the field in the older photograph. The 'Quarters' buildings were a temporary measure, constructed from wood, for the Landmark Trust labourers and tradesmen who were brought over to carry out the major works in the village. They still house employees in the buildings with a holiday cottage for rent at the far left.

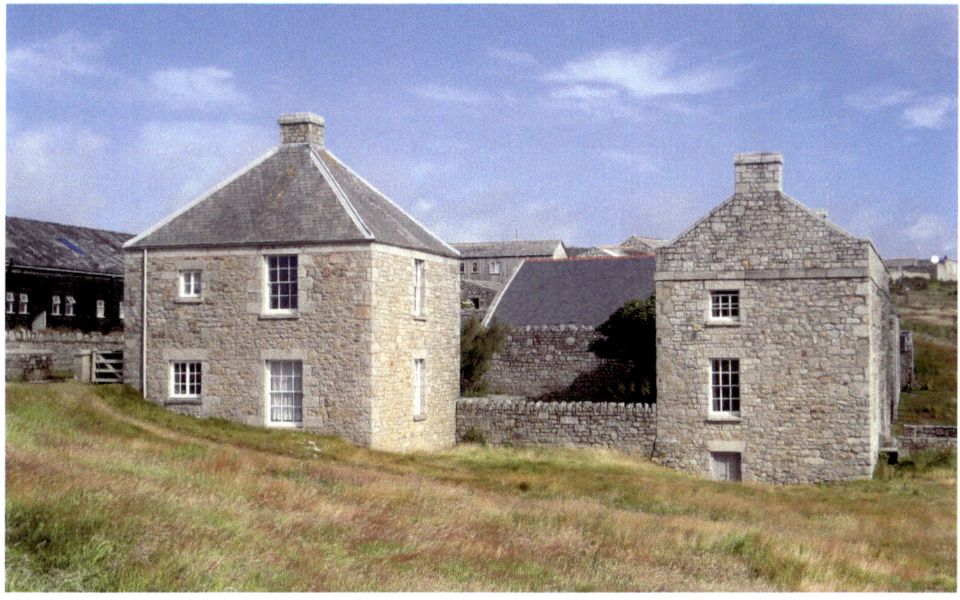

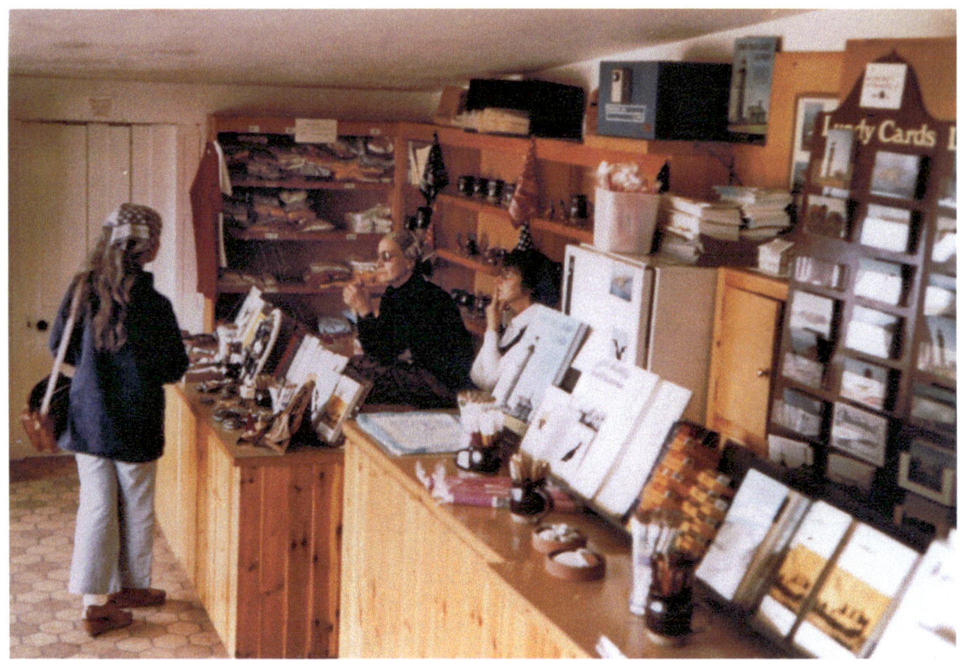

Shopkeepers – Open All Hours!

The island shop, which still occupies the same building, has significantly altered. In the upper photograph, the seated lady wearing the headscarf is Gwendolyn Morrow, a nurse who lived on the island and helped on the premises. The customer is an island resident, Pam Darlaston. In the lower image Nigel Dalby, on the right, runs the modern-day shop with the postmaster for the island, Reg Tuffin, on the left.

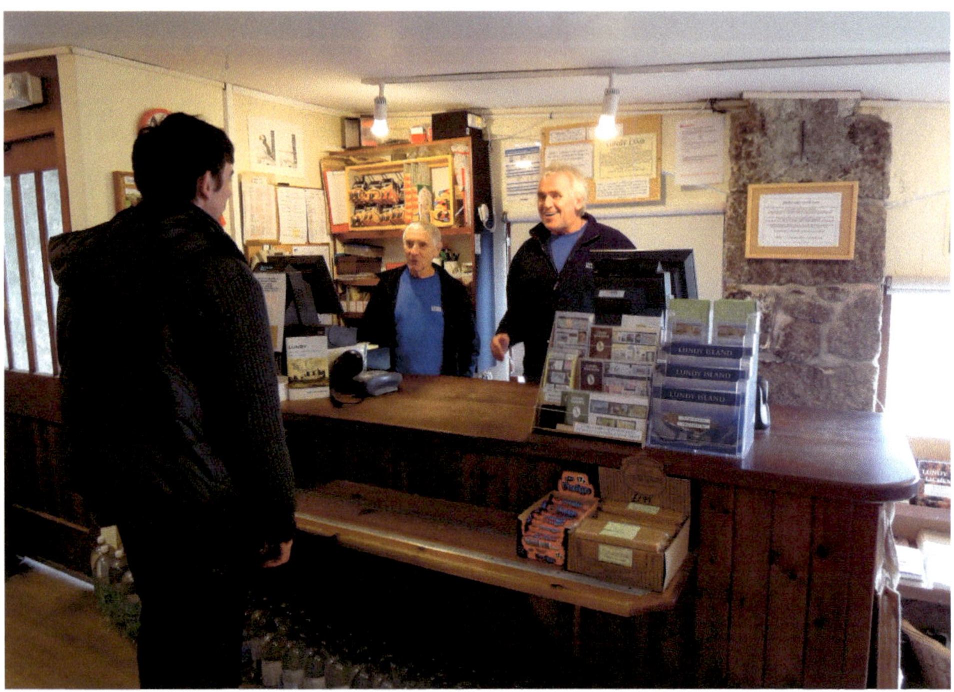

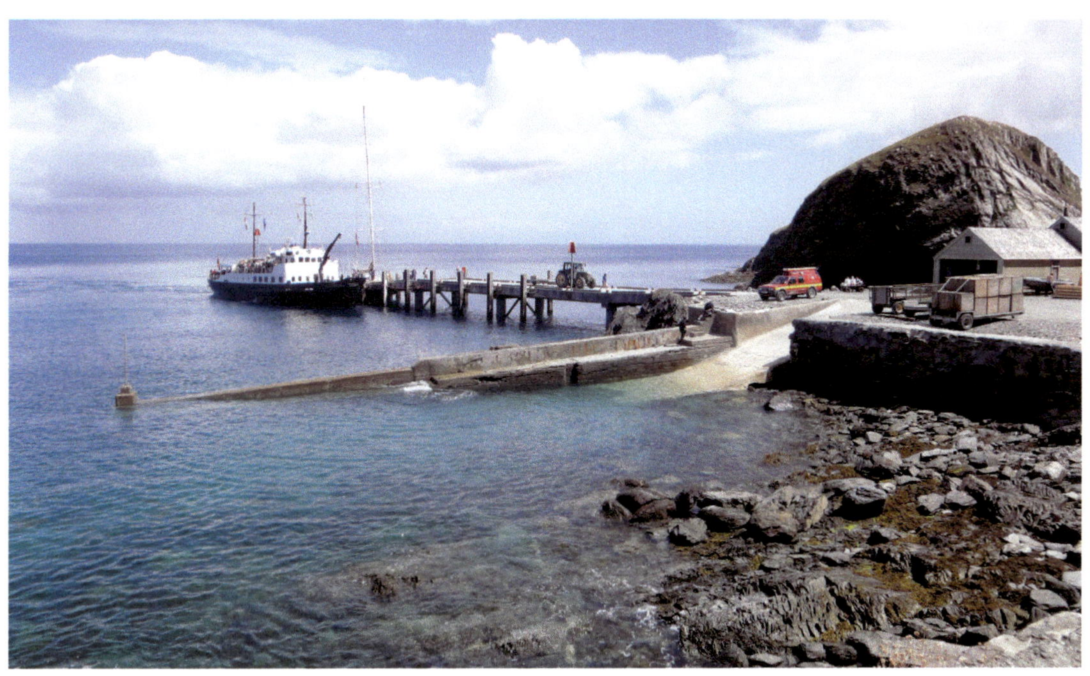

Ships Delivering Cargoes

The *Oldenburg* (*above*) is the vessel owned by the Lundy Company and used to service the island. Built in 1958, for the German Railway Services to ply between the Frisian Islands, she entered service on Lundy in May 1986 to replace the *Polar Bear*. The vessel in the lower photograph is a flat-bottomed ship used to transport cargo and deliberately 'beach' so that a horse and cart could unload stores. The owner of the vessel was Miss Grace Balley of Ilfracombe, who is standing on the ladder at the front of the boat.

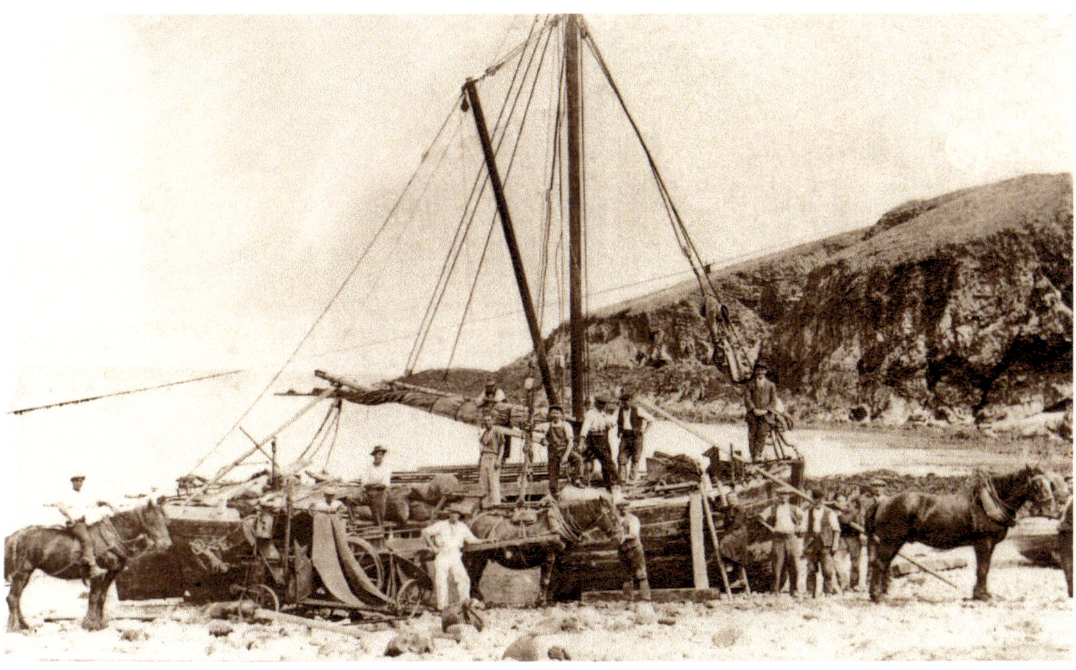

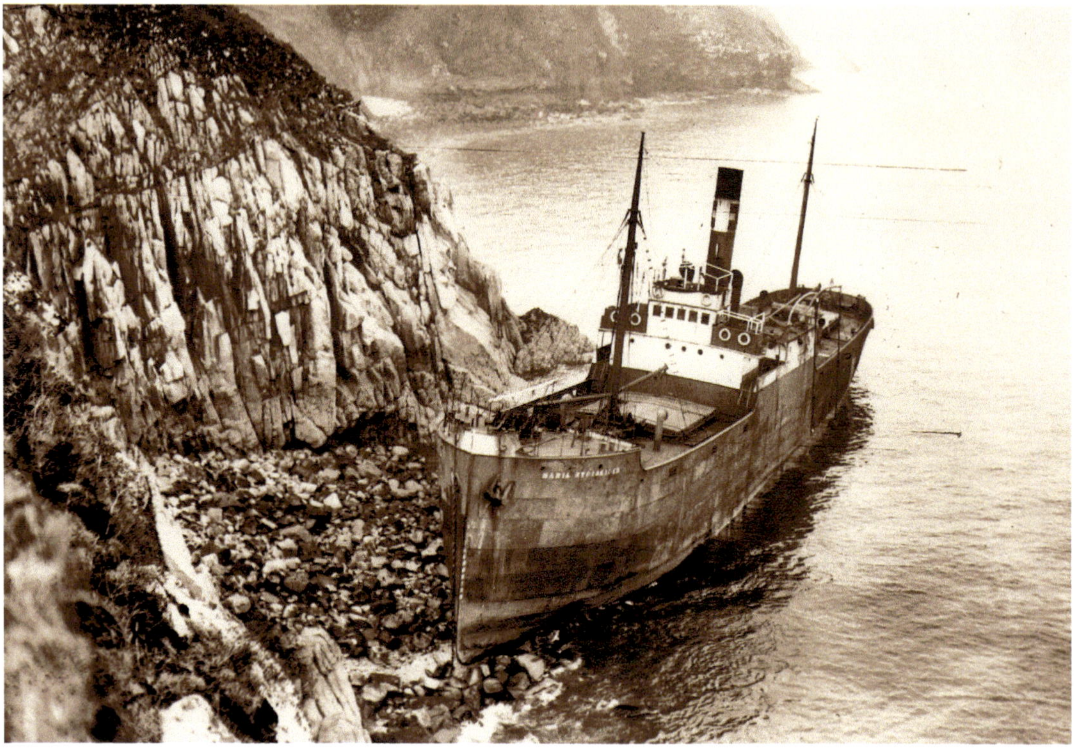

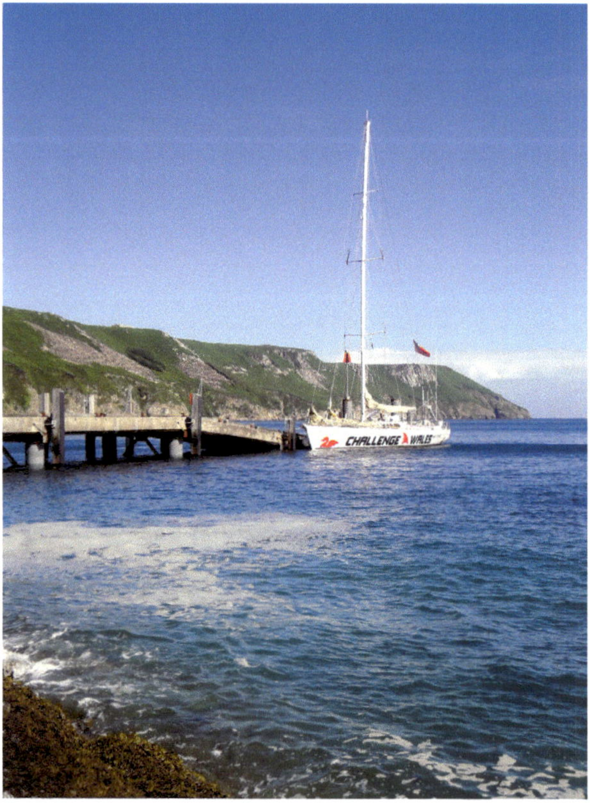

East Side Vessels

In the older photograph (*above*) the Greek steamship *Maria Kyriakides* went aground at the quarries on the east side of Lundy in March 1929. All eighteen crew were saved. About eighteen months later, she was refloated and towed to Ilfracombe. In the lower image, the 'Challenge Wales' ocean-going yacht has made a brief visit to the island, with the site of the wreck of the *Maria Kyriakides* immediately behind her. Challenge Wales is a charity dedicated to providing young people with a chance to develop their self-esteem and the life-skills of team-working and communication, through the experience of sailing a 72-foot round-the-world yacht, the largest sail training vessel in Wales.

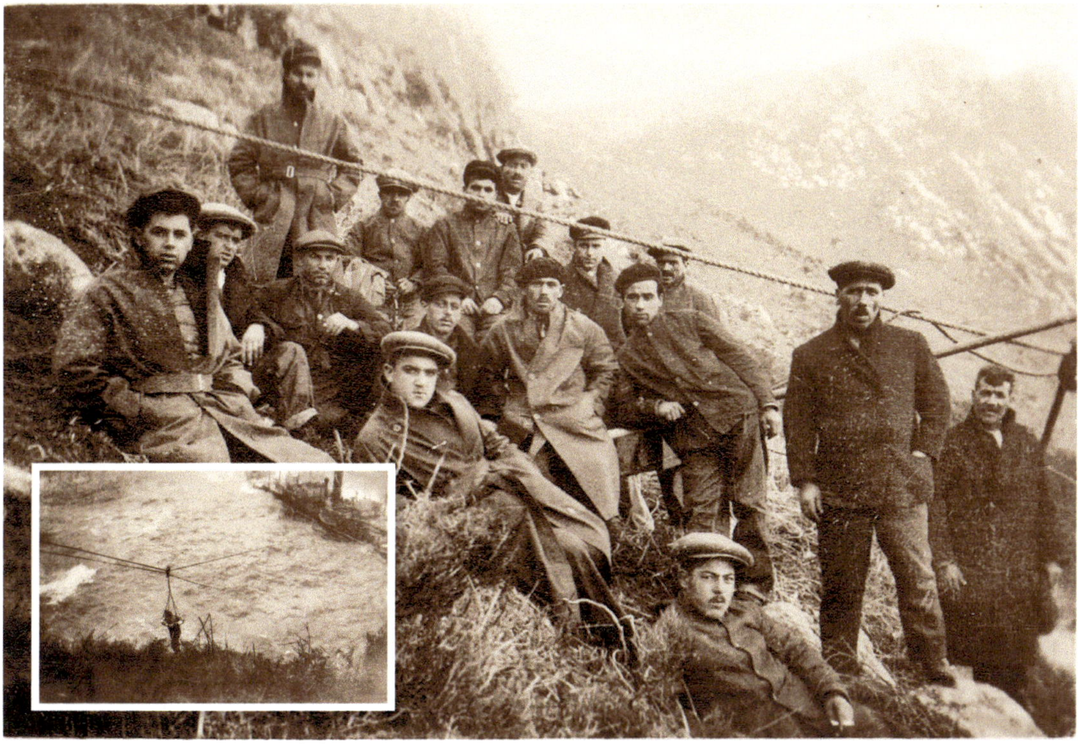

The Wreck of the *Taxiarchis*

In 1931, another Greek steamship, the *Taxiarchis*, was wrecked on Lundy. She was recovered in 1933 and towed to Ilfracombe. All the crew, pictured above on the clifftops at the site of the wreck on the east side, were saved. The small insert shows the breaches buoy rescue equipment, being used to great effect recovering the shipwrecked crew. All that now remains on the island from the ship is a lifebelt hanging (*right*) in the Marisco Tavern, above the stairs.

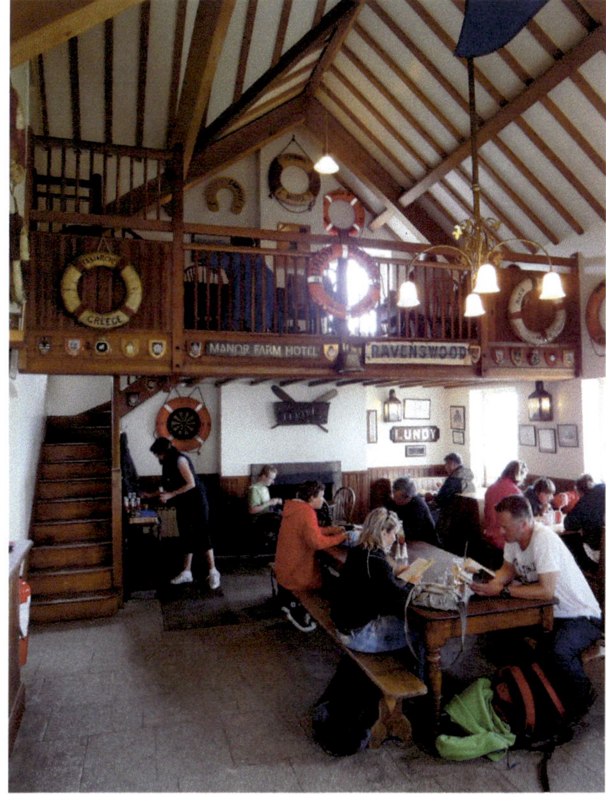

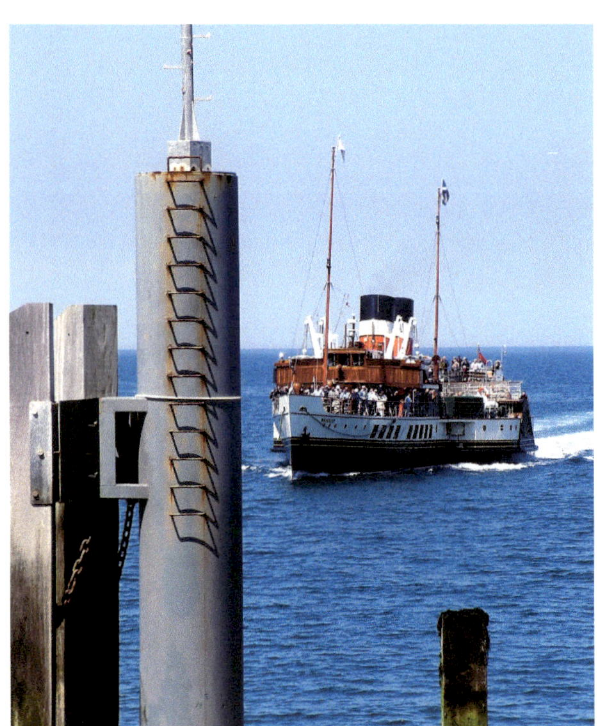

Large Boats in the Landing Bay

Above, the paddle steamer *Waverley*, from 'Waverley Excursions', sails in onto the Lundy jetty. The *Waverley* is the last seagoing paddle steamer in the world. Magnificently restored, with towering funnels, timber decks, gleaming varnish and brass, she is a colourful visitor to the island. Photographed below, in almost the same location near the end of Rat Island, is the stranded wreck of the Italian *Carmine Filomena* of Genoa in July 1937. She had collected a cargo of coal from Cardiff and was heavily laden. A minor disagreement with the captain of the ship was resolved when he and other officers were transported to Ilfracombe, leaving the wreck for 'lawful salvage'. Lundy residents didn't go short of coal for some time afterwards!

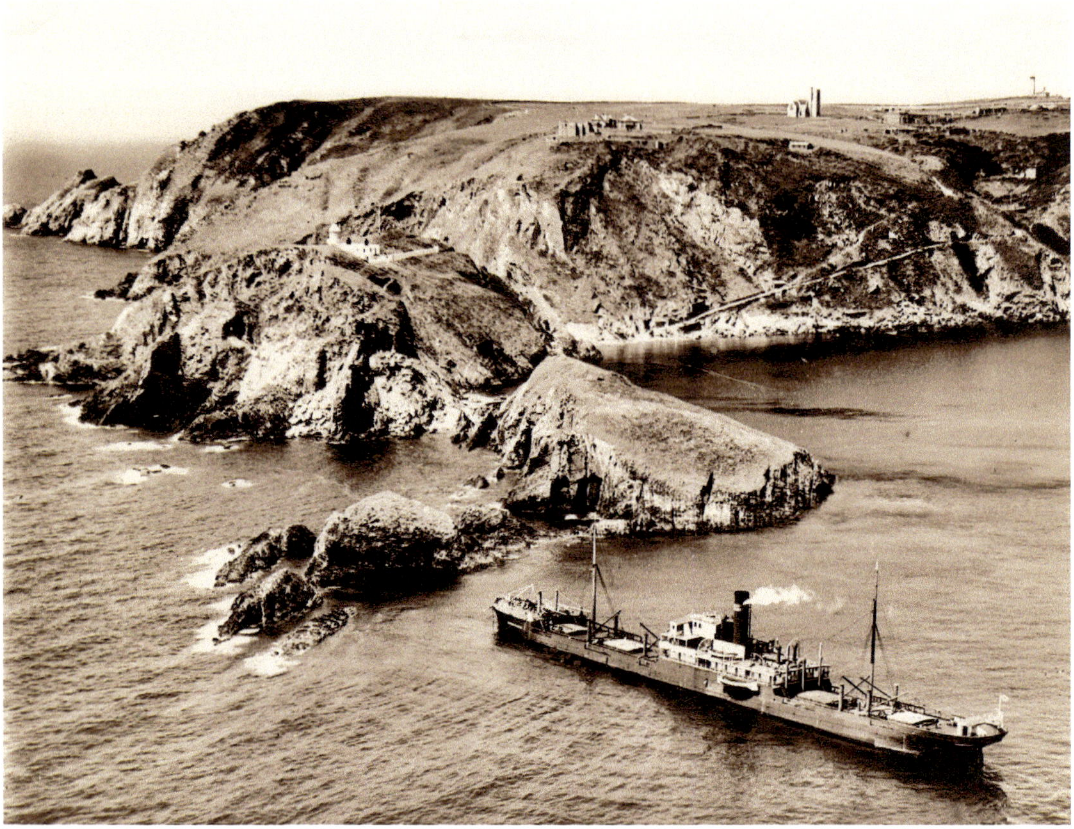

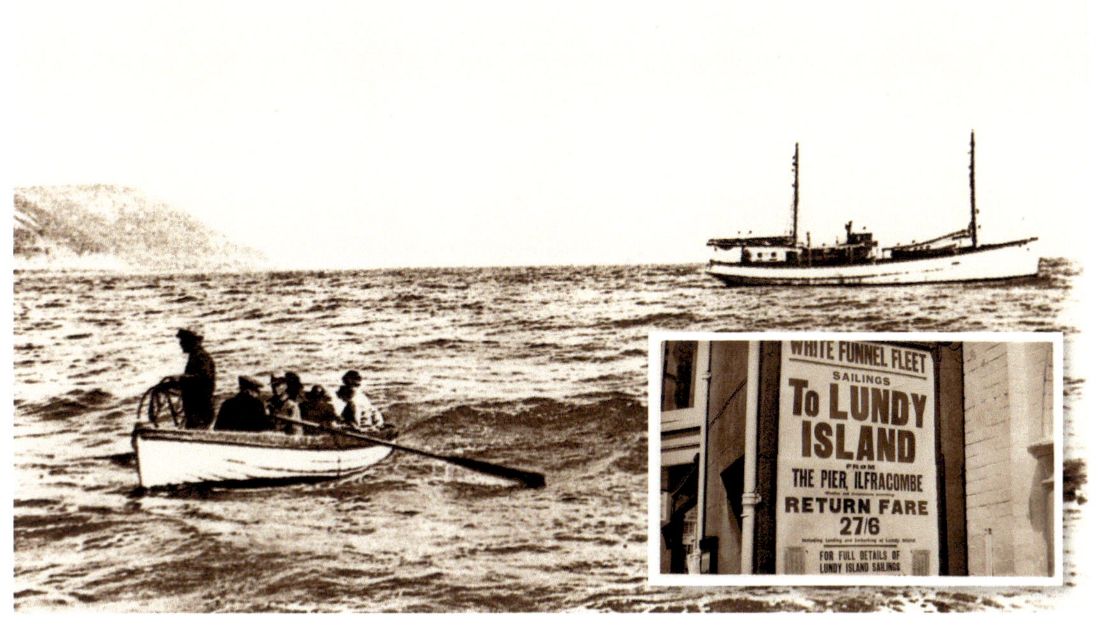

Regular Visitors

There are very few photographs of one of the most famous of the Lundy vessels, the *Lerina*, in existence. Here she is seen moored off the landing slipway in the late 1920s, having been built in 1917. She was 'dandy-rigged' with a semi-elliptical stern, and sailed out of Instow on the River Torridge. Her crew, including her Captain Fred Dark, were laid off in 1950 when she ended her association with Lundy. Another vessel, also pictured in the landing bay below, is still a frequent visitor – the Trinity House service vessel the *Galatea*. She comes in to the island with her crew of service engineers to deliver stores and work at the North and South Lights. The small insert image is a poster from the 1950s, advertising day trips to Lundy on board the White Funnel Fleet.

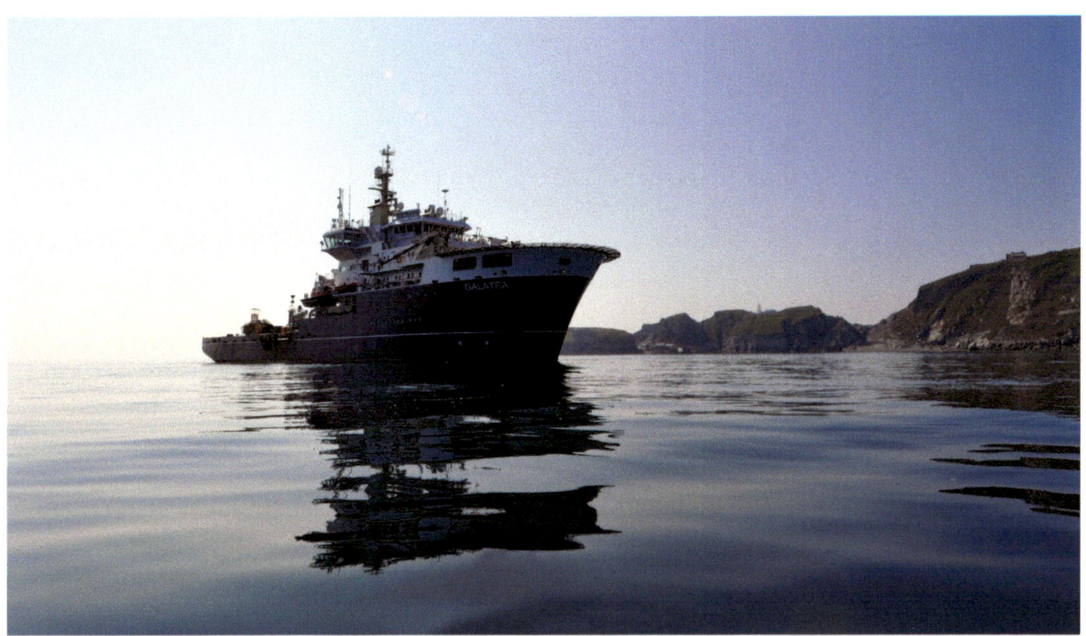

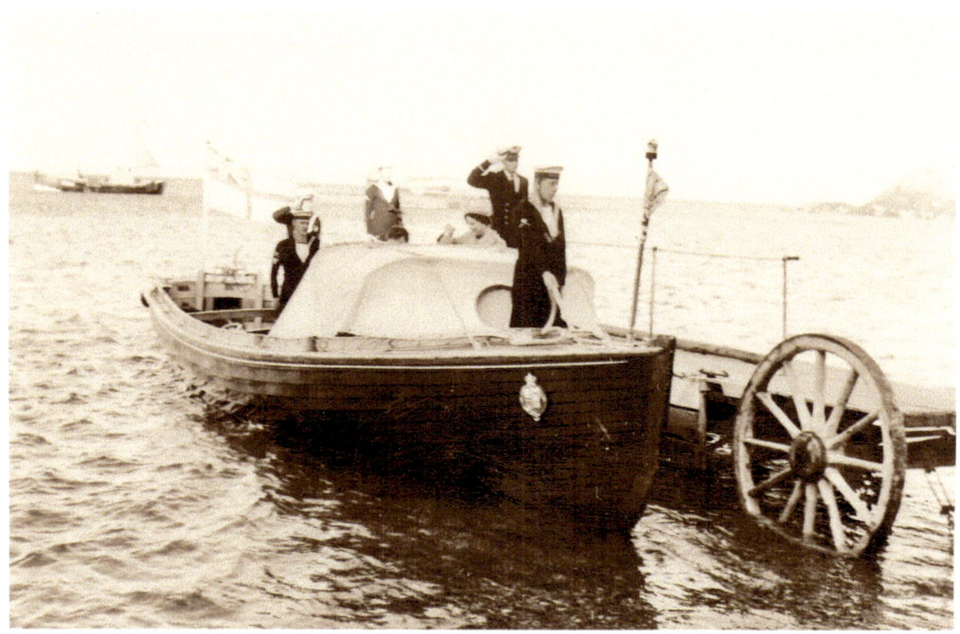

Small Boats

In 1958, Her Majesty The Queen Mother visited Lundy, on her way home from Northern Ireland in the Royal Yacht *Britannia*. She was delivered to the landing beach in one of the royal barges (*above*). Equally small but a regular visitor is the *Jessica Hettie,* with its master Clive Pearson from Clovelly, seen here approaching the Christie Quay to moor up. Clive brings out divers and fishermen, and while on Lundy is happy to take day trips around the island. It is interesting to compare this lower modern photograph with the older one on page 5, especially in respect to the buildings near the castle.

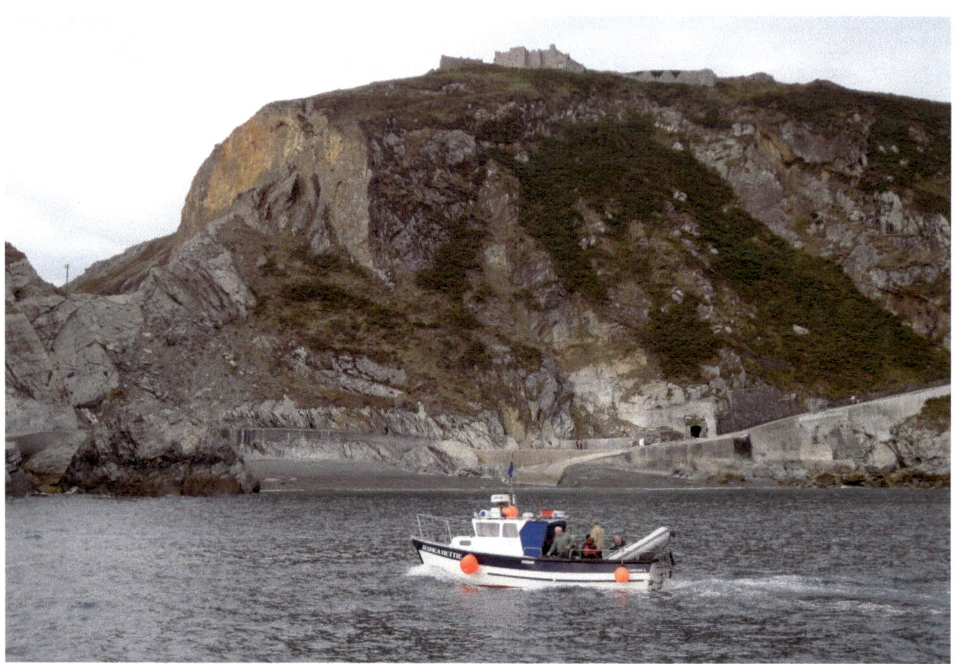

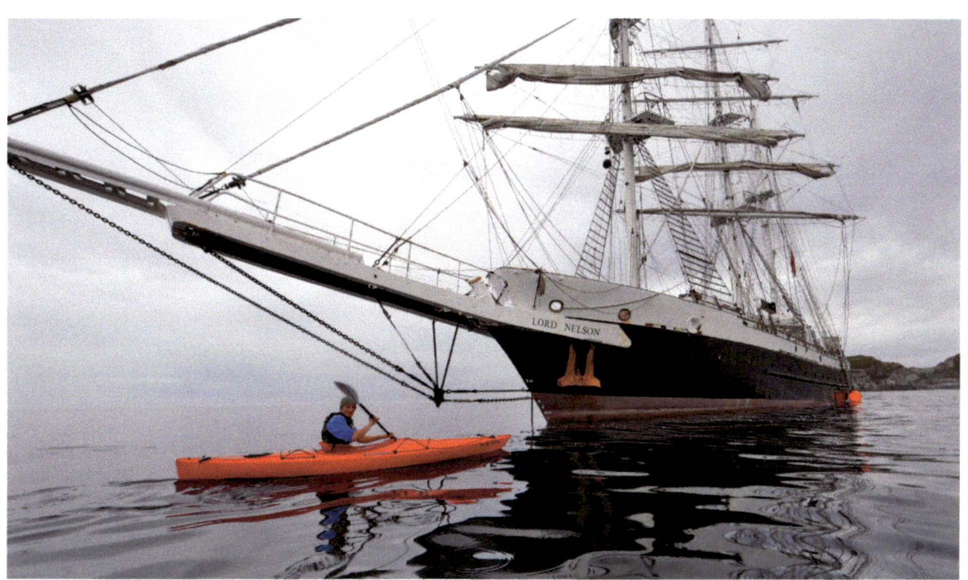

Big and Small Sailing Ships

Moored in almost the exact same spot are the *Lord Nelson* Sea Training Tall Ship (*above*) and the *Lundy Gannet* (*below*). The *Lord Nelson* is fitted to accommodate crews of mixed abilities, including those who are in wheelchairs, or those who are blind, to which a normal sailing ship would provide difficult obstacles. Below is the much smaller vessel, the *Lundy Gannet*, moored in front of Rat Island. Originally called the *Pride of Bridlington* (retaining her local H57 registration number) her captain was Trevor Davey, the nephew of Fred Dark – captain of the *Lerina*. Trevor was coxswain of the Clovelly lifeboat. The *Lundy Gannet* remained in service right up to the end of the 1960s when she was transferred to the Lundy Company once the island was leased to the Landmark Trust.

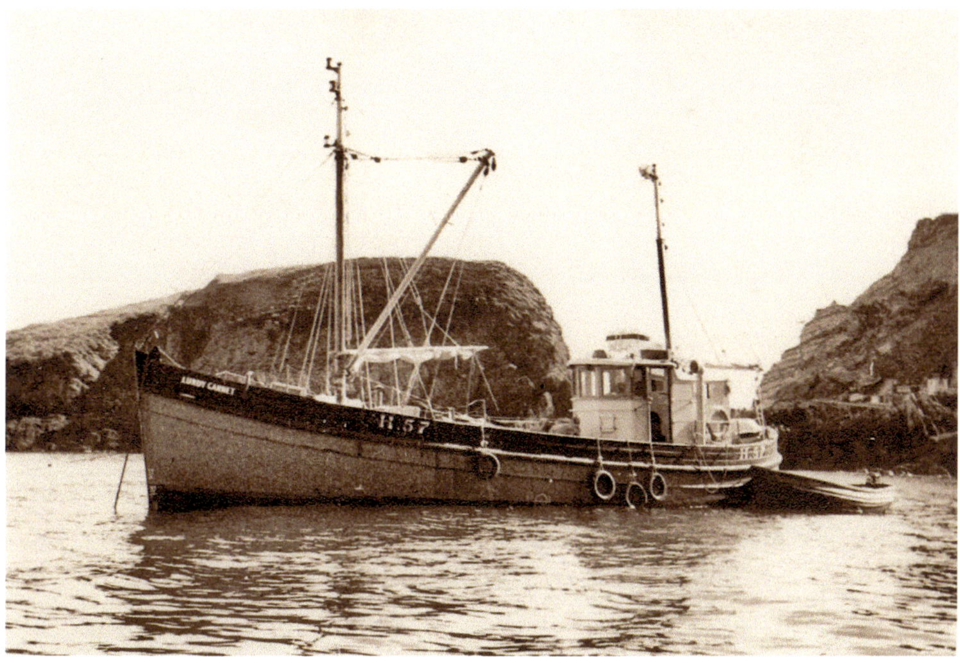

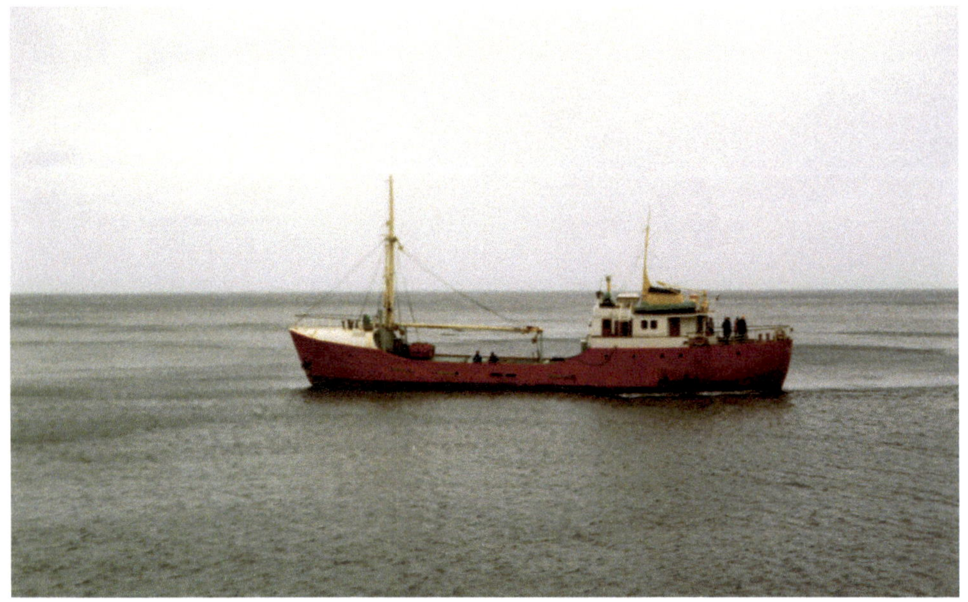

The *Polar Bear* and the *Balmoral*

Above is pictured the island supply vessel, the *Polar Bear*, in the late 1970s. She was formerly a Greenland coaster called the *Agdleq*, and was bought to replace the *Lundy Gannet*, coming in to service in 1972. The *Oldenburg* in turn replaced her in 1986. Below is a photograph of the *Balmoral* in the foreground, dwarfing the *Oldenburg* behind the jetty. The *Balmoral* of 'Waverley Excursions' is the sister-ship to paddle steamer *Waverley* and calls in to Lundy during the summer months with day-trippers.

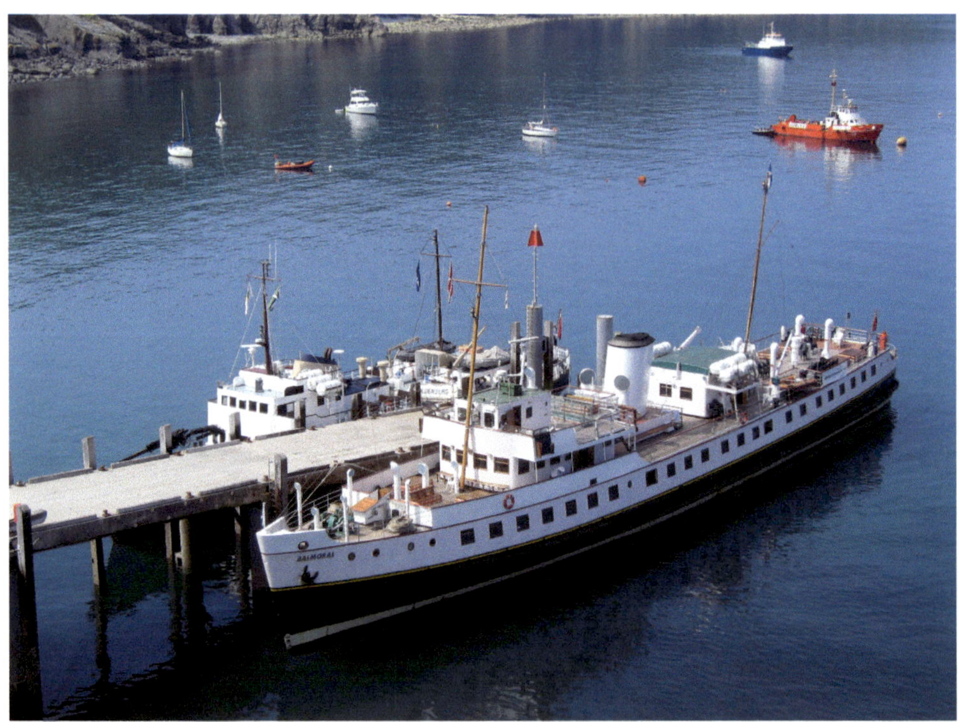

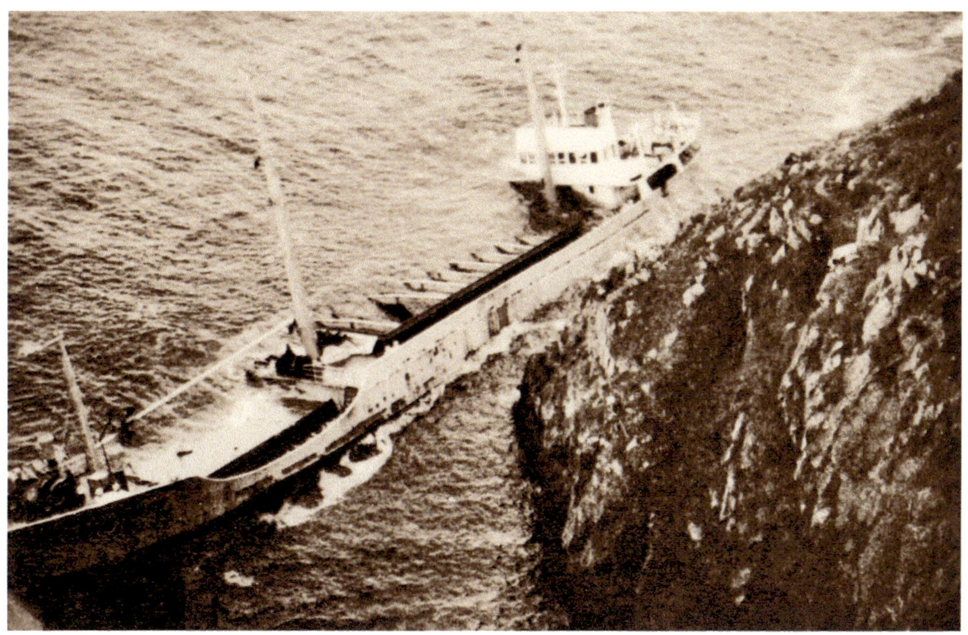

The Wreck of the *Kaaksburg*

Early in the morning of 6 November 1980, the 486-tonne *Kaaksburg* ran into Lundy Island on the east side near the quarries. Luckily, the crew escaped unhurt and were airlifted to safety by rescue helicopter. The vessel eventually broke up, and much of the stern section slipped away and sank into deep waters. Only the bow section, as seen below, remained tucked into the cliffs, left at the mercy of the tides and weather. It is impossible to see the wreck from land, and it is only from a passing boat that you have any view of the rusting remains. In the photograph (*below*) a member of staff from the island is enjoying a day off in his kayak.

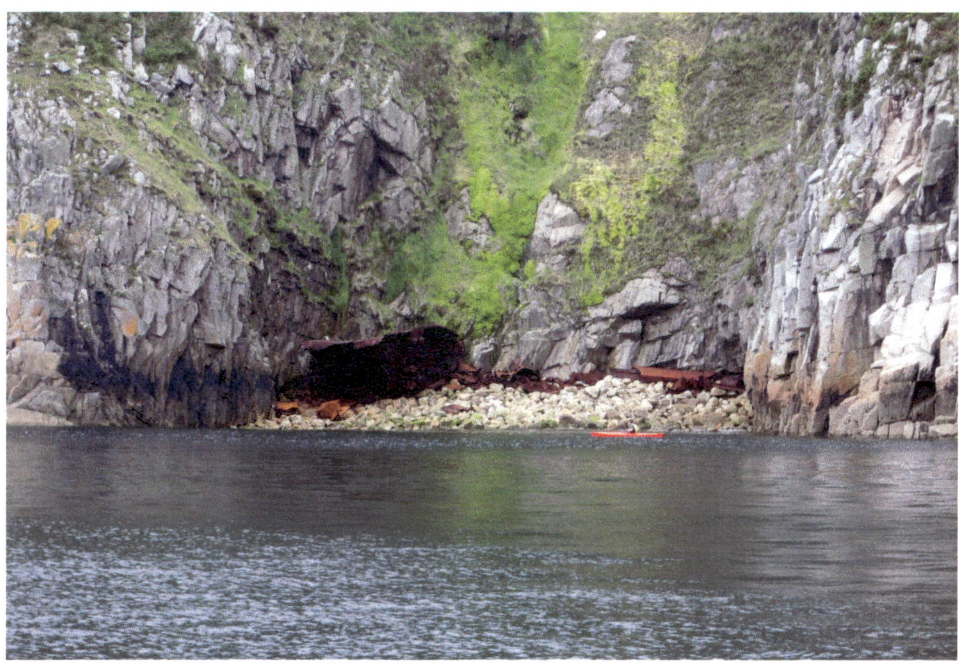

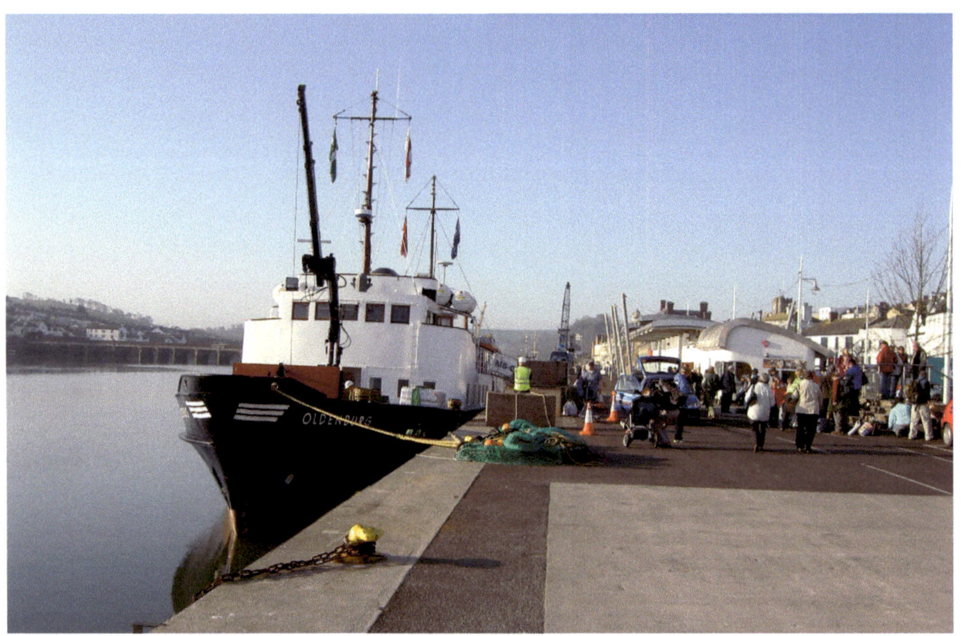

The Bideford Quayside and the *Oldenburg*

The *Oldenburg* (*above*) has its home-port at Bideford, and is seen here on a gloriously calm day loading day-trippers for a fine crossing to Lundy Island. Half an hour of the journey from Bideford is taken up by a river cruise along the Torridge. A slightly more tempestuous journey, however, used to be made in the *Shearn*, a small flat-bottomed landing craft built by John Shearn in the 1970s. The *Shearn* was used to transport passengers for many years from visiting vessels to the landing beach in the days before the jetty was built. She is now used to transport heavy equipment to an island in the River Thames in London.

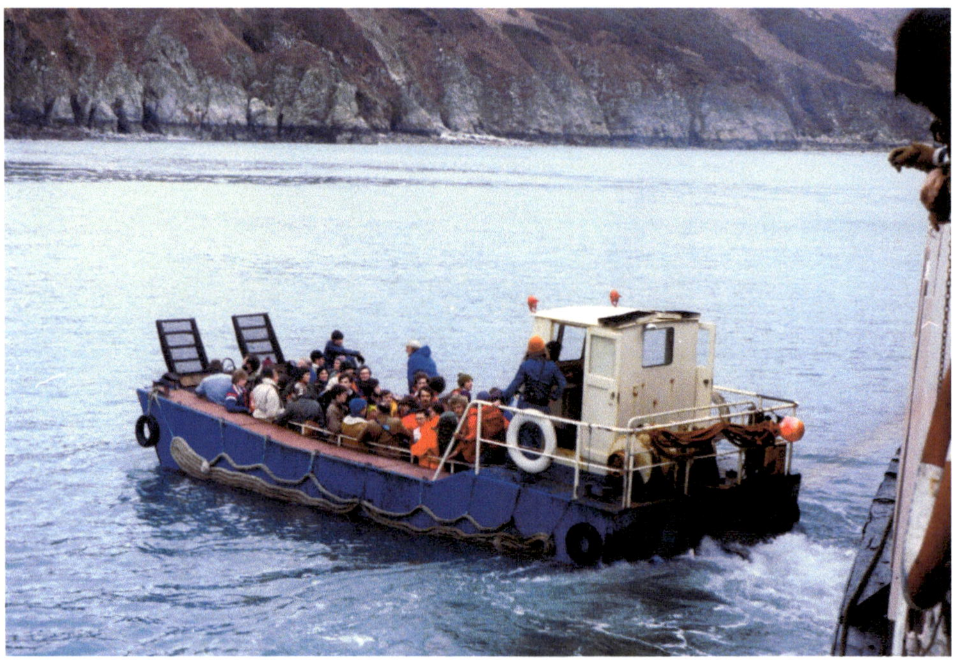

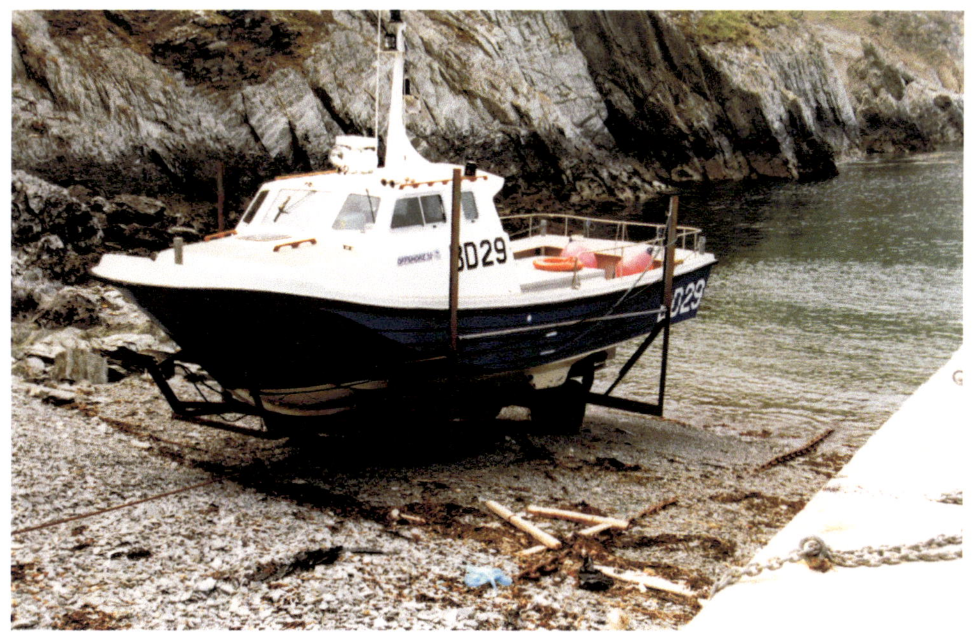

Lundy's Little Boats

Above is the *Islander*, which is shown hauled up in Christie's Quay in 1985. The *Islander* was used as a general-purpose small boat by the island staff around the close confines of Lundy. Nowadays, a fast and manoeuvrable rib is used by the island employees for various activities, and is usually kept in the summer season on the jetty, as can be seen from the rather busy quayside photograph below.

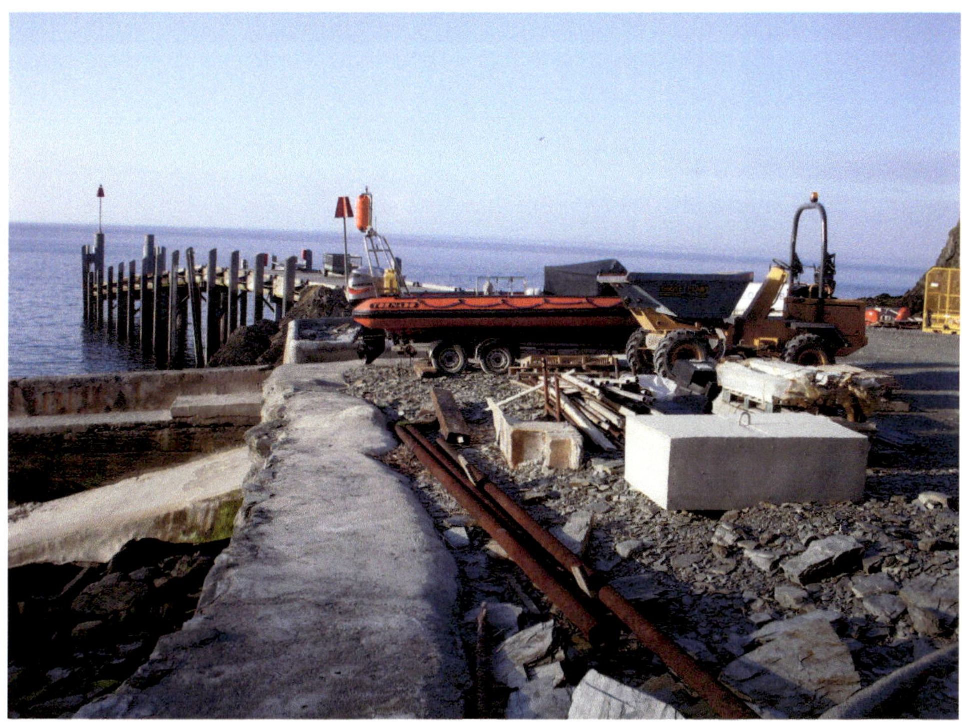

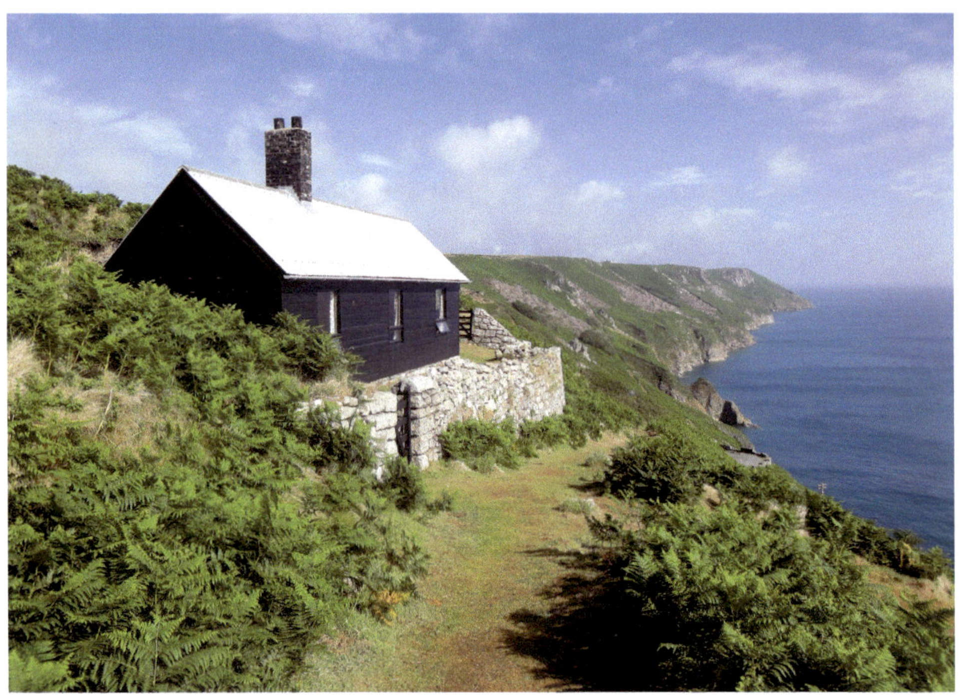

Hanmers' Cottage

In 1899, Mr George Thomas, fisherman and island handyman, built himself a house here, of timber overlaid with corrugated iron, which became known as 'the Palace'. In 1927, a Miss Wilda Gee (*below*) visited Lundy, decided she would like to live there for long periods and subsequently hired the Cliff Bungalow. She had been a militant suffragette and had served a short prison sentence for chaining herself to the railings at the Houses of Parliament. In 1939, the Hanmer family leased the bungalow and the name stuck!

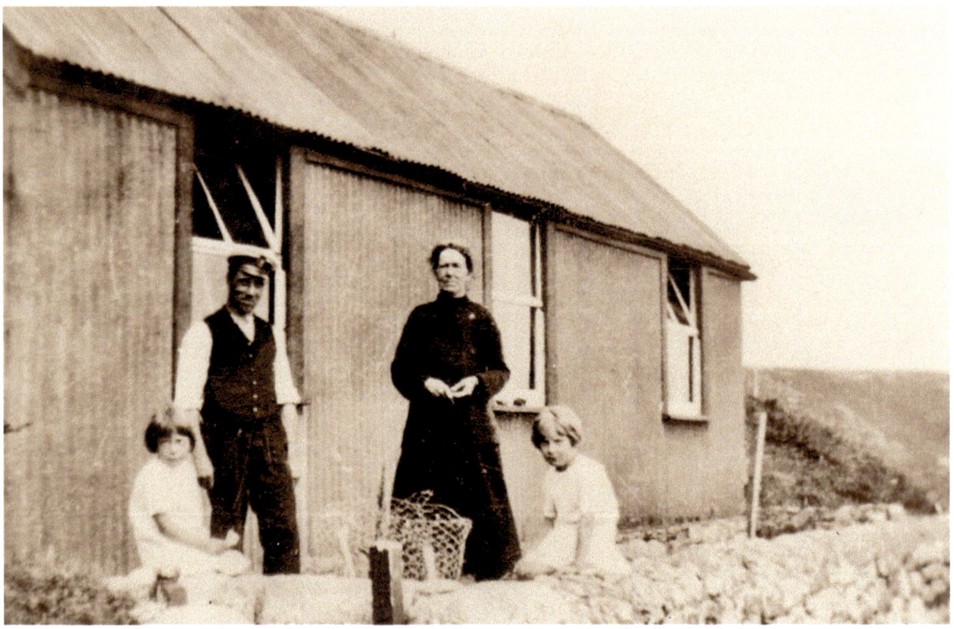

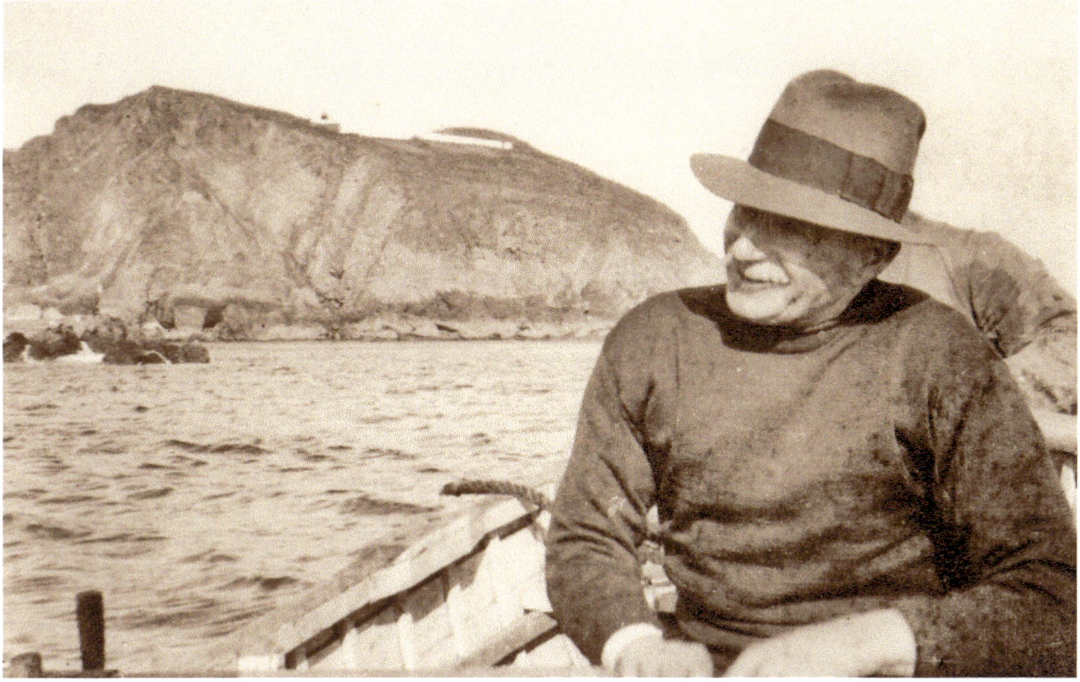

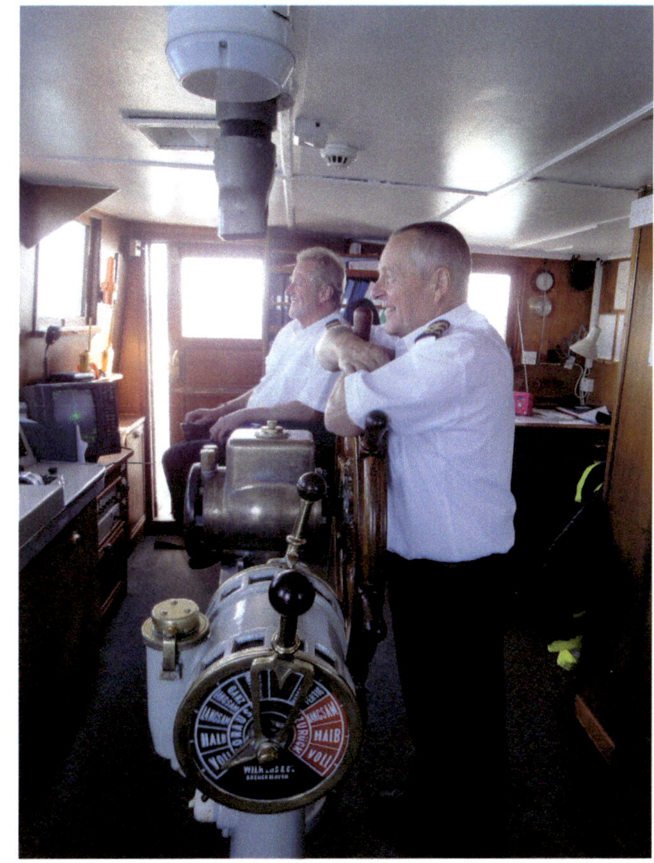

Sea Farers

Above, pictured before the Second World War years, is Captain Fred Dark, master of the *Lerina*, at the oars of a small rowing boat as it passes the South Light. He was the son of Captain William Dark, the master of the vessel that was originally called the *Gannet*, used before the *Lerina* arrived on Lundy. Captain Fred Dark's nephew – Trevor Davey – became the captain of the *Lundy Gannet*, which replaced the *Lerina*. Below are two men equally experienced in the voyage to Lundy Island – the captain of the *Oldenburg*, Jerry Waller, seated in the bridge along with First Officer / Relief Master Brian Slade, who has worked on the *Oldenburg* for almost twenty years.

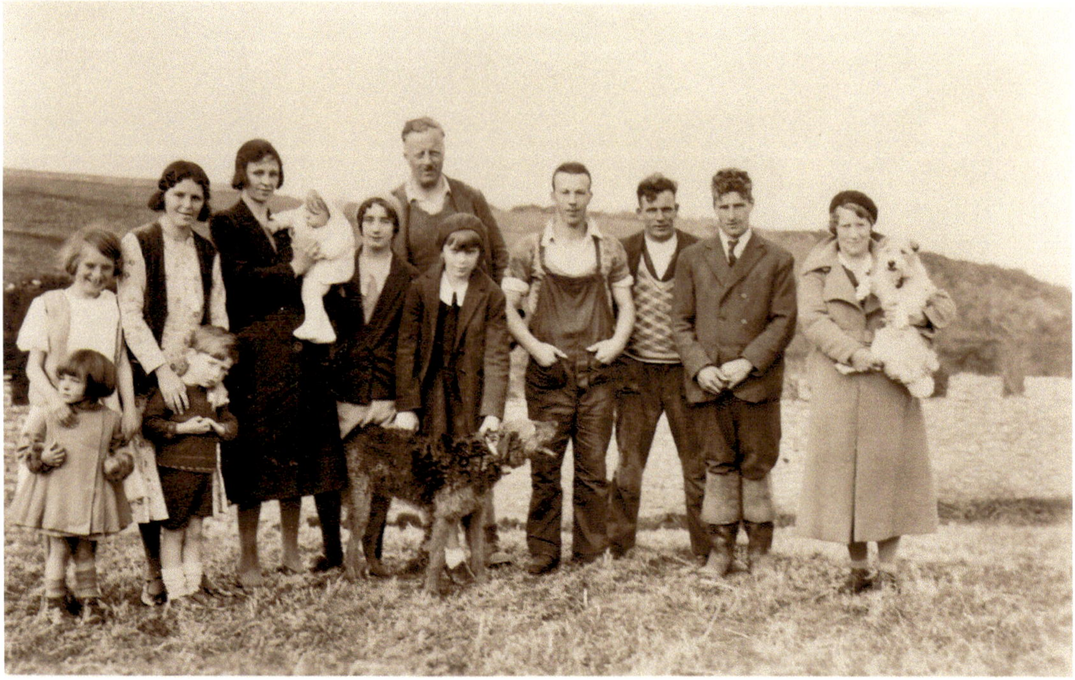

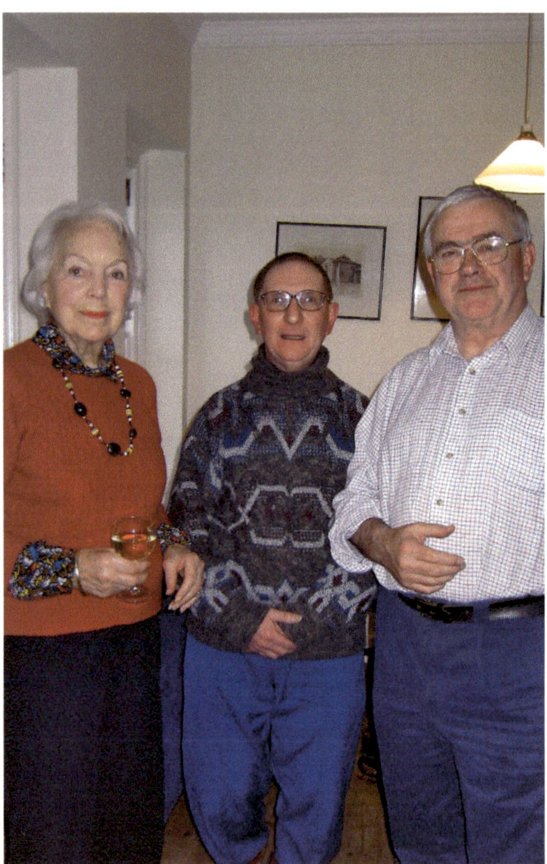

An Island Family

Pictured above is the tall figure of Mr Felix Gade – simply known as 'Giant' or 'Gi' by his friends on the island. Mr Gade was the land agent for Mr Harman, and lived almost continuously on the island for over fifty years. On the right side of the photograph is Mrs Gade, holding her dog. Second from the right is Charlie Smaldon, the island horseman. Mrs Smaldon is pictured, left of centre, holding her baby. Her two small children are standing in the front, on the left. Charlie had no love of the sea as he was unable to swim, and was unfortunately drowned when he fell overboard from a dinghy taking men back to a boat in the landing bay. In the centre of the photograph, in front of Mr Gade, is Diana Harman, daughter of the island owner – Martin Coles Harman – with the dog. In the modern image is Diana, the last joint owner of Lundy before it passed into the hands of the National Trust in 1969. This photograph was taken in 2006 on the occasion of the sixtieth anniversary of the Lundy Field Society. Pictured with Diana is Barry Branch (a society member) along with Roger Chapple, the chairman at that time.

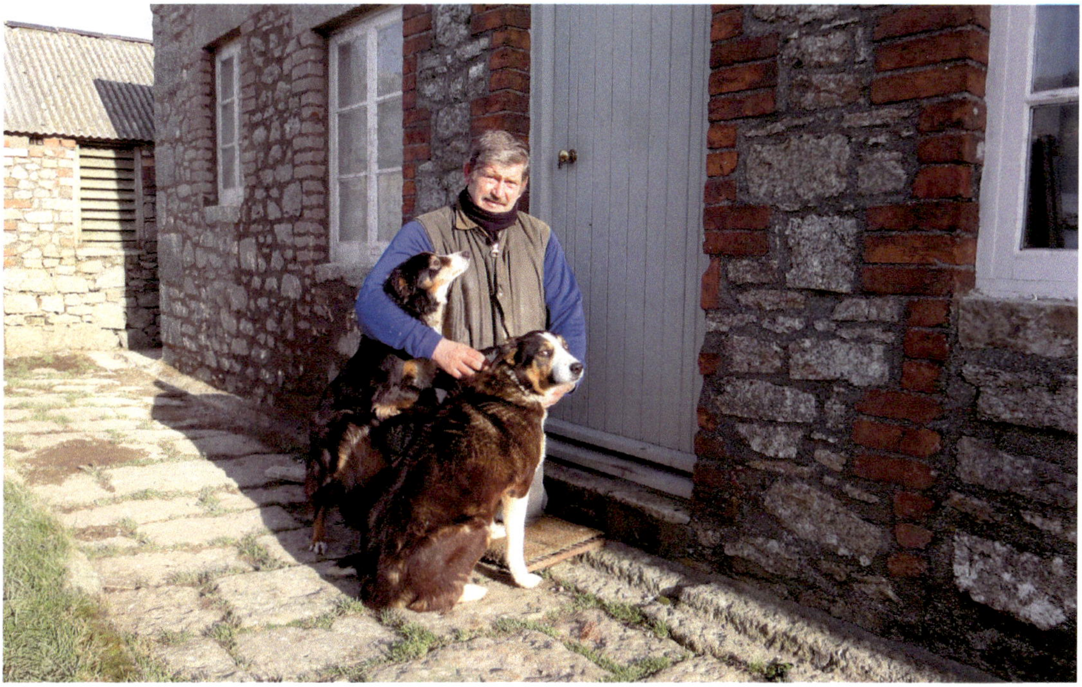

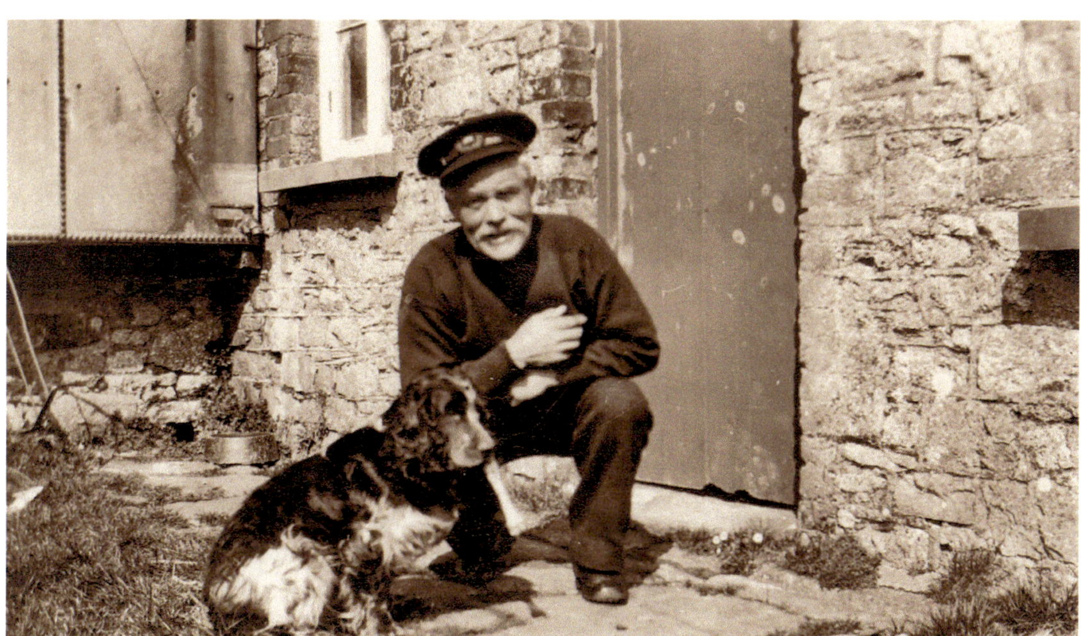

Island Men and their Dogs

The above photograph is of the farmer and island foreman Kevin Welsh outside his home at Barton Cottages along with his sheepdogs Bert and Wis. The lower photograph, also taken outside one of Barton Cottages, is of Bob Helson, who was one of the boatmen and a jobbing builder from Appledore. He was also an experienced quarry worker who did a lot of repair work on the beach road, usually in company with a dog called Simon. Bob had previously lost the sight in one of his eyes and was later totally blinded by an accident with a blackthorn briar.

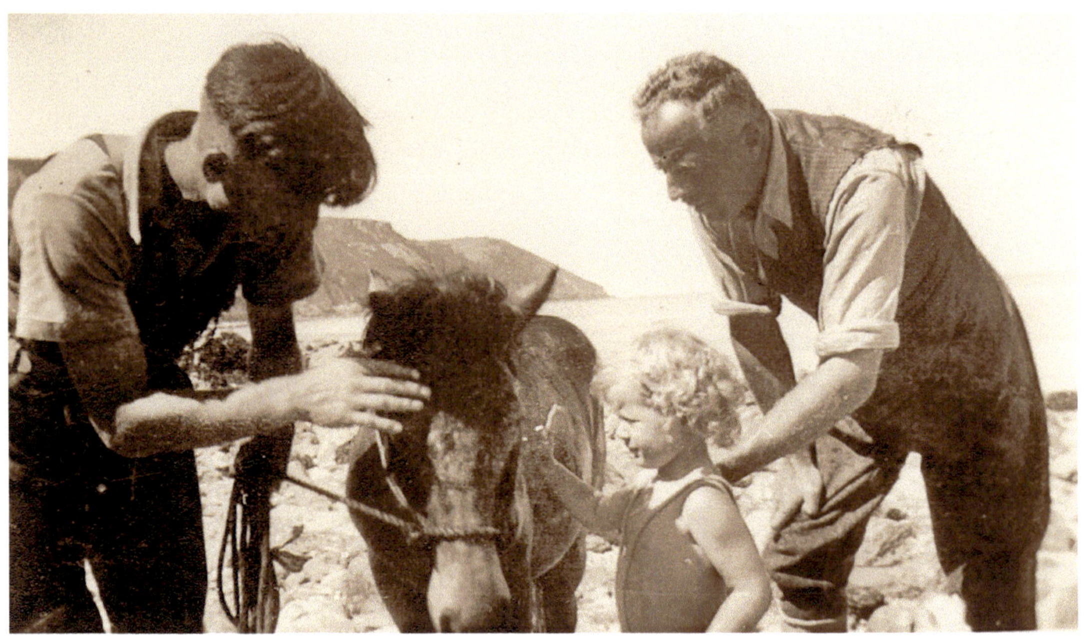

Lundy Horses

The above photograph, in the 1930s, shows Mr Gade on the right with his young daughter Mary and 'Tuppy', the 'smallest racehorse in the world'! Tuppy had been in a circus and had learned to walk on his hind legs. The lower photograph is of Mary's daughter, Annie Alford, with her horse 'Lundy Stonechat' pictured on the island, where her horse is kept.

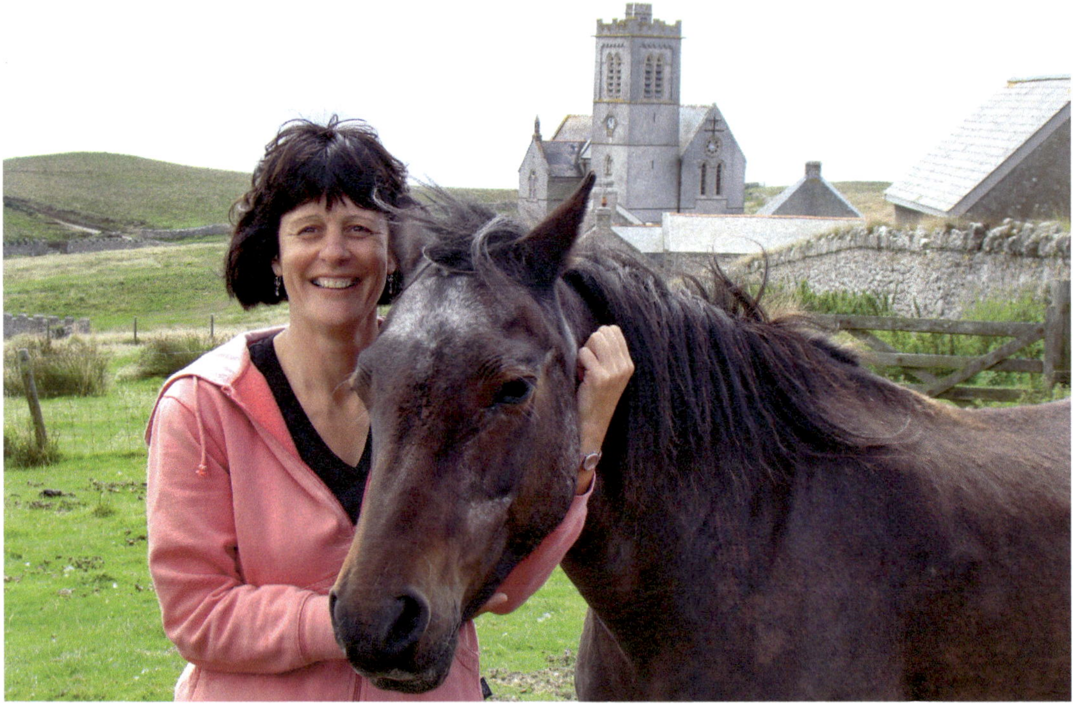

The Island Radio Equipment

The island was kept in daily communication, morning and afternoon, by the use of the radio transmitter (*right*) which had been installed during the war years. Mr Gade spoke daily with the coastguard station at Hartland and transmitted requests for routine deliveries as well as emergency calls for help. He is pictured with John Ogilvie, the island farmer, who married Penny Ruddock. The radio equipment, although no longer in use, is still situated as a small piece of island history in the Radio Room (*below*) where the author is a frequent visitor!

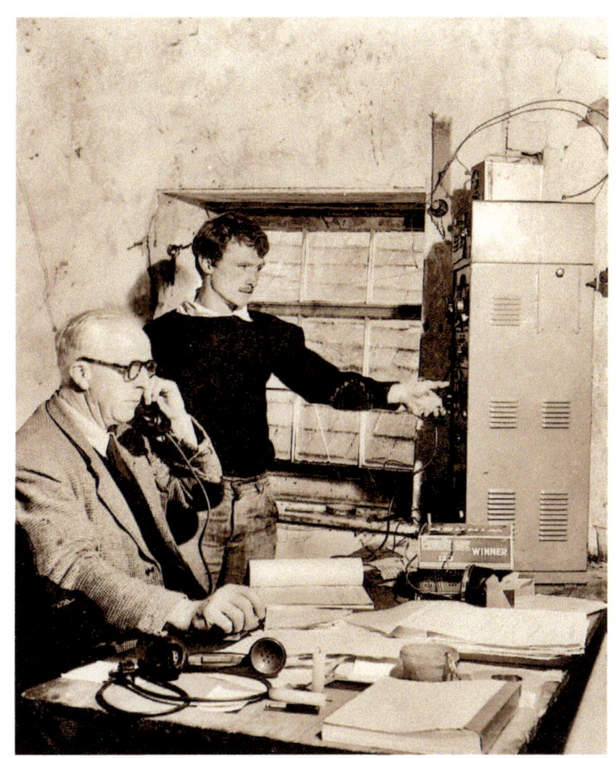

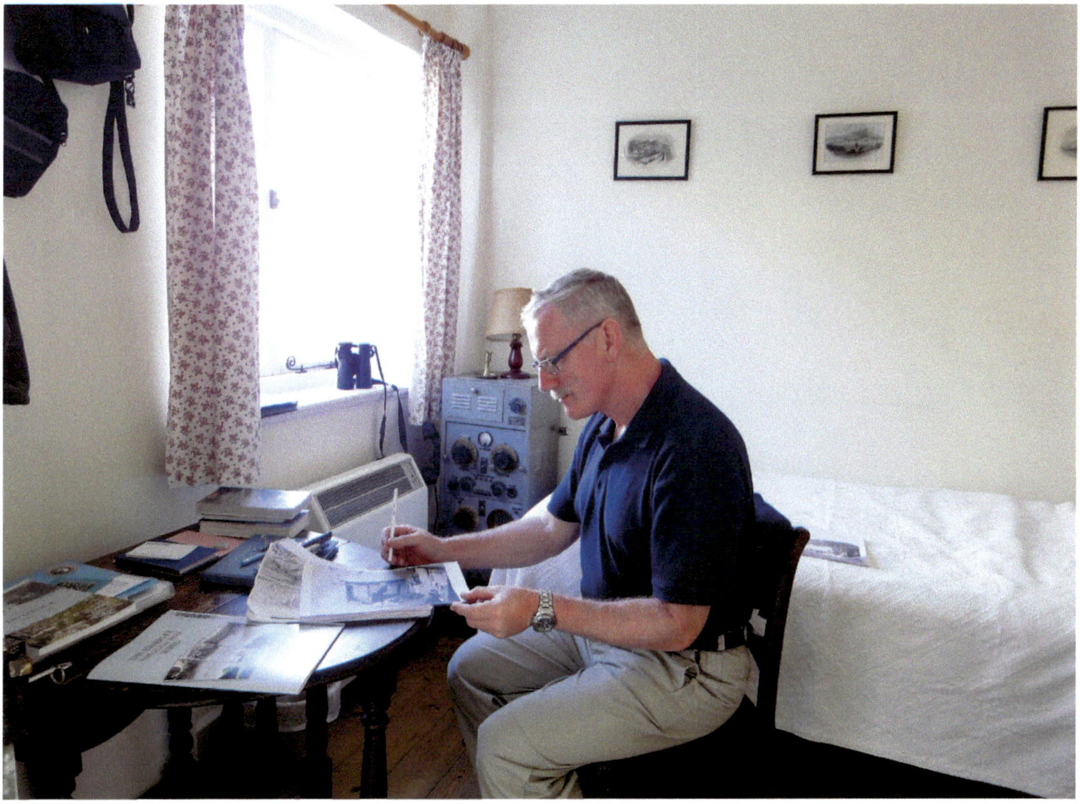

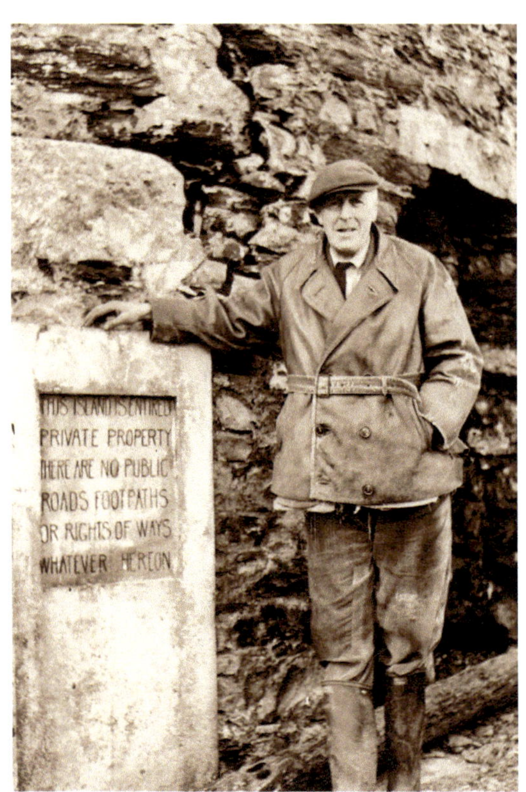

Island Agent and Island Manager

Felix Gade leans on the island landing-bay stone, which was erected at the time of the Heaven ownership in the nineteenth century. The stone and nearby limekiln were swept away in a landslide in 1954. After his retirement as Island Agent, Mr Gade remained on the island until his death in 1978, and lies buried with his wife in the island cemetery near the Old Light. The lower photograph is of the current Lundy General Manager, Derek Green, next to the National Trust Lundy sign on the beach road slipway where Mr Gade stood over fifty years before. As soon as Derek arrived on the island he was instrumental in raising funds to restore the beach road, thus ensuring the future economy of the island.

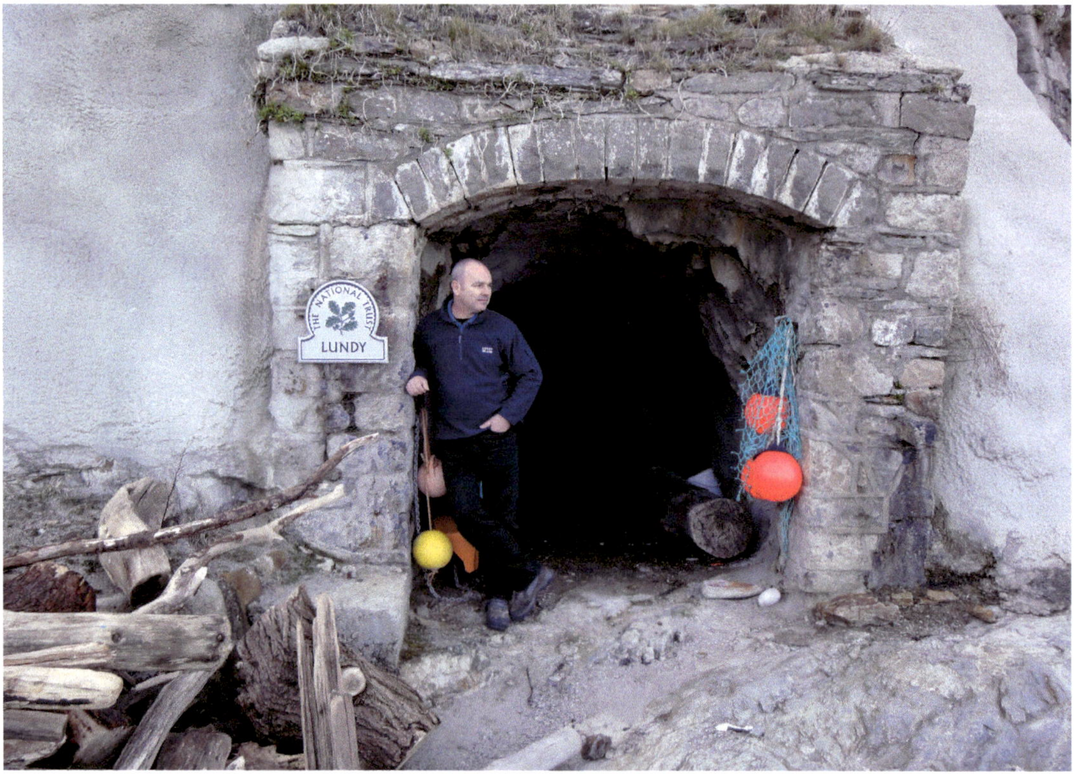

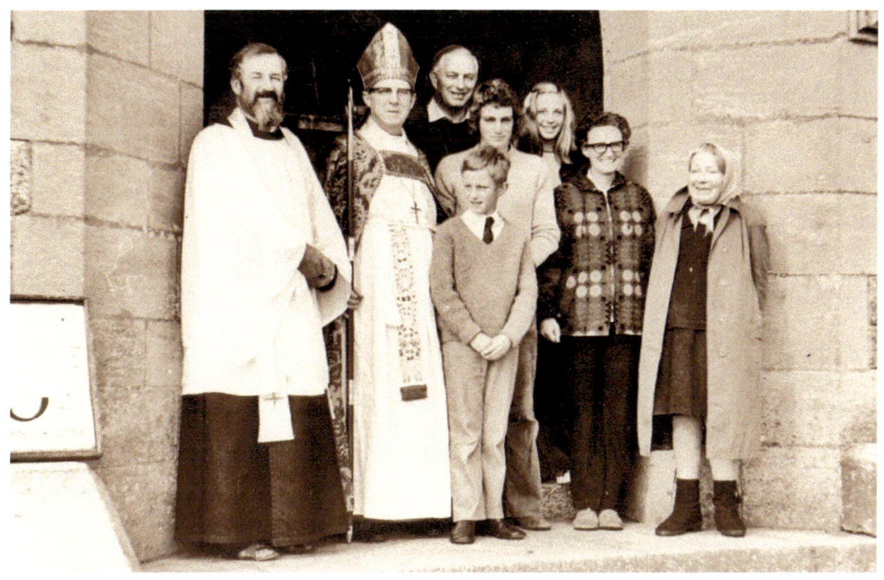

The Clergy, a Bishop and the Bell-ringers

Above, a rare visit by a Bishop to Lundy in 1974. Taken on the occasion of the confirmation by the Bishop of Plymouth, at the front is Tom Grainger, the son of the Island Manager Ian Grainger, at the rear. Also pictured is Major The Revd Donald Peyton Jones, Vicar of Appledore and priest in charge of Lundy. In his obituary in *The Times*, he was described as the 'Unconventional Royal Marines officer who became a vicar with an idiosyncratic priestly style'. When the author was a schoolboy in Appledore, he recalls the vicar riding a horse to church! Also worthy of note is the lady on the right, Ms Sylvia Heaven, who also appears in the photograph on page 26 as a young girl. The lower photograph is a group of bell-ringers in the St Helen's church tower; one of the most frequently visited bell towers in the county!

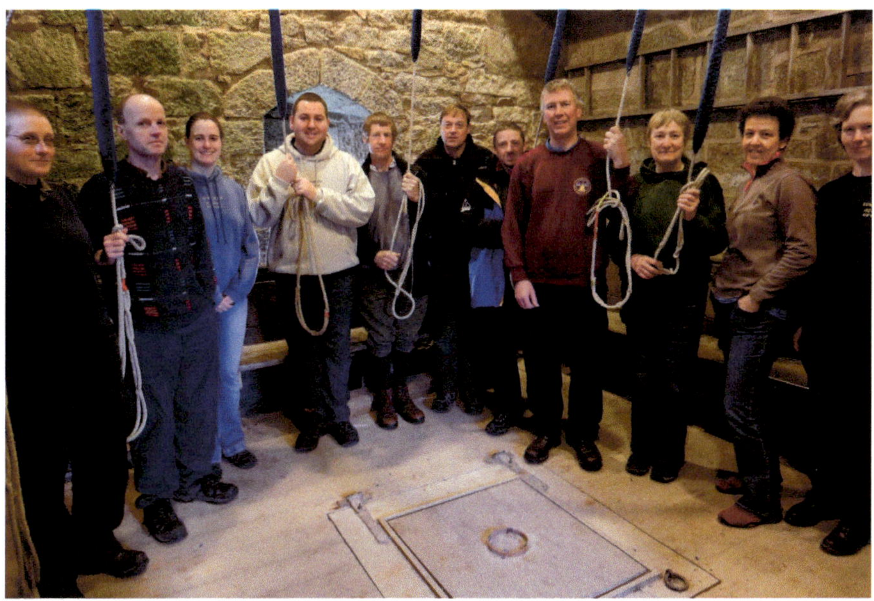

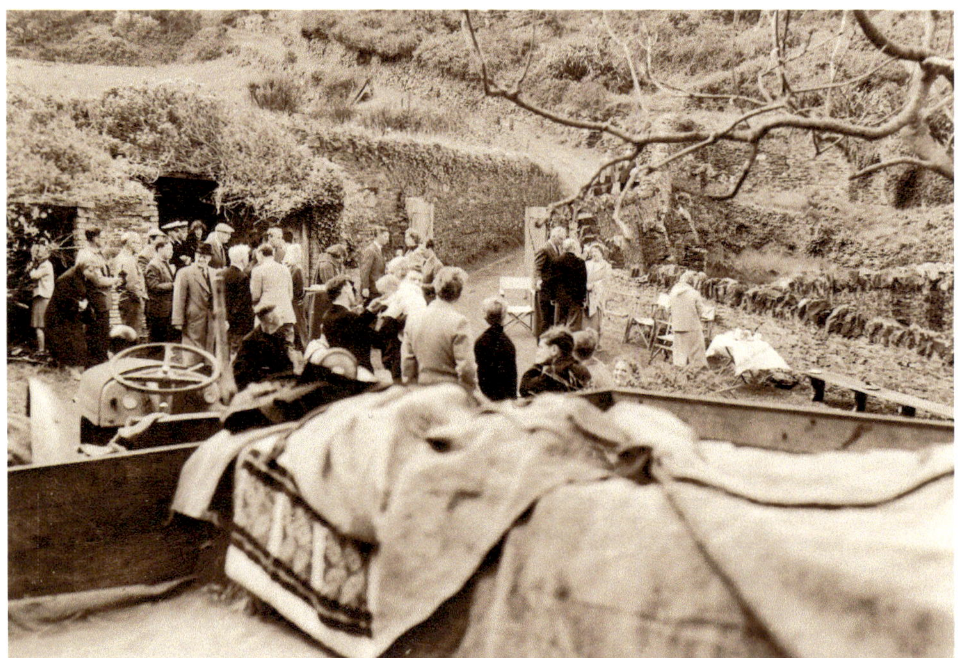

The Gateway to Millcombe House

The gateway to Millcombe House in 1958 (*above*) was the scene of the Queen Mother taking tea with island residents during her brief visit. An equally enjoyable occasion is pictured (*below*) during a brief rest in warm weather, as a group of day-trippers make their way up to the village from the landing bay below.

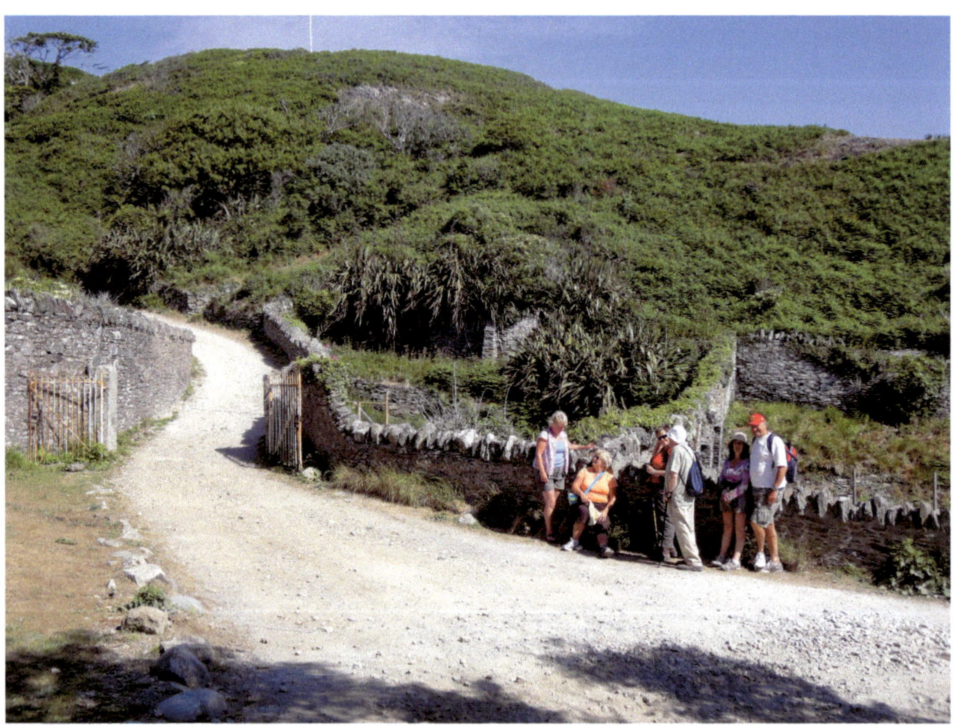

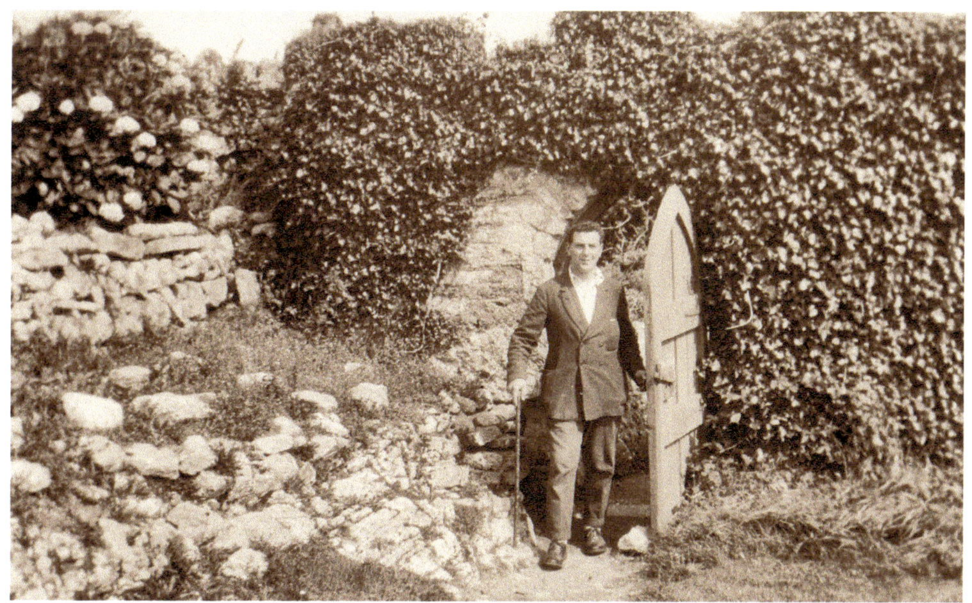

The Monastery or Gothic Gate

The blue gate in the wall at the rear of the tavern was installed to allow guests to attend services at the little iron church, situated behind the wall, before St Helen's church was built in 1896. This prevented visitors having to go all the way through Millcombe House gardens to gain access. In the photograph (*above*) Mr Alfred Blackwell, a frequent visitor and photographer in the 1920s, is seen coming through the doorway. He had been a Metropolitan policeman before retiring to Instow, where he became the shore agent, selling tickets and arranging transportation from the home-port of the *Lerina*. The lower photograph is of the author, who leads guided walks on Lundy and who, by coincidence, has also been a member of the local police service for over thirty-five years!

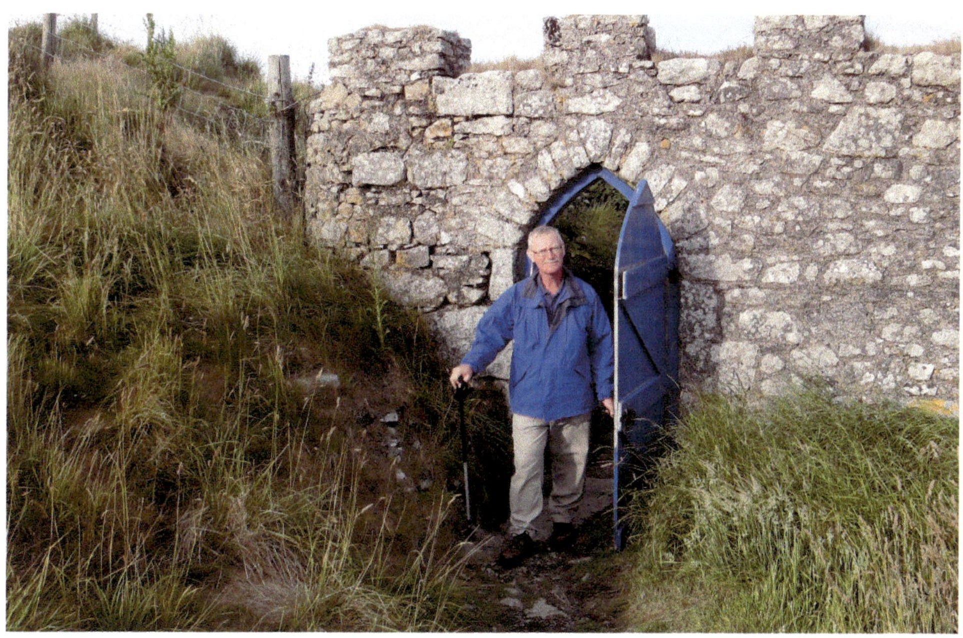

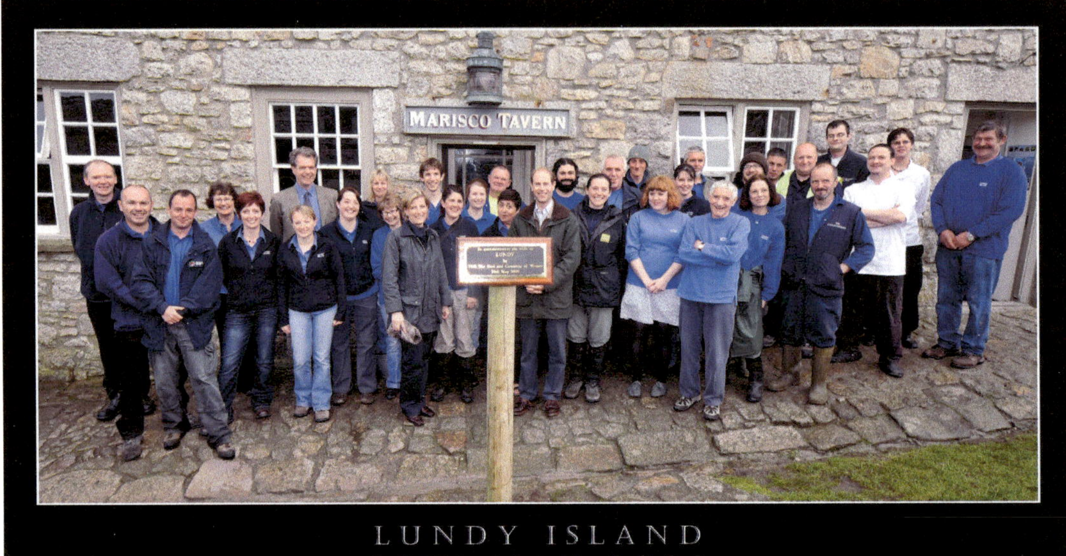

Royal Visit
The visit to Lundy of the Earl and Countess of Wessex, on 20 May 2009, to commemorate the fortieth anniversary of the National Trust and the Landmark Trust acquiring Lundy Island.

Acknowledgements

Such a book would be impossible to produce without the assistance of many people involved with Lundy Island. Firstly, to Myrtle Ternstrom, author of innumerable books on Lundy, my thanks for your overwhelming enthusiasm for such a project, for sharing your knowledge and a wealth of photographs. Alan Rowland, the Lundy Field Society archivist, for sharing his own private collection with me and pointing me in the right direction for other sources. Tom Baker, whose incredible Lundy collection was made freely available to me. The memory and personal experiences of Mary Squire (the daughter of Felix Gade), who herself lived on Lundy for many decades, has provided so much information for the captions and put right so many assumptions and errors on my part, along with the more recent memories of Annie Alford – her daughter. Steve Knight, for sharing the historic archives of R. L. Knight Photographers, of Barnstaple; Jonathan Evans for his lovely photograph on the title verso page, and Stuart Leavy for many of his images, taken while living on Lundy. Finally, a huge thank you for the support of Derek Green, Lundy Island General Manager, and his staff, which has been magnificent – thank you everyone, one and all (*pictured above*).